Groupwork Volume 10

In this series

Published Spring 2007

Groupwork: Volume 1
ISBN 9781861770554

Groupwork: Volume 2
ISBN 9781861770561

Groupwork: Volume 3
ISBN 9781861770578

Groupwork: Volume 4
ISBN 9781861770585

Groupwork: Volume 5
ISBN 9781861770592

Groupwork: Volume 6
ISBN 9781861770608

Groupwork: Volume 7
ISBN 9781861770615

Groupwork: Volume 8
ISBN 9781861770622

Groupwork: Volume 9
ISBN 9781861770639

Groupwork: Volume 10
ISBN 9781861770646

Groupwork: Volume 11
ISBN 9781861770653

Groupwork: Volume 12
ISBN 9781861770660

Groupwork: Volume 13
ISBN 9781861770677

To be published Autumn 2007

Groupwork: Volume 14
ISBN 9781861770684

A full contents list for volumes 1-13 will be found at the back of t

Groupwork

An Interdisciplinary Journal for Working with Groups

Volume Ten

edited by

Nuala Lordan, Tara Mistry & Claire Wintram

Whiting & Birch Ltd
1998
Reprinted 2007

Notes from the Publisher

Citation
This volume comprises, without any amendment, all material published in *Groupwork* Volume 10, 1998. It is advised that authors citing material in this volume should recognise this original date and journal provenance in the manner indicated by the house style of the publication for which they are writing, either by citing material as the original periodical article, or, if citing this volume, by clearly indicating the original date of publication of the material both in text references and in the bibliography.

Reproduction
For technical reasons, the typesetting files of some early volumes of *Groupwork* are no longer usable. We have therefore scanned early volumes in this series from the original journals. This inevitably results in reproduction which is less than ideal. Material is available in some other formats.

Editorial contact details
We have reproduced volumes in their complete original format including notes to contributors and advertising. It should be remembered that editorial contact details and manuscript preparation requirements have changed. Current contact details and notes for contributors are available at www.whitingbirch.net.

Published by Whiting & Birch Ltd,
Forest Hill, London SE23 3HZ

ISBN 9781861770646
ISSN 0951-824X
Printed in England and the United States by Lightning Source

Groupwork
An Interdisciplinary Journal for Working with Groups

Volume 10, 1998

Contents

Preface

Since its first issue in 1988, much interesting and inspiring material has been published in *Groupwork*. Most of this still says much of use to today's groupworkers. We are therefore delighted that back volumes of Groupwork will in future be readily available in convenient form.

Mark Doel and Pamela Trevithick
Co-Editors *Groupwork*

GROUPWORK

Volume 10 Number 1 1997-98

SUBSCRIPTION, ADVERTISING AND BUSINESS ENQUIRIES
Should be addressed to the publishers, WHITING & BIRCH LTD, PO Box 872, Forest Hill, London SE23 3HL. TEL: 0181-244-2421 (Int'l +44181 244-2421). FAX: 0181-244-2448 (Int'l. +44181-244-2448)

SUBSCRIPTION RATES
British Isles £37.50, North America US$85, Elsewhere £47.50
Special reduced rates apply as follows: Individuals to private address: £19.00 British Isles, North America, US$37.50 Elsewhere £25.00.
Special reductions for members of AASWG.
Groupwork is published three times a year.

PAYMENT
Should accompany order. Cheque or banker's draft (made payable to WHITING & BIRCH LTD) may be in any convertible currency to the relevant amount. Direct transfer can be made to our Girobank account (no. 5440564). The following credit cards are also accepted: Access/Mastercard, Visa, Diners Club, American Express. Quote card number, expiry date and give cardholder's name and address if different from delivery address.

GROUPWORK is cited in: *Applied Social Sciences Index & Abstracts, Sociological Abstracts, Bibliographie Zeitscriftenliteratur aus allen Gebieten des Wissens, Social Care Update, Social Work Research & Abstracts, Special Educational Needs Abstracts.* and *Studies on Women Abstracts.*

PUBLISHED BY WHITING & BIRCH LTD, LONDON. ISSN 0951-824X
Printed in the UK by Watkiss Studios Ltd

Editorial

This issue provides yet further proof of the dynamic growth of groupwork internationally. It is heartening to be able to read, on the one hand, about the specifics of groupwork within the Probation Service in England and, on the other, about the mechanics of establishing group support to young people at risk of substance abuse in the US. This issue contains accounts of work in England, Australia, the US and Canada. Thereby reminding us that the principles of sharing and co-operation continue to survive against the odds in systems that would still deny their value.

This issue demonstrates the enormous breadth of imagination used in applying groupwork principles, whether it is with children who have survived the loss of a father, or women who are at risk of different forms of violence. We learn here not only about the empowering and liberating experiences of the groupwork participants, but also about the learning and self-development that takes place in the facilitators. Groupworkers have been honest about the need for self-criticism and self-appraisal and about the need for change in themselves. All of this has brought about positive developments in their ways of working as they discuss their self-analysis in a creative and instructive way. These changes have led to greater autonomy and decision-making potential for group participants, thereby enhancing their experiences of personal growth and support. There is much to take away and reflect on in the accounts here for those of us who may be seeking new ideas for practice and research. Each paper gives us evidence of the growth of self-awareness and confidence, of the recognition of the value of change and of its limitless possibilities. Workers have shown courage in stepping outside tried and trusted methods in order to create environments in which participants' strengths and abilities can flourish.

One of the strong impressions gained from reading all of these papers together is of the care and concern expressed by all the authors for the people with whom they work, their recognition of shared humanity, whether with colleagues or with group members. It feels highly significant to us in the current political climate, to be editing an issue which contains such a strong element of care. We are well aware of the negative, patronising connotations such words have carried in the last two decades, in the West in particular.

Positive steps are being taken in some areas to challenge the prevailing spirit of individualism (even though some would still have us believe that this is the only philosophy of life worth having). These challenges are crucial as proof of the fact that collective innovatory practice, use of imagination and working through problems and traumas can occur in virtually any setting with beneficial consequences for the participants.

In this issue, we are presented with an account of work with a small, closed group of very young women whose lives have been changed by the loss of a parent. The intensity and depth of the content of sessions are vividly conveyed, bringing to life the group and the work as it is carried out, and enabling readers to feel part of the changes that occur in each young person's life. At the opposite end of the spectrum lies the account of establishing a teleconferencing counselling group in Australia, the vastness of the geographical area to be served ceases to be an obstacle when such an imaginative approach is adopted. People are brought together across distance to explore shared problems and difficulties without having to engage in complex arrangements. The advantages of this way of working are clarified both from a practical and emotional point of view.

We hope readers will derive as much pleasure from and find as many sources of interest as we have in the varied and stimulating content of this issue of the Journal. The scope is as broad as it is deep, reinforcing the value and adaptability of groupwork approaches.

Claire Wintram
Nuala Lordan
Tara Mistry
Co-Editors

Teleconferencing Group Counselling: Pre-Group Public Phase

Sandra Regan[1]

This paper introduces the reader to teleconferencing group counselling (TGC) and then focuses on the pregroup public phase of group development which is fundamental to the successful establishment of a teleconferencing counselling group. This includes: keeping records, the role of the agency, theoretical perspective, co-leadership, preliminary decisions on selection, recruitment, composition and structural aspects, initial contact with potential group members, practical arrangements, what happens in the fifteen minutes prior to first teleconferencing counselling session and awareness of potential technical problems.

Introduction

As helping professions move towards a new century, it is important to consider the use of technology and how this might influence or enhance practice. The telephone itself is not a new technology, but what can be done with it has changed dramatically, even over the last five years. Now with a mobile telephone one can be reached in virtually any location by telephone, and a wider number of people can be reached through the use of teleconferencing technology, computer link-ups, or interactive video. Technology does not stand still. Helping professionals need to expand their horizons and be proactive in their use of technology.

1. Senior Lecturer in Groupwork,
Address for correspondence: School of Social Work, University of New South Wales, Sydney, NSW 2052, Australia.

While recognising the contributions of these variations on the use of the telephone, for the purposes of this paper I will be dealing with audio teleconferencing only. This is for practical reasons. The telephone is accessible to the widest number of people. Although computers are becoming common for many families, there are still many people for whom the costs are prohibitive. Interactive video may be the way of the future, but again costly. The people I am most interested in reaching may not have access to such expensive technology.

Teleconferencing allows a number of people, in different locations, tied to a common telephone line to connect and hear everyone else's comments and each person can contribute as in a face-to-face group.

Teleconferencing has been used to provide socialisation experiences, break down isolation, offer support and meet short term educational/therapeutic needs (Albertson and Bearlin, 1977; Evans and Jaureguy, 1981; Galinsky, Rounds, Montague and Butowsky, 1993; Gibbons, 1982; Ritter and Hammons, 1992; Trang and Urbano, 1993; Tropp, 1987).

Teleconferencing group counselling (TGC)

My interest in teleconferencing is in its potential for group counselling. Understanding the difference between teleconferencing as it is used for business, educational or support purposes and when it is used for group counselling is important.

This article assumes a knowledge of groupwork skills and theory in face-to-face group counselling. As with therapeutic face-to-face groups, TGC requires the expressed intent to use it for therapeutic purposes. This must be acknowledged by leader and participants before group begins. The same groupwork principles and ethics are used as in face-to-face group counselling.

In other words, TGC, as with face-to-face groups, has a therapeutic focus engaging people experiencing problems in specific areas of their life, whether these be personal, relationship or practical aspects of life. In the process of helping people to cope with their current situation, TGC, as in face-to-face groups also offers the opportunity for growth so that participants may handle similar situations in a more beneficial manner.

Teleconferencing in the area of groupwork is a means of making contact with people who may be excluded from face-to-face group counselling experiences. This exclusion may be based on limited access, inability to break isolation or fear of exposure in face-to-face groups. Otherwise, the differences between face-to-face and teleconferencing group counselling are technological, not theoretical. The focus of this paper is to explore the differences that result from the use of this technology, differences which need to be considered in preparation for TGC.

Preparation for teleconferencing group counselling

From my experience of a range of groupwork models, the one that seems to stand out as having particular application to TGC is Hartford's model (1971). This is because she made specific divisions in the pregroup phase into: private, public, convening. She recognised the importance of each and how significant the entire pregroup phase is to the establishment of a group.

The pregroup private phase starts when the leader has to make a personal decision as to whether to establish a group. The pregroup public phase is initiated when the decision to have a group is shared with others such as: potential co-leaders, fellow workers who may refer participants, agency staff who will provide support and/or backup for the new service, and possible group members who may become part of the process. The pregroup convening phase occurs when the group physically comes together for the first time (Hartford, 1971). In TGC pregroup convening occurs when the teleconferencing link up is made.

This paper specifically focuses on the *pregroup public phase*. It is here that decisions need to be made about the potential of TGC. There are additional factors that need to be considered in setting up a teleconferencing counselling group compared with a face to-face-group. While acknowledging the similarities in setting up both kinds of group, this paper focuses on differences encountered and how to prepare for them.

In TGC major consideration needs to be given to the use of technology in a manner with which many people are unfamiliar. Even though some may have used it for business or education purposes, once it takes on a counselling focus one encounters different challenges.

Careful preparation ensures that TGC has a high probability of success. Poor preparation means loose ends and things that go wrong which could have been avoided with a little effort. Participants can only tolerate so many mistakes and eventually begin to think the leader does not really care about them if mistakes happen frequently. Good preparation helps establish credibility and gives the impression that an effort has been made to make the groupwork.

In face-to-face groups physical presence in the pregroup convening phase, can sometimes initially help overcome problems resulting from poor preparation in the pregroup public phase. In TGC one cannot rely on physical presence to solve these problems. It is important that everything comes together in the first session and that nothing is left to chance.

The pregroup public phase is a very active process which will contribute to the success or failure of your first teleconferencing counselling group. The areas to consider in the pregroup public phase up to the point when the group is actually linked together in pregroup convening phase will now be discussed. In summary:

- keep records of teleconferencing group counselling related materials;
- think out the role of the agency;
- be clear about theoretical perspective;
- decide whether to work alone or with a co-leader;
- make preliminary decisions on selection, recruitment and composition of the group;
- make preliminary decisions on structural aspects;
- initiate contact with potential group members;
- make all practical arrangements;
- the fifteen minutes immediately prior to start of first teleconference session;
- awareness of potential technical problems.

Keep records of teleconferencing group counselling related materials

It is important to *keep records of TGC related materials* for future reference as consulting with a number of people will be necessary. These include formal records, minutes or notes from planning meetings and consultations. This enables reflection on the process involved in starting a teleconferencing counselling group, especially if this is the first one in the agency. In all probability it will take a while to get going and people's memory of previous meetings and consultations can fade, thus it is necessary to have something concrete to refer to. My first teleconferencing counselling group took two years from preparation to running the group. This was partly because TGC had never been used before and time was spent identifying a theoretical perspective for use within TGC as well as trying out new ideas. It was also a reflection of staff turnover in the agency. Acknowledging and consolidating thinking about TGC during this initial experience as well as subsequent experiences is important. Personal notes help this to happen consistently.

With experience, the process may take six months from start to finish, because one acquires a theoretical perspective and a better understanding of what is required by way of preparation. In an agency which has never used teleconferencing, it may take a year for its acceptance. It is better to invest this time and get it right. Once teleconferencing has worked, subsequent groups for other populations are much easier to pursue and take less preparation time.

Initially it takes longer to set up a teleconferencing counselling group than a face-to-face group because there is a transition period in which leader and agency need to develop a belief in the possibility of TGC. If TGC is not a well-established method of group intervention, tried and tested by others, it is easy to resist it as too hard or not possible. There seems to be such an overriding commitment to face-to-face group counselling that it may be difficult for TGC to be accepted. It takes some effort on the leader's part to make the shift and then to convince others about the efficacy of the technology.

Think out the role of the agency

The TGC will not occur in a vacuum. The environment in which the group will occur is significant, and part of that environment is the agency which provides the service. *Think out the role of the agency* in relation to the members of the intended teleconferencing counselling group. Make sure the group can be justified within the mission statement of the agency and be aware of any legal or technical aspects in dealing with specific client populations. If it cannot be justified, TGC will be viewed as draining agency resources and will be the first to go if there are cutbacks or downsizing. TGC requires agency commitment. For example, training others in TGC is necessary, otherwise there is no backup and, if the identified TGC person leaves, TGC stops by default. Although initially support was minimal from the first agency I worked with, the success of the first teleconferencing counselling group led to a training program for other staff members. Initiating new services becomes easier because of past successful experiences.

Just as it is difficult for leaders to make a shift from traditional face-to-face group counselling to TGC, this is also true for agencies. They need to go through a shift in belief system too. Agencies seem most receptive to TGC because it lowers costs and increases access. Their decision making is usually based on these two aspects, not on TGC per se.

Be clear about theoretical perspective

Although a range of groupwork models could be suitable, the model I have used consistently is the theme-centred interactional model (Anderson, 1984; Cohn, 1970; 1972; Regan, 1992; Shaffer and Galinsky, 1974). This model seems particularly applicable to short-term time-limited groups and very adaptable to the unique aspects of teleconferencing.

The theme-centred interactional model has a specific focus on content and process: process being the attention to the individual 'I' and the group as a whole 'We', and content being the attention to the theme 'It':

> The present model's proponents see as one of its major contributions the explicit attention given to both the emotional-experiential-interactional aspects on the one hand (the 'I' and 'We'), and to the group's cognitive task-learning function on the other (the 'It') (Shaffer and Galinsky, 1974, p.249).

This model also identifies the environment of the group as the 'Globe'. This is a particularly useful concept. It helps to make explicit that the teleconferencing is part of the environment as well as encompassing the location of participants.

Decide whether to work alone or with a co-leader

Once the support of the agency is gained, and a clear theoretical perspective identified, it is important *to decide whether to work alone or with a co-leader*. If a decision is made to work with a co-leader, that person needs to be involved in preliminary decisions regarding the group and be clear as to what theoretical perspective directs practice. Co-leading can be a positive aid in the balance between content and process. One leader can take primary responsibility for attending to the theme or task aspects of the group process, and the other to the interactional, maintenance or socio-emotional aspects. Initially when adjusting to lack of non-verbal communication it is useful to have this backup. One can also work with a co-leader to create strategies to handle differences encountered in TGC.

There is no need for rigid adherence to co-leader roles. There is in fact much cross-over between the two roles. However, when undertaking a first teleconferencing counselling group there is security in knowing what role each will take. Experience allows co-leaders a wider degree of flexibility. Switching roles is also a useful learning device.

Co-leaders provide support and, when new to teleconferencing, being able to consult before and after sessions to discuss group process is important. Co-leaders also provide different kinds of input. In my first teleconferencing group, having a leader with background knowledge of the client population and an awareness of resources available was essential. A co-leader can share the preparation tasks, whereas when working alone one is responsible for all the preparation.

Co-leaders also need to consider how it feels to be linked by optic fibres. Initially there is a sense of wonder that an optic fibre can contain so much emotion. As leaders should be familiar with the counselling process, it is the technology and its implications that requires additional debriefing. The leaders will be more concerned about the technology and the counselling process than members because of a feeling of responsibility for the group as a whole.

Working with a co-leader may also create interest in staff not included in the TGC. When two or more people are involved in TGC a sense of team builds around these people. Other staff may like to be connected with something that is innovative. It is the technology aspect that generates the interest, not the counselling per se. Staff are often interested in how it will work in practice and like to keep in touch with the process.

Make preliminary decisions on selection, recruitment and composition

Once a decision is made whether to involve a co-leader or not, begin considering the target population and *make preliminary decisions on selection, recruitment and composition* of the group.

In considering *selection*, participants must be able to understand and hear each other. If a participant has difficulty in hearing, one should check the possibility of special equipment. This should be made available and tried out before the teleconference. If there are still problems, this person should not be involved in a teleconferencing counselling group. Difficulty in hearing creates problems for the participant as well as the group. The individual misses the group interactions and group members are frustrated as they can't improve the situation.

Participants need the ability to verbalise their thoughts as well as to take in the comments and ideas of other group members. This is all without the availability of non-verbal communication. In TGC one only has what is said in the group, so participants need the ability to concentrate and remain focused.

Disabilities affecting speech, which create difficulties in a one-to-one telephone interaction, will not improve in TGC. The individual tries to get a point across, but others still may not understand. The group may then become centred on helping one participant, not on the group as a whole. Participants may pretend they understand rather than continue the struggle. In a face-to-face group, non-verbals make up for some of the loss of hearing, difficulty in verbalising and speech but this is not true in a teleconference.

However, in an on-going teleconferencing group, when members are connected, if at a later stage group members have problems, participants will tolerate a wider range of behaviours. Ritter and Hammons (1992) found this to be true in their work with people with end stage AIDS:

> Members were remarkably tolerant of painfully slow speech patterns, lost words and trains of thought, frustrations, irritability, distractibility or tendencies to convert abstract material into very concrete and literal terms (Ritter and Hammons, 1992, p.65).

Although TGC can be used with a wide range of clientele, it is of particular significance to those who in the past have been denied services because of lack of access, those experiencing isolation, or where anonymity is a strong determining factor.

Access difficulties may result from geographical separation, disability, lack of transport or limited time. Isolation may be experienced in both rural or urban areas. In both instances TGC links people going through the same experiences, and helps them to share.

TGC also offers anonymity and allows people to come together who may not be willing to participate in a face-to-face group. This may be because clients don't want others to know their situation, the topic is too painful to confront in person, or they don't want to be seen by others. Teleconferencing is not a place to hide, but it can provide transition space in these circumstances so that participants can move on, if they choose, to a face-to-face group with confidence or to other services if available.

As this is a counselling group, *recruitment* will be from personal caseloads or by referral from other workers. If the agency becomes committed to TGC, one needs to flag possible group participants and start a waiting list from which participants are selected depending on what specific needs the group is being formed to address.

TGC can handle a range of diversity in group *composition*. The teleconferencing counselling group members seem to search for what they have in common rather than differences. Members do not have as much information about each other as they would in a face-to-face group. Because members cannot see each other, physical differences are not as significant. Members are judged strictly on what happens in the group and not on other aspects which may be irrelevant. The ability of group members to see members as themselves seems to be greater, perhaps because it's easier to ascribe different attributes to a voice. A similar process can also occur in relation to group leader, as Williams and Douds found in one-to-one telephone interviews:

> The important point is that the telephone contact, much more than the face-to-face interview, permits the patient to make of the therapist what he will. This has the crucial implication that he can make of the therapist what he needs (Williams and Douds, 1976, p.85).

Make preliminary decisions on structural aspects

Once the composition and who will be recruited into the group have been decided, *preliminary decisions on structural aspects* can be made, e.g. size, number of sessions, length of sessions, time of day, closed group, location of group members, and cost.

Size. Teleconferencing technology can handle a number of participants with conventional receivers and more with speakers. However, when TGC is chosen other aspects need to be considered. A counselling group implies that all participants have time to express and meet their own needs and feel part of the group. A group consisting of eight, including leader(s) seems to allow each member the opportunity to speak and feel connected to the group. The internal process of the group redistributes the time and each week one person seems to become the special person who gets extra time.

At present I am only aware of short-term teleconferencing counselling groups, but there is no logistical reason why they couldn't be long term. However, my preference would be to reconstitute a short-term group and redefine the purpose

This paper focuses on teleconferencing counselling groups that are *short-term* with a specific purpose. Eight sessions on a weekly one hour basis have proved sufficient to develop continuing group process, to maintain the momentum of the group and to move through the stages of group development. These sessions offer the opportunity for intense involvement, recognition of gains and a springboard for future work. One still needs to be realistic as to what can be achieved in eight sessions.

Clients are aware of *time limits* from the outset. Teleconferencing time is measured in minutes and seconds. *It is not u*nusual for a teleconference to run 59 minutes and 2 seconds. However, there is a difference between real and subjective time:

> To the degree that a group is greater than the sum of its parts, it is not unusual to expect that given the presence of personalized subjective times, in interaction where there is the sharing of values, the emergence of a group culture, norms, contagion, etc. a common subjective group time could evolve. It is conceivable that members who share similar experiences are more likely to share a common 'time' clock, although, of course, it should not be taken for granted that a common frame of reference will have similar influences on all members (Alissi, 1985, p.9).

There is another aspect of time that goes beyond group subjective time. Telephone subjective time links to the awareness of being on a telephone and linking to past telephone experiences and not to group experiences. Telephone time is also linked to 'time is money', in that everyone is used to receiving telephone bills and aware of the costs involved in the use of the telephone. Group and telephone time weave together but in fact are quite separate. When the two overlap it is a very different sense of time than occurs in a face-to-face group.

The selection of the *time of day* for the teleconferencing counselling group is based on group members' need and agency policy. There is more flexibility because one can be at home or in a convenient location and does not need to consider time getting to and from group, transport and safety factors. This is particularly important with night groups. Some people would not attend evening groups because of concerns about safety. TGC eliminates these concerns.

The group is *closed* because of its counselling focus. By week two of teleconferencing counselling groups, participants begin sharing very private information. If an additional member is expected to join the group for the second and subsequent sessions, the group should be prepared in the first session. No new members should be allowed after the second session. To have a new member at later stages would disturb the process and slow down the momentum of the group.

Anonymity and previous lack of services seem to combine in such a way that individual participants and the group as a whole take risks very early in the life of the group. The leader must be prepared for this, for one can be caught unawares. Given the populations being serviced, many have stored up their concerns and when they are asked to share they seem to erupt. They are not interested in waiting. They want to get on with it. Their waiting time was in waiting for TGC to be available.

Integration of a new member would also be difficult because it takes time to get used to the technology and the lack of non-verbal communication, whereas the other group members have moved beyond this stage by the third session.

Members can be in a wide variety of convenient *locations*. The locations may be as diverse as: home, office, hospital, respite care hostel, at a relative's home, indeed anywhere in reach of a telephone. The degree of *comfort* may differ: sitting at a desk, on a comfortable chair, cushions on floor, lying in bed etc. *Refreshments* available may vary: favourite herbal tea, hot chocolate, coffee, and so on. In contrast, a face-to-face group is in one location, most likely with the same kind of chairs and refreshments are more limited. The *drop out rate* of TGC is low because of ease of access. Even if a member is not feeling well, he or she can still take the call and listen in the comfort of familiar surroundings.

In calculating the *costs* of TGC it is important to differentiate between direct and indirect costs, because the savings are made mainly in the indirect cost area. In TGC there are no travel expenditures- fares, petrol/car maintenance, time spent in travel which can't be spent working, organising travel for participants, child care, renting rooms etc. Even though TGC costs less than face-to-face group counselling, where access or distance issues are involved, there is still a cost involved. One needs to be aware of the budget allocated to TGC. It is important to negotiate for special rates for people with disabilities and to consider the advantages of evening or other special time rates when dealing with metered phone calls. Clearly it is important to check whether calls are metered as this relates to the cost.

Initiate contact with potential group members

The next step is to make *initial contact with potential group members*. In the pregroup public stage one needs to communicate to prospective members a clear purpose for the group's existence. Potential group members may be contacted personally by the leader or by other staff members. Decisions made about the structure of the group are conveyed to possible participants. What is said about composition, purpose of the group and use of teleconferencing will contribute to their initial responses and affect their expectations of what will follow. At this point expectations build and potential group members need to make a decision whether to participate and to be available at the agreed upon time.

One needs to make explicit that it is a counselling , not a discussion group that is being offered. Possible anxiety concerning the teleconferencing must be explored. Even though information is given, people have different expectations of TGC. The group experience is quite different from face-to-face counselling groups and may be hard to conceptualise. And for some who have never experienced a face-to-face counselling group, it might seem even more strange. It is sometimes helpful to compare the technology to talk-back radio or, for some, party lines provide a helpful comparison.

Even though explanations are given, when participants have been asked at the end of groups if TGC met their expectations, some have said 'no'. The outcomes were actually better than expected. There will always be an element of surprise when something new is tried. TGC initially has an amorphous quality. Participants put their own connotation on what it is to attain comfort. They begin a process of adjustment when they take part in a teleconferencing counselling group. It is a new way of working with groups and it takes time to get used to the technology and concept of TGC. However, telephones are easy to use and familiar so the transition comes about quite quickly.

As with face-to-face groups confidentiality and taping of sessions are discussed with participants both before and when the group begins. Taping occurs only if all agree. Even if all agree to taping and have given written consent, it is still raised again in the first session. In Australia if one wishes sessions to be taped there is a legal requirement that pips (the little bleeping noises that sound in the background to alert participants that time is passing) be included. This is to make clear at all times that taping is occurring. Concerns about confidentiality may also extend to the telephone company itself. This needs to be discussed openly if it is of concern to the participants. There has to be some element of trust in the technology for the group to eventuate.

Make all practical arrangements

With group membership established, ensure that *all practical arrangements* for TGC meetings are settled and fix a tentative date for the first meeting. Develop a booking form with the telephone company that meets your needs as well as theirs and try to book at least a week before the first session. Although the booking is made in advance, there is still the option of changing telephone numbers at the last minute. The booking form includes the following:

- A format in which it is possible to book *all sessions* at the same time. Although sessions can be booked on a weekly basis, if all sessions are put into the system together one doesn't have to call every week.
- *Names and telephone numbers* of all participants. It is not necessary to use names. If participants wish, they may be identified by telephone numbers or by pseudonyms. If they are concerned about confidentially they may take the telephone calls in what they consider a safe location. The leader is usually identified as the convenor or chairperson by the telephone company.
- A request for *call back* after each teleconferencing session with information on time and charges. This is an excellent way to know at any point what the group as a whole costs, as well as the cost for each session.
- If you are not taping ask that there be *no pips*. They can be distracting in counselling groups, but they do become softer and less distracting over time.
- A separate space for the *charge number* is necessary, because where the call is taken may not be where it is charged to. If an agency undertakes a large number of teleconferencing counselling groups, for accounting purposes it is much better to have all teleconferencing counselling charged to the same number.

The fifteen minutes immediately prior to start of first teleconferencing session

Some specific pregroup public preparation requiring consideration occurs in the fifteen minutes *immediately prior to the first teleconferencing session*. Anxiety levels may be high because, in addition to group considerations, concerns regarding the technology may emerge. Be aware that thought processes occur that are quite different from those before a face-to-face group. There seems to be a much higher and more focused level of anxiety, most of which is directed at the telephone

Waiting equals loss of *control*. Once given to the telephone company, the booking becomes their responsibility. One may wonder if they have forgotten the group and feel a need to check if everything is going as planned. As time passes and connections are made this need decreases. However, if something goes wrong reassurance is needed until faith in the technology is restored.

While waiting, be aware that the sudden ringing of the phone can startle. It is unwise to have spillable items in hand. Even though one knows it will ring, it still seems to startle because of concentrating so hard and worrying about not being connected. When connected one still has to wait until all members are connected and the waiting process can be tedious. The group will not be truly connected until everyone is on the line. Members do not have gradual entry into the group, it all happens at the same moment for everyone. You are all alone and then suddenly all are together. The connecting time is always shorter than it seems. Once all are connected anxiety lessens and now coffee/tea can be an enjoyable part of the process.

All *equipment* should be checked. The telephone is basic and the leader may prefer a 'hands off' telephone so that notes can be made as the teleconference progresses. If not familiar with such a receiver, do a test run. Get used to where the microphone is and how to be positioned comfortably, as the teleconference will last for one hour. Making notes with a hand held telephone is possible, but it is not as satisfactory. Participants only need their regular phones unless there are difficulties that require hearing-enhanced telephones or other technologies that overcome disabilities.

Paper is necessary to take notes. Because the telephone magnifies sounds, make sure paper is spread out close to the telephone so it doesn't have to be shuffled. Write the names of participants and leave spaces for notes. The lack of non-verbal communication makes it difficult to keep track of ideas without reference to notes. In face-to-face groups note taking can be found to be distracting to members. This is not the case in TGC. Other extraneous sounds like jangling jewellery can be magnified and distracting for the group.

A watch or clock is necessary to keep track of the time. Because so many things are happening at once, it is very easy to lose track of the time. Make sure the watch or clock is easily visible. If you go over your hour you are not cut off, but obviously it's important to keep to contracted time commitments.

If all the equipment checks out and preparation has occurred, all you need do is wait for the connection.

Awareness of potential technical problems

A few final comments about the actual connection process would seem to be appropriate here. Be aware of the possible *technical problems* that may occur that relate to the hook-up. In my experience *far more goes right* than wrong, but it is always best to be prepared for the worst. At the point of hook-up an operator is still available, try to deal with initial problems while she or he is still on the line. In different countries a variety of telephone technologies are used. Be aware of the technical problems that may arise in your own telephone system.

Now let us assume that any technical problem has been solved or, better, everything goes right. The group is now connected and ready to begin its first teleconferencing group counselling session.

Conclusion

This paper has focused on the preparation in the pregroup public phase necessary to ensure successful TGC. This includes: keeping records, role of agency, theoretical perspective, co-leadership, preliminary decisions on selection, recruitment, composition and structural aspects, initial contact with potential group members, practical arrangements, what happens in the fifteen minutes prior to the first teleconferencing counselling session and awareness of potential technical problems.

While at first sight TGC may appear daunting, there are many rewards in establishing teleconferencing counselling groups for people who might otherwise be denied services due to access difficulties, isolation and desire for anonymity. However, its success is dependent on careful preparation and planning.

TGC is in its infancy (Regan, 1992). Documentation is slight. Because of the small numbers presently involved, each group becomes a piece of action research and while some qualitative comment can be made, quantitative research and evaluation is yet to come. As more people establish teleconferencing counselling groups it is expected that a more quantitative approach will eventuate and a literature emerge.

References

Albertson, L.A. and Bearlin, K.S. (1977) *Melbourne Telelink: A Case Study.* Research Laboratories Report No. 7241. Melbourne: Telecom Australia.

Alissi, A.S. (1985) 'Time as a factor in social groupwork', *Social Work With Groups,* 8(2), pp.3-16.

Anderson, J.A. (1984) *Counseling Through Group Process.* New York: Springer Publishing Company.

Cohn, R.C. (1970). 'The theme centered interactional method: group therapists, as group educators', *Journal of Group Psychoanalysis and Group Process,* 2, pp.19-36.

Cohn, R.C. (1972) 'Style and spirit of the theme centred interactional method' in Sager, C.J. and Kaplan, H.S. (eds.) *Progress in Group and Family Therapy*. New York: Brunner/Mazel, pp.852-878.

Evans, R.E. and Jaureguy, B.M. (1981) 'Group therapy by phone: a cognitive behavioral program for visually impaired elderly', *Social Work in Health Care*, 7(2), pp.79-90.

Galinsky, M., Rounds, K., Montague, A. and Butowsky, E. (1993) *Leading a Telephone Support Group for Persons with HIV Disease.* Chapel Hill: University of North Carolina.

Gibbons, J. (1982) 'Telelink: teleconferencing and social welfare services', *Australian Educational Communications*, PLET, 21(4).

Hartford, M.E., (1971) *Groups in Social Work,* New York: Columbia University Press.

Regan, S. (1992) 'Theme centred conferencing counselling groups: working with vision impaired elderly women', *Social Group Work Monograph.* Volume 3. Sydney: University of New South Wales, pp.2-13.

Ritter, B. and Hammons, K. (1992) 'Telephone group work with people with end stage AIDS', *Social Work with Groups*, 15(4), pp.59-72.

Shaffer, J.B. and Galinsky, M.D. (1974). *Models of Group Therapy and Sensitivity Training.* New Jersey: Prentice-Hall, pp.242-264.

Trang, T. and Urbano, J. (1993) 'A telephone group support program for the visually impaired elderly', *Clinical Gerontologists*, 13(2), pp.61-71.

Tropp, D. (1987) 'Teleconferencing: supportive group work by telephone', *Australian Social Work,* 40(4), pp.31-44.

Williams, T. and Douds, J. (1976) 'The unique contribution of telephone therapy' in Lester, D. and Brockopp (eds.) *Crisis Intervention and Counseling by Telephone.* Springfield Illinois: Charles C. Thomas.

Suddenly the Light Went On: Using Groupwork to Empower Returning Students

Roni Berger[1]

This paper presents, illustrates and evaluates the use of a mutual support group to address unique needs of returning social work students. Returning students, who comprise a considerable part of the social work student body, are older, need to balance more responsibilities than their peers and share unique needs. A short-term open group was used to help them cope with their issues. Main topics were performance anxiety, fear of success, unrealistic expectations, guilt and the impact of returning to school on inter-personal relationships. Participants reported satisfaction with the experience and its results. Research is necessary to evaluate the effectiveness of support groups for returning students and shape specific guidelines for developing them within social work education.

'In the morning following our last meeting as I was standing in front of the mirror in my bathroom I felt like a bright light bulb started shining just above my head. It suddenly hit me that I do not 'have to'. I need to do what I can do, this is me and this is OK. I felt relieved and calm and that light bulb followed me for a couple of days'. The speaker is R., 46, who participated in a group for returning students in a School of Social Work.

A recent inquiry by the writer with colleagues on faculty in a dozen schools of social work across the country indicates that 30-50 per cent of the student body are returning students. These students pursue a

1. Roni Berger, PhD, CSW, Assistant Professor
Address for correspondence: Adelphi University School of Social Work, Garden City, NY 11530, USA

Groupwork Vol. 10(1), 1997-98, pp.21-29

degree in social work after they have been away from academic studies because they had another career or have been raising a family. The vast majority of them are women. They are older than the traditional student (Hovey, 1988; Johnson and Schwartz, 1989). Many of them are married, hold a job and have complex and sometimes conflicting responsibilities of running a family and of child care, often combined with caring for elderly parents. They are faced with the challenge of balancing school, work, parental, homemaking and marriage responsibilities. When they return to school they meet computer savvy students the age of their own children in campuses different than what they experienced in their college days and high demands for technical academic skills. While returning students have advantages because of their life experience and maturity, they also have unique problems. Some of the problems are directly related to re-entering school while others are indirect consequences of returning to the status of a student (Johnson and Schwartz, 1989).

Overwhelmed by the changes in role and status they are often intimidated, anxious, ambivalent, fearful, uncertain, helpless, lonely and with a shrunken self esteem (Erikson et al., 1976; Claus, 1986; Johnson and Schwartz, 1989). Consequently these students need programmes designed to address their unique issues and help them to adjust to a new career.

In spite of their considerable number among social work students, little has been written about their situation, strengths and issues and a review of the literature reveals paucity of reports on programmes designed to address their specific needs (McGraw, 1982; Wheaton and Robinson, 1983; Griff, 1987; Khan and Donlevy, 1991). Even though mutual support groups were recommended as a means to smooth the transition, only one report of such an endeavour has been published recently (Crampton and Holm, 1993). However, as this project was not designed exclusively for returning students and targeted also transfer students, it focused on a common goal of enabling participants to build an academic and social community but did not address the unique concerns of returning students.

The purpose of this paper is to present and illustrate how a short-term mutual-support group was used as a vehicle to empower returning students to help them effectively and efficiently cope with the stresses involved with their career change. The group was initiated by a collaborative effort of the Students Association and the faculty of the School of Social Work. It was designed to help participants enhance their coping skills and sense of competence by creating a safe environment in which they could share their experience of transition with understanding peers, validate each other's emotional reactions, reduce loneliness and discuss adjustment strategies.

The article includes three parts. First, the programme will be presented, then an evaluation by participants will be reported and finally, implications for social work education will be discussed.

The programme

Returning students were invited to participate in a short term open group. All returning students in all academic status were welcome. The group met six times bi-weekly for an hour in the evening and was facilitated by the writer of this article who is an experienced groupworker and groupwork teacher. Scheduling proved to be of utmost importance as it became quickly clear that there are three major populations: students who are available in the daytime because in the evening they have family or fieldwork commitments, those who work during the day and come to school at night and those who study mostly in the weekends. The existence of the group was announced on the voice mail of the school by the Student Association with recurrent reminders prior to each meeting.

Two to seven graduate and undergraduate social work students and one psychology student participated. A core of four permanent members was soon established and five additional members attended on a rotating basis. All participants were women in their late twenties to early fifties.

The group was designed as a mutual help group that constitutes 'people sharing certain characteristics who get together to provide one another with advice, emotional support, information and other help' (Barker, 1991, p.149). It was guided by a strength perspective that assumed the participants are functional, mature and capable individuals who are experiencing an existential temporary adjustment-related stress and can unite their abilities to effectively support each other to cope with their situation (Katz and Bender, 1976).

The open group model was chosen to accommodate needs of over-burdened participants and allow them to monitor their use of the group (Galinsky and Schopler, 1985). This format is appropriate for people whose life circumstances require more flexibility and people who feel over committed (Glassman and Kates, 1990). This choice proved to be compatible with the needs of some participants as expressed by one member 'it's good to know you can come whenever you feel you need some support and everything about school is overwhelming and yet not to have to come, it's like a present you can give yourself when you want it'. However, other members commented that 'the varied attendance made it more difficult to bond with some of the members and could block opening up'. The open format required addressing each session as a single session group. Leading a group within an educational setting posed unique issues regarding confidentiality and role confusion. Participants experienced diverse types of out-of-group relationships such as sharing classes and students' social activities. Moreover, participants and the facilitator had (and could have during the following semesters) contacts in their students-teacher roles. These potential obstacles, were used by participants as a means of tightening mutual bonding and helping each other to feel comfortable in the group by referring to a class they had together, common assignments and exams.

Nevertheless, the group quickly developed a sense of intimacy, warmth and bonding that was sustained throughout its existence. Participants were active, shared personal experiences and feelings and offered support and advice from their own experience.

During the work of the group several topics evolved that proved to be of common concern to the participants. Performance anxiety was a major issue. Participants expressed their expectation to be perfect spouses, super mothers and top students to justify the tremendous financial and time pressure required to enable them to go to school: 'I must be a strait A student. Otherwise how can I justify to myself spending with my daughter less time than she needs me?', 'I know I should allow myself and it is not the end of the world if I will not get a B, but...'. Self doubts and fears about 'not making it' have been recognised as typical of women who re-enter school and have been attributed to guilt and anxiety (Weinstein, 1980; Dickstein, 1984; Johnson and Schwartz, 1989).

Group members shared their specific experiences of unrealistic expectations of themselves and their ways to cope with them. Sharing is a powerful means of mutual help as it enables members to acquire a broader perspective and practical advice regarding their issues (Shulman, 1992).

As all group members acknowledge that this self expectation is not functional, each made a specific commitment to change their level of anxiety, developed a plan to achieve it and used the group as a sounding board for their ideas. Members helped each other by mutually validating feelings, offering practical advice about establishing reasonable goals and strategies to reach them. This led to a decline in self imposed stress. For example, one group member reported that she allowed herself to go to sleep the night before a test knowing that she is reasonably prepared but does not master the material 'I knew I will get a B and I felt I could live with that. When I will submit my resume nobody will ask me about my grade in Human Development'. One group member expressed letting go of her extreme self expectations in the words quoted in the beginning of this article and another participant reacted by asking 'where do you get your light bulbs?'. The speaker answered after some thought 'I don't get them, I make them' followed by a discussion of how each of them can create her own light bulb, being less demanding of herself and more accepting of her right to fulfil her needs free of guilt feelings.

Combined with the drive to succeed was fear of success: 'I constantly get top grades but I get depressed because I feel I do not deserve them... I think it's a mistake', 'I also feel that I steel the grades', 'on one hand I must succeed, but I must not be too successful to preserve my relationship with my husband'.

Guilt about going back to school was not uncommon 'It is not the fault of my family that I have a mid-term. They still should get a hot dinner'. However, these obligations created enormous stress that brought some of the participants to doubt their decision to pursue graduate studies, as P. expressed it: 'why do I need all this? I had a good career, a family. When I shared this with my husband he told me that this is not something I have to do but I chose to do and I can quit any day. This convinced me not to quit'. Group members shared experiences of coping with extreme difficulties, mutually validating their power to do things for themselves rather than allowing others to run their life and supported P.'s decision.

Following the group discussion, P. was able to report in the next meeting: 'For the first time I allowed myself to put my needs first. I did not spend all my time taking care of my husband who was sick and my children. I was home, everybody needed something from me and I sat there and wrote my paper'.

As group members started to trust each other more they shared issues related to the impact of going back to school on relationships with spouses and boyfriends and to express anger towards significant people in their life: 'my family does not accept the 'new me', they try to push me back to where I have been'. Even spouses who supported their wives' studies did not always provide much needed help: 'he complains that now I do not have time for him like I used to and blames me because now we cannot afford things we could before I dropped my job to go back to school'. Such complaints were identified by several participants as fear of the spouse's success: 'he is afraid that now that I am more educated than him I will leave him'. Disempowering was not limited to spouses. One group member described how her parents refuse to acknowledge her advice about a psychological problem of her brother, 'because they still see me as the little girl playing in the living room'. Participants encouraged each other's 'personal right to be the new you', 'to do what you have to do and not feel guilty about it. You cannot and should not take responsibility for your husband's issues' offering practical ways to address complaints assertively.

Each participant chose a specific goal towards which she wanted to work. Group members used feedback to help each other shape achievable goals and develop strategies to accomplish them and to cope with possible obstacles. Members reported that they made progress with their goals and pointed out that knowing that they have to report to the group and being prepared for diverse scenarios helped motivate and follow through.

As the semester neared the end participants expressed their feeling that the group had accomplished its purpose and time pressure because of finals and term papers led to group's termination.

Evaluation

Nine participants were asked to respond to six open questions regarding their experience in the group:

1. What was the experience of the group like for you?
2. What did you expect to gain from the group?
3. What did you actually get? What worked best for you?
4. Which of your expectations did the group not meet? Why? What could have helped to meet them?
5. What needs to be done in future groups to improve the experience?
6. Any additional ideas, thoughts and feedback?

Responses indicated an overall satisfaction with the group. It was evaluated as 'serving a much needed purpose'. Participants reported that the group helped them to relieve their anxiety regarding school related assignments and enabled them to be more efficient in writing papers and preparing for exams. One group member reported that she realised how common her concerns are among returning students and changed her previous intent to quit school. The group was perceived as a supportive experience in an accepting and intimate atmosphere as one participant said: 'I knew I will get empathy, I will be able to identify with others and I will have people who genuinely are interested and capable of helping me to figure out what to do and how to do it in a way that makes sense'. One member suggested that 'commonality of concerns that transcended age and life circumstances' made it easy to share and made the burden feel lighter. Another reported about the all-in-the-same-boat phenomenon: 'it was helpful to see that there are others with similar concerns and that with changes in life-style and making certain choices they could be overcome'. Sharing experiences enabled participants to better mobilise themselves to deal with problems productively (Shulman, 1992).

Group members reported that they gained better acceptance of their accomplishments and their limitations. As one member expressed it: 'I understood and came to peace with the fact that I can't do it all, no one can.. and it's OK'; another wrote: ' I learned to be proud of myself and my achievements'. Participants emphasised gaining legitimisation and effective skills to limit demands on them by others, to take time for themselves and to request help and consideration for their own needs without feeling guilty.

Several participants wished to see more people and more consistent attendance.

Discussion

A short-term open-ended mutual-support group was offered to returning students in the School of Social Work. Participants were women in their late twenties to early fifties who focused on discussing exaggerated self expectations, fear of success, performance anxiety, personal and family price of success and related guilt.

The group proved to be a positive and empowering experience. It included components of providing mutual support, sharing of useful information, skill development and was perceived by participants as therapeutic albeit it was not a therapy group. By sharing mutual concerns, validating feelings and giving support and advice, participants helped each other in a short time to gain higher self confidence and self acceptance, diminish guilt and develop better skills to request help and consideration of their needs.

The experience presented to the facilitator several questions. First, normative situation-specific issues of returning students may be 'contaminated' by personal clinical problems related to divorce, alcoholism and so forth. The facilitator is faced with a dilemma of navigating between diverse roles and balancing his/her prerogative in this specific type of group with professional ethical commitments as a therapist. Second, the issue of maintaining the boundaries between the different positions of a group facilitator and of group members proved to be very challenging and intricate, requiring the facilitator to be alert to where each group member comes from at any given moment as well as aware from which position s/he reacts. Third, cultural characteristics of participants need to be considered, since cultural factors have been proved to hinder development of the necessary levels of openness and willingness to share that are at the core of mutual aid (Liu Lo, 1993).

Based on this experience preliminary recommendations seem to emerge. First, it appears that there is a need for a support group for returning students. Offering it at different times will accommodate better the needs of diverse student populations. Information about the group should be included in the material provided to students in registration and introduced in the beginning of the year orientation and in practice classes. Facilitators of these groups should be extremely sensitive to covert messages because the double role of a group member-student may impact on participants' willingness to self disclosure. It is also suggested that short-term open-ended groups can be used to empower people who experience other types of stressful transitions.

Because this group is a pilot designed to open the field for systematic and comprehensive exploration it limited the scope of the current article to descriptive and anecdotal data, based on a small number of students. However, it raises questions to be studied by means of systematic research. First, it is of utmost importance to assess the impact of the group within the student body of the school. Exploring if participation in a group impacts on academic achievement or field work performance and examining effective models for such groups will enable us to enrich our understanding of group dynamics and develop more effective strategies for using groups to empower returning students. Also, a comparative analysis of different types of groups is anticipated to yield valuable and useful guidelines of responding to unique needs of returning students. Specifically, developing groups for specific populations such as closed women only groups for female students from a working class background. Such groups will enable us to look in depth at issues regarding gender and culture in their broader sense that were raised by this pilot. Lastly, evaluation could be developed to measure expectations of participants in the beginning of the group and the degree of meeting these expectations at the end.

Note

This paper was first presented at the 42nd Annual Meeting of the Council on Social Work Education, Washington DC, 15-18 February 1996.

References

Barker, R.L. (1991) *The Social Work Dictionary*. Second Edition. Silver Spring, MD: The National Association of Social Workers.

Claus, J.K. (1986) *Adult Students in Community College: Learning To Manage The Learning Process.* Paper Presented at The 70th Annual Meeting of The American Educational Research Association, San Francisco.

Crampton, B. and Holm, K. (1993) 'A learning community program for transfer and returning students', *Journal of College Student Development,* 34(6), p.439.

Dickstein, L.J. (1984) 'Psychiatric issues of women college students today', *Psychiatric Annals*, 14, pp.653-660.

Erikson, L., Kimmel, E.W., Murphy, M.T. and Newcomer, W.J. (1976) 'Back to school: the older than average student', *College and University*, 51, pp.679-692.

Galinsky, M.J. and Schopler, J.W. (1985) 'The patterns of entry and exit of open ended groups', *Social Work With Groups,* 8(2), pp.67-80.

Glassman, U. and Kates, L. (1990) *Group Work: A Humanistic Approach.* Newbury Park: Sage.

Griff, N. (1987) 'Meeting the career development needs of returning students', *Journal of College Personnel*, 28(5), pp.469-470.

Hovey, S. (1988) 'College degree programs for working adults', *On Campus* (Magazine of the American Federation of Teachers), May, pp.8-9.

Johnson, E.A. and Schwartz, A.J. (1989) 'Returning students' in Grayson, P.A. and Cauley, K. (eds.) *College Psychotherapy*. New York: Guilford Press.

Katz, A.H. and Bender, E.I. (1976) *The Strength in Us: Self Help Groups in The Modern World.* New York :Franklin Watts.

Khan, Z. and Donlevy, J.G. (1991) 'The college classroom and non-traditional students: employing effective adult learning principles and practices', *Journal of The Indian Academy of Applied Psychology*, 17(1-2), pp.51-53.

Liu Lo, F.W.C. (1993) *Is It Possible to Achieve Mutual aid in Groups in a Chinese Society?* Paper Presented at the XV Annual Symposium, Association For The Advancement of Social Work With Groups.

McGraw, L.K. (1982) 'A selective review of programs and counseling interventions for the reentry woman', *Personnel and Guidance Journal*, 60, pp.469-472.

Shulman, L. (1992) *The Skills of Helping Individuals, Families and Groups.* Itasca, Ill: F.E. Peacock.

Weinstein, L. (1980) *The Counselling Needs of Re-entry Women: Field Evaluation Draft.* Washington DC: Association of American Colleges, Project on the Status and Education of Women.

Wheaton, J.B. and Robinson, D.C. (1983) 'Responding to the needs of re-entry women: a comprehensive campus model', *National Association of Student Personnel Administrators Journal,* 21(2), pp.44-51.

A Group's Journey Through Separation and Loss: Therapeutic Groupwork with Children as a Social Work Intervention

Maria Neary[1] and Geraldine Brandon[2]

This article seeks to explore groupwork as an effective method of direct work with children. In order to examine this we have drawn from our experience of planning, running and evaluating a therapeutic group for girls aged 9-11 years while on placement at Thamesmead Family Service Unit.

The focus of this group was the difficulties these children experienced through separation and loss. Taking this as a central theme, we outline the importance of the need for groupwork to be firmly rooted in a theoretical base. In this case, the group has taken a psychodynamic model, drawing on a knowledge base of child development theory, concepts of attachment and mourning theory.

This piece of work analyses the relevance of direct work with children to help them express their feelings. We outline some of the techniques of play and activities used in the group which helped the process. Through evaluation methods, we conclude that groupwork is an effective method in direct work with children. We advocate groupwork with children as having the potential to tackle issues in a child centred way, being an essential support service for children in their communities.

The group captured the participant's - Michelle, Laura, Helen and Sharon's - journey through grief.

1./2. At the time of writing, the writers were on placement at the Thamesmead Family Service Unit
Address for correspondence: 104a Burnt Ash Road, Lee, London SE12

Background to the group

'The pain of separation from those we love is, for all of us, a devastating experience, but for the dependent child the whole of his or her world collapses and everything loses meaning (Fahlberg, 1994, p.133).

The work of the group focused on exploring the painful issues of separation and loss for children. The Family Service Unit in Thamesmead is a voluntary sector social work agency offering support to individuals, children and families in need in their local community. As a result of feedback from a previous children's group, where the girls said they felt the boys demanded too much attention, the need for a girls group was identified, to create a safe place for girls to express their feelings and have their needs met.

Planning began by initially defining our aims and objectives, making our value base and the legal context explicit, and setting up a referral procedure. Practical arrangements of dates, times, length of sessions, resources and supervision arrangements were organised. Planning the venue was particularly important as it was vital it became a safe and consistent space for the children.

The initial assessment was based on the referral criteria, and home visits where individual time was spent with each child and parent. This was vital in ensuring that each child was listened to and her wishes and feelings considered in relation to the planning of the group. These visits served to get a picture of the child's life in her environment, family dynamics and a view of the child's development, needs and strengths. Another important element was discussing with the parent the possible effects the group may have on the child, on their relationship and on the parent themselves, in stirring up painful issues which may not be fully resolved.

The group was made up of four girls who shared a common thread of experience; the separation from and loss of their fathers. Their home life meant that they were unable to explore the issue of separation and loss openly in a supportive and sensitive environment. The group was a closed structured group running for twelve sessions, each two hours long. We explored three main themes - identity, feelings, separation and change - with four sessions set aside to address these themes. Each session was structured using Randall and Southgate's (1980) creative cycle of a nurturing, energising and relaxing phases. The familiarity of following this structure each week had a containing effect on the group, as a means of making each child safe.

Theoretical framework

The theoretical framework underpinning the work was that of a psychodynamic approach, exploring key relationships, past and present experience, inner and outer reality. This approach:

> ... implies a recognition of the psychological forces motivating human behaviour and the importance of feelings in the client's life and in the client/worker relationship (Lishman, 1991, p.49),

We drew on the work of Bowlby (1961) in relation to stages of mourning, Fahlberg's work on children coping with separation and loss. We also used the theory base of direct work with children (Aldgate and Simmons, 1989). Another vital aspect was that of anti-discriminatory practice in groupwork, particularly challenging racism and sexism. The group was established taking into consideration the legal frame work of the Children Act, 1989, by devising clear child protection procedures, which were discussed with parents and with the children in negotiating ground rules in the first session.

In working directly with children, we felt it was important in the group situation to remember children are unique, and despite sharing similar experiences, these may have very different meanings for each child. Taking an overview on approaches to direct work with children, this group has taken guidance from Oaklander's (1978) interpretation in taking an active role in helping children express their inner feelings. As workers we took on a directive approach, seeking to provide the children with a means of expressing painful feelings safely. The groupworkers' role also rested on the reflection and understanding of the children's wishes, thoughts and feelings through the group process.

The activities used proved to help engage the children by creating interest and motivation. We felt it was important not to participate in the activities, but to facilitate, thus not distracting the children from their input. It was important also to be sensitive during activities, not to force the pace of work and to persevere with children looking at painful experiences. We planned and prepared carefully in relation to the games and activities used, considering issues of the children's development, concentration span and relevant emotional and interactional issues. We also endeavoured to use activities which allowed the group to reflect on and address the issues of difference and sameness in terms of race and family diversity.

The techniques used were selected according to the following structure:

1. In the nurturing phase a game was played which focused on building trust and developed listening skills.
2. In the energising phase a game was played designed to motivate the children and to develop co-operation skills. The main activity followed this which reflected on the theme for that session.
3. In the relaxing phase an ending game was played which served to bring the group together and to say goodbye constructively.

A range of techniques was used in the main activity to explore the theme of each session, for example, working with clay, artwork, collage, body painting, eco-map. How a particular session worked is described below.

In Session 6, on the theme 'How I feel as a girl' the children made a body painting, which proved to be a dynamic way of helping the children understand their feelings. A worksheet was used to help the children identify the feelings common to them, with a colour code to paint each feeling.

A worksheet was used to help the children identify the feelings common to them, with a colour code to paint each feeling, including: happy, unhappy, excited, angry, unloved, jealous, loved, guilty, confused, nervous.

The children then took turns to paint in the colours on a body shape, locating in their body where they felt each particular feeling. This involved considerable discussion about real events when they had experienced the feelings.

The children

The children in the group had different experiences of separation and loss, although all related to their fathers. It was helpful to locate the children within the grief process and try to understand the many behaviours and emotions displayed in the group.

Laura

Laura is aged 9 of white UK origin. Her parents separated four years ago, she lives with her mother and younger half-sister. Laura's contact with her father is irregular. He is now in another relationship through which Laura has two half-siblings. Laura was accommodated briefly by the local authority when her mother had a breakdown. Laura's mother has had other relationships since the separation, having another daughter, but this relationship has also ended. This man had been a significant father figure in Laura's life, and she now has no contact with him.

Laura's principal response to what has happened has been to become more adult like. She reflected this in the group with her preoccupation with adult concerns, for example, tidying the room, concern about other children's behaviour. Laura is the eldest child in her family and often cares for her sister at home. Laura's mother treats their relationship very much like a friendship.

Kroll identifies this behaviour in the early stages of grief, adding:

> ...an adult persona effectively provided a carapace, representing what I felt to be a manic defence in the form of a denial that had been lost, as well as a way of demonstrating how powerful and important a child still was (Kroll, 1994, p.96).

This behaviour may protect Laura from knowing or dealing with some of the more powerful feelings she may be experiencing towards her parents. Assuming responsibility for a parent over time could have serious consequences, where the child's own needs have not been met, due to the needs of the parent (Kroll, 1994).

In Session 3 - on the theme of 'My Family' - Laura found it extremely difficult to draw any representation of her family. Laura described the pain initially as a toothache, but later disclosed it was 'inside' which was hurting so much. The group helped her release some of this pain and she became less adult like. Laura was able to express how much she missed and thought about her father. In Session 6 on the theme of feelings, Laura was enabled to disclose feeling jealous, unloved and guilty due to her younger sister receiving attention and gifts from her dad.

Sharon

Sharon is aged 11 and of Afro-Caribbean origin. Given she was the only black child in the group, this was given consideration, acknowledging it was not an ideal situation. Sharon's parents divorced three years ago, following the death of her grandmother. Sharon remains in regular contact with her father, seeing him each week. Sharon's mother displays many unresolved feelings about the divorce, which has affected her relationship to both parents. She lives with her mother, older brother and sister.

Sharon exhibited immature 'babyish' attention seeking behaviour in the group, reflecting how she behaves at home and in school. Her participation needed much encouragement and motivation. Regression to an earlier stage of development in response to a crisis and as part of the mourning process is well documented (Bowlby, 1961; Murray-Parkes, 1972; Jewett, 1994; Kroll, 1994). It was hoped that the group, in providing a safe space with her peers, would help Sharon express some of her feelings. Sharon enjoyed regular contact with her father, although with him she also exhibited signs of regression through 'baby talk', thumb sucking and wanting to sit on his knee. Jewett advises:

> ...visiting allows the child, through trial and error to work not only towards accepting the situation, but making the best of it - through repeatedly being frustrated and letting go, the child gradually understands the reality of the loss (Jewett, 1994).

It was significant that in Session 7, Sharon introduced her father to the group, having been previously unwilling or unable to speak of him, by getting him to bring her to the group. From then on Sharon was more able to talk about her father, and her behaviour became more age appropriate.

Michelle

Michelle is aged 10, of white UK origin. Michelle's father committed suicide three years previously. Prior to this her parents had been separated and reunited. During the separation, her dad had a child, Michelle's half-brother, with another woman, with whom Michelle had developed a relationship. On her father's death, Michelle lived with her mother, older brother and younger sister. As workers, we acknowledged that Michelle's experiences of loss through death were significantly different to the other children's experiences; this was discussed on an ongoing basis in supervision to ensure the group was sensitive in meeting her particular needs.

Michelle's appearance was unkempt and she had difficulty in sustaining eye contact, using her long fringe to hide behind. She appeared to have a wall around her, expressing much of her feelings through anger. Anger is seen as an essential part of the mourning process and a healthy, necessary form of release, although through time it becomes a defence against acknowledging and expressing sad feelings (Fahlberg, 1994). Michelle expressed anger in the group, frequently directed at other children. She also had difficulties with this at school, being involved in fights with other children, and often came to the group displaying the scars of her confrontations.

Michelle was unable to talk to her mother about her father's death. Her exclusion from the cremation ceremony caused her much pain and in effect stole her opportunity to say goodbye, with her family. The chance to say actual thought out goodbyes has been seen as among the most healing things a child can experience (Jewett, 1994). Michelle's difficulty in coming to terms with her father's death was compounded by her mixed feelings towards him, as she had witnessed him being violent to her mother.

Michelle showed positive steps in making sense of her bereavement in the group. In Session 3 - 'My Family' - she drew a large tree with a bird sitting on a branch. She explained the bird was her father, as both she and her father believed in reincarnation. Her picture showed how she had fitted this loss into her understanding of life. Despite this positive step, her tree had a large hollow, a possible representation of the gap that remains. In Session 6 on the theme of feelings, Michelle disclosed her feelings of sadness, writing:

> I am sad my dad is not here today, it isn't fair other girls and boys in my school have got their daddies and my daddy's gone to heaven and he can't play with me today or tomorrow. I will never see him again, never, never again. I am sad today and I can't tell my mummy.

Helen

Helen is aged 10 of white UK origin. Helen's parents divorced four years previously. Contact between Helen and her father has been irregular.

Helen presented very much as a child in despair, showing indifference when the subject of loss was raised in the group. She frequently seemed passive and fatalistic about life. She showed difficulty in concentration, apparent forgetfulness when between her thoughts and words. In Session 3 - 'My Family' Helen was overcome by the task of drawing a picture of her family, drawing a picture would not be valued, and was surprised at group support and encouragement.

Helen's lack of display of emotion about loss seemed to point to a tendency for her to turn angry destructive feelings inward (Kroll, 1994). Helen's mother was unavailable at an emotional level to Helen, unable to bear any mention of her ex-husband. The outcome of children's experiences of loss is directly related to whether adults are able to tolerate their expression of strong feelings in a supportive way (Jewett, 1994). Helen's difficulties were also compounded by inconsistent contact with her father and his inability to keep promises. Helen awaited her birthday gift for months with an air of resigned hopelessness. This is identifiable with the second phase of grief - despair - which is also characterised by high levels of parental conflict (Kroll, 1994). Helen also demonstrated her preoccupation with death and destruction in story games where her stories were filled with blood and death. It was significant that Helen showed a preoccupation with food in the group; it is recognised that food can become a focal issue for children at this stage as such children can have difficulty in differentiating between feelings and hunger and emptiness (Jewett, 1994). In Session 6 - 'How I feel as a girl' in the body painting exercise, Helen located many feelings in the stomach area including feeling unloved, angry, nervous, and unhappy. this graphically displayed the range of painful feelings she experienced.

Working with the issues of separation and loss

The four children had a range of experiences of separation and loss, all having a degree of commonality but also significant diversity, as outlined above.

Jewett (1994, p.34) outlines the experiences of child coping with divorce:

> Separation and divorce involve both death and loss; the death of the family unit and the loss of the normal expectations for what life would be. But because there is neither a body nor mourning rites, the grief following a separation often becomes convoluted and fantasies abound.

In this way Laura expressed hopes that here parents would get back together, and Sharon was in some way required to take sides, making her father the 'bad' parent. Failure by their fathers to maintain contact with Laura and Helen left them feeling abandoned, with all the pain this involves.

With regard to death from suicide, Jewett (1994, p.30) states that this is particularly difficult:

> ...because of ingrained social stigmas and taboos about taking one's own life... children often feel that if the individual truly loved and cared about them he or she... would have made a different choice.

Self blame was a feature of Michelle's response, with her having difficulty in expressing anger and building trusting relationships.

Given the focus of the group on separation and loss, the ending of the group itself was structured to help avoid unresolved emotional cut-offs, and to allow the children the opportunity to work through a positive ending. The ending of the group was marked throughout the whole process by the use of a group calendar on the wall, which was referred to each week. Session 11 and 12, the last two sessions, focused on the task of ending the work successfully, to ensure the change and learning could be sustained beyond the life of the group.

In Session 11 each child made an individual group book, by which to remember the group. Each book contained a list of sessions, photos of the group, extracts as reminders of topics covered, and each child had the opportunity to write, draw and add to their books. This involved everyone writing in each other's book a 'goodbye' comment. This work was continued in the last session, which was partly to celebrate the group ending. Ritualised ceremony was used; the usual session ending game, and a cake divided into six sections, each with a candle which was lit and blown out, to take away. The use of ritual is helpful in managing loss and endings, but it has been eroded in British society today, resulting in endings and the grief process being more difficult. There was a great deal of anxiety, sadness and pain in the last sessions. This was highlighted by Michelle refusing to participate in the ritual of the candles and cake, or in the final ending game, instead hiding under the table in the room, watching from a crouched position. This was discussed, noting how sad and painful endings are for everyone at times, and each child managed to leave the group holding the ambivalent feelings and saying goodbye in a constructive way. the ending was important for us as workers and to the children as:

> [a] demonstration that people can say goodbye in a non-destructive way without a residue of angry or bitter feelings (Aldgate and Simmonds, 1992).

Given the central theme of separation and loss in the group, the ending of the group itself was of particular significance. This was invoked by structuring the ending of each session, and using the ending of the group as a process to understand and come to terms with other endings.

Evaluation

Evaluation was a continual and integrated part of the group, which helped highlight the achievements and limitations of the work. We received positive feedback from the children and parents in an evaluation game and final home visit, which established that the group aims and objectives were met. the children fed back that by being in the group they made more sense of the loss of their fathers.

Michelle explained this by saying that before she went to the group she had many questions about her dad, and at the end of the group some questions remained but others were answered. All of the group members fed back that they were glad to be given a chance to talk about their fathers. They also enjoyed being part of a group, in particular the games and activities. The group facilitated children meeting other children who shared similar experiences, and enabled all the children to realise they were not alone in their experiences and feelings. Indeed, the high attendance rate and active participation reflected the children's commitment to and benefit from the group.

One identified limitation was that there was only one black child in the group, which was acknowledged from the outset as far from ideal. Both groupworkers were white Irish women, and shared a strong commitment to anti-discriminatory practice. It was vital to ensure this child's needs were met, by incorporating activities and discussion which embraced difference. Sharon's participation was encouraged and racism challenged through discussion and setting clear boundaries in terms of ground rules on behaviour and language.

The fact that the group was a 'girls only' group was an essential element in its success, allowing an ethos which centred around the celebration of being a girl, as well as acknowledging the difficulties it presents and the diversity of experience.

A final limitation we acknowledged on completion of the evaluation centred around recording. The FSU has an open files policy, whereby users have access to their files. Recording the group proved to be essential for reflection on the group process and children's needs in supervision. A limitation in the recording was that the children were not involved in this process and did not see the records, as this was not addressed at the planning stage. This has led to a broader discussion in the staff team on how groupwork should be recorded, how group members should be involved, and some of the restrictions in the current system which are now being reviewed.

Conclusion

Through the experience of this group it is clear that children voyage through the grief process, in order to make sense of their experiences of separation and loss. Through groupwork, children can be helped to deal with the feelings of sadness, anger, denial and final acceptance in a sharing and supportive group environment. The group was a place where the children were accepted and helped to understand their many feelings.

It was of paramount consideration to keep the interests of the child in mind at all times and to listen to the children, particularly within the framework of the Children Act 1989 and the ratification of the UN Convention on the Rights of the Child. From our experience, we advocate groupwork as an effective approach to direct work with children. Groupwork with children has the potential to tackle issues in a child centred way, being a crucial support service to children in their communities.

As workers it has been a significant learning experience to share the joy and pain walking alongside these four children, on their journey of coming to terms with their experiences of separation and loss.

Acknowledgements

We wish to thank Mark Peak, Senior Social worker, for all his expertise and support as our supervisor. Also, to thank the children who participated in the group.

References

Aldgate, J. and Simmonds, J. (eds.) (1992) *Direct Work with Children*. B.T. Batsford Ltd.

Bowlby, J. (1961) 'Processes of mourning', *The International Journal of PsychoAnalysis*, XLII(4-5), pp.317-340.

Fahlberg, V. (1994) *A Child's Journey Through Placement*, British Agencies for Adoption and Fostering.

Jewett, C. (1994) *Helping Children Cope with Separation and Loss*. B.T. Batsford.

Kroll, B. (1994) *Chasing Rainbows: Children, Divorce and Loss*. Russell House Publishing Ltd.

Lishman, J. (ed.) (1991) *Handbook of Theory for Practice Teachers in Social Work*. Jessica Kingsley Publishers.

Murray-Parkes, C. (1972) *Bereavement: Studies of Grief in Adult Life*. Tavistock Publications.

Oaklander, V. (1978) *Windows to Our Children*. Real People Press.

Randall and Southgate (1980) *The Creative Cycle of Groups*.

Implementing a Novel Groupwork Model: Application of an Innovation-Developmental Process

Jerome R. Kolbo[1], Kimberly Horn[2] and Elizabeth Randall[3]

The best laid plans of group work innovators often go astray due to insufficient appreciation of the systemic complexities of implementing group models, once planned. Practitioners may spend considerable time and energy conceptually refining new group work models in order to meet the special needs of a particular target population. Yet those whose primary interests reside in the direct service arena may find their training and practice experience of limited value, as they attempt to negotiate for the variety of resources needed to deliver group services in accordance with the model they have laboured to develop. The innovation-developmental process described herein provides a framework to assist group work practitioners with transforming their innovations, specifically novel group work models, from conceptualisation to implementation. In order to illustrate the utility of this framework, we describe our efforts to develop, implement, and enhance adoption of groups for children at high risk for substance abuse.

Novel and specialised models of group work often result from practitioners' careful assessments of the needs or problems of specific target populations. Unfortunately, practitioners skilled in group work theory and technique are not likely to be equally skilled in the implementation of their models following conceptual development. The need for referrals, funding, space, staff support, documentation, training, evaluation, and other factors may create obstacles. These

1. Associate Professor of Social Work, University of Southern Mississippi
2. Adjunct Assistant Professor in Community Medicine, Prevention Research Center, West Virginia University
3. Assistant Professor of Social Work, West Virginia University
Address for correspondence: University of Southern Mississippi School of Social Work, PO Box 5114, Hattiesburg, MS 39401-5114, USA.

Groupwork Vol. 10(1), 1997-98, pp.41-54

Figure 1. Seven phases of the Innovation-Developmental Process.

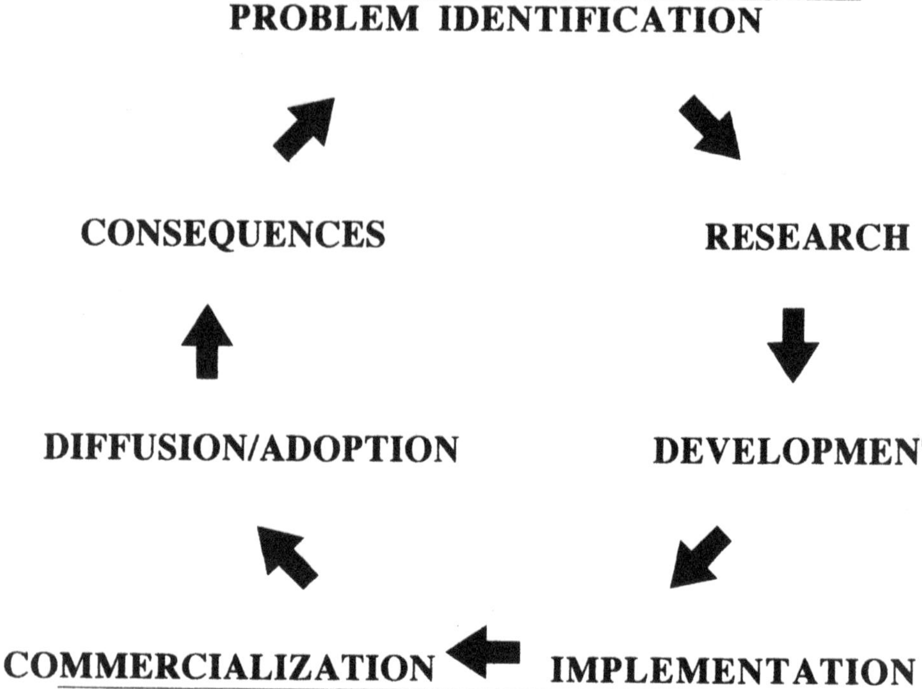

factors associated with implementation necessitate a series of negotiations within the economic and sociopolitical arenas in which group work practitioners may have far less comfort, familiarity, and training than they have in direct practice. Moreover, a fledgling new model that does make it off the drawing board and into practice may not readily garner the external support necessary for long-term maintenance. As such, its operational life span may be all too brief, however promising the approach.

The innovation-developmental process (IDP) (Rogers, 1995) described herein provides a framework to assist group work practitioners with transforming their innovations, specifically novel group work models, from conceptualisation to implementation. The IDP process, an extension of earlier empirical and theoretical work on diffusion theory (Rogers, 1983), delineates the decisions and activities that occur upon the recognition of needs or problems, toward goals of resolution and amelioration. Successful innovations move through a process of *problem identification, research, development, implementation, commercialisation, diffusion and adoption,* and *consequences*. This seven phase process is presented in Figure 1.

In order to illustrate the utility of IDP as it applies to group work innovations, we describe our efforts to develop, implement, and enhance adoption of a novel group work model for children at high risk for substance abuse. This group work innovation is a theory driven, risk-based primary prevention program for elementary age children of substance abusers. CHOICES (Children Having Opportunities In Courage, Esteem and Success), is a school-based program that supplements mainstream substance abuse education with peer support groups, peer mentoring groups, and academic networks (Horn and Kolbo, 1995; 1997). These program elements are designed to forestall maladjustment caused by exposure to familial substance use and abuse, and to prevent or eliminate increased likelihood of substance abuse by the children themselves. A major goal of the program is to promote general adjustment, emotional well-being, and social competence in children. In the following sections, examples of 'lessons learned' from the implementation of CHOICES over the past several years are shared as an example of IDP applied to social group work. We hope other group work innovators will find these examples helpful as they confront various systemic obstacles that may arise during the process of trying to implement new models of their own design.

Problem identification

The first phase in the IDP is identification of a need or problem. Group work practitioners are generally well-equipped to identify and define problems or needs through multidimensional assessments using clients, agencies, communities, and/or other group workers as additional sources of information.

> Four years ago, a group of school and community practitioners participated in a series of meetings to discuss escalating health and safety issues caused by the early onset of substance use in our community (as well as nationwide). Practitioners were concerned and frustrated by the lack of substance abuse prevention services available to young children in the community, particularly children who were at high risk for substance abuse. Although no specific target high risk population was defined during the initial discussions, everyone seemed eager for innovative prevention approaches. The developer (and now director) of CHOICES was a participant in these discussions and had experience working with children of people with

> alcoholic-related problems . She was aware that this population was underserved and at high risk for substance abuse. She proposed an innovation, a structured support group designed specifically for children of substance abusers. Upon hearing this proposal, other practitioners overwhelmingly agreed this was a population they felt most inadequately equipped to assist. An informal poll and assessment of the practitioners' collective experiences with children of substance abusers validated the need for services for the identified target population.

Even though there may be agreement about a specific need or problem, it is necessary to seek further clarification. Specifically, locating empirical support for an identified need or problem leads directly to the initiation of activities designed to create an innovation. This begins the second stage of the IDP, which is research.

Research

For the purpose of the IDP, research might include gathering information about the extent or scope of a problem; the history of previous attempts to resolve the problem; and the strength and valence of correlations assumed to be causally associated with the problem. Research may facilitate the production of theoretical models, clarify the nature of a problem and how it affects populations of interest, or delineate specific practice technology. Accordingly, it is important to determine 'state of the art' approaches to the identified problem. This may be accomplished through an evaluation of the existing literature.

While a particular group work innovation may be supported by published reports of successful efforts using a conceptually related approach, the absence of empirical findings in the literature need not necessarily result in setbacks. Gaps indicating the absence of services successfully addressing the problem may also support the need for an innovative group approach. Lack of empirical data may foster attitudes that practitioners must begin somewhere lest the population continue to go unserved. Furthermore, an absence of empirical findings does not preclude one from basing a group approach on theoretical models. Accordingly, group workers have opportunities to shape and mould group approaches by selecting and integrating the most relevant theoretical models or strategies.

> After identifying a need for prevention services for children of substance abusers in our community, we sought literature that

would support our assessment, facilitate the development of the novel group work model, and generalise to the community at hand. In order to learn more about the current state of knowledge, we spent several weeks reviewing relevant research findings at a local university library. There was a dearth of empirical information regarding primary prevention efforts with elementary age children of substance abusers. Thus, during the initial conceptual development of CHOICES, the majority of time was spent examining various theoretical perspectives and interventions with related at-risk populations, which were the primary influences on the emerging design of the model.

Since understanding the current state of knowledge does not guarantee the successful implementation of groups, research does not end with a review of the literature. IDP requires an assessment of potential sources of support or resistance, existing and available resources, and potential financial costs and benefits. Internal and external support for the group is necessary to increase chances of successful implementation. This is consistent with Rogers' (1995) core premise that widespread acceptance and adoption of any innovation occurs in a complex sociocultural matrix, frequently influenced more heavily by considerations of social desirability and custom than by any objective appreciation of the excellence or utility of the innovation.

Prior to implementation, novel group work approaches are most vulnerable to political, economic, and administrative influences (Gilbert, 1990). During efforts to foster internal support, group workers should anticipate and identify potential concerns, such as reservations expressed by directors or administrators in the host settings (where the innovation is to be implemented). Internal support must also be obtained from direct-line staff (individuals who deliver the group model) and any other personnel who will be involved in the implementation and delivery of the innovation. This might include clerical or support staff, records technicians, security or physical plant personnel, or others depending on the setting.

Our desired host settings were the public elementary schools. Individuals most likely to serve in direct-line roles (implementors) were school counsellors. Before implementing CHOICES groups in any school, we arranged inservices for the teachers, principals or other school personnel who were to be indirectly involved in the implementation process. During the inservices, we provided basic information about the target population, goals and objectives of

> CHOICES, and approaches for working with the target population in the classroom. We tailored the inservices to fit the needs and concerns of our audience by indicating how the benefits of the program extend beyond the students to the teachers and the schools. For instance, we pointed out that children who feel better about themselves tend to perform better in the classroom, and that student performance parallels teacher satisfaction. We observed that teachers who received inservices were more supportive of the program.

Early in the innovation-developmental process, perceived concerns and interests of external constituents, such as consumers, community leaders, and community agencies should also be recognised (Abramson, 1983). Determining the concerns and interests of these constituencies is crucial in order to identify potential external sources of ideological support or resistance. Further, some sources may possess assets such as potential funding, personnel, equipment, supplies, and physical space.

To attract ideological or financial support for the innovation, gaps between existing needs and available resources should be documented (Glisson, 1981). In addition, potential costs or benefits (that is, public relations, visibility, tax deductions, free services) for target populations, agencies, and communities at large should be determined. The assessment of resources not only serves to avoid the duplication of services, but may provide additional rationale for implementation of the group, particularly if there is a void.

> The director of CHOICES aligned herself with various committees in the community addressing substance abuse and related issues. Committee involvement allowed opportunities to initiate contacts and receive valuable information on pertinent policies and agendas in the community. Further, committee participation presented opportunities to discuss the innovation and generate support from key players in the community. As a result, both the director and the program became more visible and accessible to community agencies and practitioners.

Development

The third phase of IDP, development, is defined as the process of putting new ideas into forms that meet the needs of potential adopters of the innovation (in the present example, potential users of CHOICES in additional school systems and other communities). Many of the decisions about the form the innovation needs to take will grow directly out of the research activities undertaken in the previous phase. Yet much more information in which to make decisions is obtained through an ongoing information exchange with the potential adopters.

This phase of the IDP can be one of the most difficult and yet rewarding times for both the group worker and potential adopters. Innovation development is, most of all, driven by the exchange of technical information in the face of a high degree of uncertainty (Rogers, 1995). The struggle of the innovation-developer to explore, understand, and even meet the needs of potential adopters is necessary in order to make improvements in the innovation.

> As initially proposed, a structured support group (SSG) was developed and delivered to three elementary schools. The SSG was designed to provide emotional and informational support in structured peer groups led by trained facilitators (i.e., social workers or school counsellors). Through ongoing discussions with direct-line staff and review of the literature during the piloting of the SSG in the three schools, additional strategies were identified for better serving these children.
>
> The two additional components that emerged through these discussions were designed to enrich the original group work model . The first of the two new components was an academic support network of teachers designed to supplement primary classroom instruction and home study time. The second new component was a mentoring group composed of children who successfully completed the SSG. Mentors were matched with younger children participating in one of the SSGs, and served as facilitators of healthy and productive peer relationships within the school setting.
>
> A continual review of the literature, regarding technological advances in prevention strategies with this and other at-risk populations, validated the changes in the form of the CHOICES program that occurred through the exchange of information between the group worker and the direct line staff. Specifically, the empirical literature suggested that successful prevention strategies consisted of multiple components designed to address specific risk factors, with two or more strategies employed conjointly to address each individual risk factor (see Horn and Kolbo, 1995, for a review). Consequently, we felt the innovation was ready for the next phase of the IDP.

Implementation

Prior to this point, the IDP has been 'a strictly mental exercise' (Rogers, 1995, p.172). Implementation involves behaviour change; here, the innovation is actually put into use. It is important to package the innovation in a way that is 'user-friendly' and generalisable.

> The direct-line staff received detailed manuals for facilitating each component of the program and at least 15-20 hours of hands-on training. Training was provided by the CHOICES director in the host settings. Counsellors entered a co-facilitating role with the director in each school. After co-facilitating at least 10 sessions, counsellors were permitted to proceed with other groups independent of the director. Some counsellors, however, preferred to continue co-facilitative relationships with the director.

Regular consultation with direct line staff promotes integrity of implementation (Corey and Corey, 1992). Constructive and positive feedback to staff about their efforts help to maintain staff commitment to the group work innovation. Moreover, enhancing their knowledge and providing consistent feedback may increase the likelihood that plans and procedures are carried out as indicated.

> The social worker who developed and initiated the CHOICES innovation maintained leadership of the program. Direct-line staff in the schools brought CHOICES - related issues or concerns directly to her. If further consultation was needed, other channels were engaged, such as respective principals or teachers. Regular meetings were held with counsellors individually and together to discuss progress and give and receive feedback. This created a sense of unity in the implementation process.

Commercialisation

Commercialisation is defined as the production, manufacturing, packaging, marketing, and distribution of a product that embodies an innovation (Rogers, 1995). The analog of this process for social group work is the dissemination of information concerning the availability and performance of an innovative group work model to potential adopters. Innovations should be put into tangible forms for this audience, such as structured manuals or curricula.

Each component of CHOICES includes a facilitator manual. SSG curricula (Horn, 1996) are provided to counsellors; Academic Channels to Ensure Success (ACES) manuals (Horn, 1997a) are provided to academic tutors (usually teachers); and Healthy Lifestyles Peer Mentoring (HeLP'M) manuals (Horn, 1997b) are available to other designated facilitators.

Although most group workers neither maintain proprietary interests in their innovations nor charge for materials beyond production and mailing costs, the fundamental principles of commercialisation remain useful for 'selling' novel ideas to potential referral and funding sources. Given current political and financial realities, funding for novel group approaches is limited (and competitive). Groupwork models based on demonstrated need, sound theory, empirical support, and goals consistent with the host settings are more likely to be supported (Turnbull, Galinsky, Wilner, and Meglin, 1994). It may be important to present an innovation as a product that encompasses these factors. Presentation of an innovation as a product is enhanced by an effective written proposal or brochure. These materials increase an audience's (i.e., potential users, host settings, or funders) understanding of the innovation, render the innovation more defensible, and project an image of long-term investment. A proposal or brochure is most convincing when it is adapted to each specific audience.

We developed a variety of printed materials describing CHOICES - each geared toward a particular audience. For instance, detailed and extensive proposals (inclusive of research and evaluation) were presented to funding agencies; program summaries (inclusive of program goals and objectives and general outcomes) were provided to school personnel and parents; brief program descriptions (inclusive of goals and objectives) and referral forms were provided to school and community practitioners; and one-page flyers were available to the children. We also developed a program brochure for general audiences. The reading levels, graphics, and stylistic elements in each printed format were adjusted for each particular audience.

Diffusion and adoption

Diffusion is the process by which an innovation is communicated through relevant channels over time among the members of a social system (Rogers, 1995). Adoption is the decision to put ideas to use; to implement the innovation in a new setting or context. Five attributes of innovations have been associated with higher rates of diffusion and adoption: *relative advantage; compatibility; complexity; trialability;* and *observability.*

Relative advantage

Relative advantage refers to the degree to which an innovation is perceived as better than the approach it supersedes. If practitioners in the host settings view the proposed innovation as more beneficial than existing services, the adoption is more likely to occur. Moreover, the rate of adoption may be even higher if there are no existing services for the identified need. It is important to note that innovations involving prevention are adopted more slowly because of the hosts' difficulty perceiving an immediate relative advantage. Non-preventive innovations are associated with more immediate results and adopted sooner.

> We were fortunate that our innovation, although preventive, addressed highly prioritised concerns on the part of practitioners in the host settings. Counsellors identified children of substance abusers as being at risk for both the early onset of substance abuse and immediate adjustment difficulties. When presenting CHOICES to the host settings or others, we emphasised the potential, immediate advantages of the program, such as improved academic performance, self-esteem, and social and coping skills.

Compatibility

Compatibility refers to the degree to which an innovation is perceived to be consistent with existing values, past experiences, and cultural contexts shared by potential adopters of the innovation (Garland, 1992; Glisson, 1981). For instance, a women's group may not be accepted if based on feministic ideology to an extent that is intolerable in a strongly patriarchal society. Effects of previously introduced innovations (i.e., groups) will also have carry-over effects as new models are introduced. For example, a therapy group for clients with chronic mental illness which may have been too stimulating or confrontational may dampen adoption of new group work models thereafter. Compatibility of a novel group model may be affected by how the innovation is named or framed. The group worker may need to think how to position the innovation, point out similarities to other well-received programs, and make sure that ideological or methodological distance is maintained from models that have not been valued by potential adopters.

The director of CHOICES was affiliated with a respected agency in the community; a local drug and alcohol partnership project. This project was widely visible in the community, and since the community partnership project and host settings had similar agendas around substance abuse prevention, CHOICES was viewed as a compatible service.

Complexity

This refers to the degree to which an innovation is perceived as difficult to understand and use. Quality and integrity are more likely to be maintained where a clear, standardised process has been articulated. Procedural guidelines are helpful to direct line as well as administrative staff. Group participants are also more likely to have positive experiences if they are oriented into the group's process and socialised into their role as participants (Corey and Corey, 1992). All should know the goals, objectives and procedures, as well as their rights and responsibilities at a level of understanding appropriate to their level of involvement.

We provided school counsellors with READY, SET, GO Checklists. The checklists reduced the program delivery process to four manageable phases with clearly defined steps. Phase one included pre-selection procedures while phase two covers methods for the screening and selection of participants. Phase three described the actual delivery of the group services, and the final phase outlined steps for evaluation. Children were also informed about the goals and objectives of the program during a private pre-group orientation interview.

Trialability

Trialability is the degree to which an innovation may be tested on a limited basis (piloted). Potential adopters are far more comfortable considering an innovation if they need not make a complete commitment (of time, hope, or resources) in the absence of encouraging preliminary data. If possible, the data should be gathered experientially (i.e., via a positive personal experience with the innovation). Similarly, as consumers, the patterns of selection and acquisition of all sorts of goods in our society would be dramatically altered if retailers across the country rescinded their relatively liberal return policies.

Once approved for implementation in the selected host settings, CHOICES was implemented on a trial basis. The 'trial run' (pilot) of CHOICES originally occurred with 20 children in three schools. Each school had the option of continuing or discontinuing the innovation after the trial period, as CHOICES was never a mandated program in the school system. As mentioned previously, the trial period provided opportunities to further develop the innovation, as well as conduct a preliminary evaluation and modify the group curricula. Findings from the trial period were sufficiently favourable that the initial host schools adopted the program.

Observability

This is the degree to which an innovation's results are visible to others. These results stimulate enthusiasm, creating a ripple effect which helps spread the word. Depending on the innovation, this process may develop more or less naturally due to substantive numbers of people who have been influenced by the model, either as facilitators, supporters, or clients. Smaller scale groupwork models with fewer participants, while of significant benefit to their clientele, may be disadvantaged in this regard and tend to go unrecognised. Groupwork practitioners finding themselves in this position may need to consider increasing levels of activity such as preparing articles, leading workshops, or conducting inservices for related agencies in order to increase the regional visibility of their models.

Upon the adoption of CHOICES by the original hosts, other schools began requesting the program. The counsellors who assisted in its delivery began talking to other counselors about the positive impact of the innovation. By the second year, CHOICES expanded into ten schools. In fact, word began to spread about CHOICES at various levels in the state and requests were made by schools in several other counties. Due to the growing awareness of the program and discussions among direct line staff in numerous county systems, statewide expansion is presently being explored.

Consequences

The final phase of the IDP includes monitoring the changes that occur as a result of the adoption or rejection of an innovation (Rogers, 1995). The analog of this concept for human services is program evaluation. For our purposes, this is divided into three factors: the evaluation of process, outcome, and impact. Process evaluation is intended to determine whether the groups were implemented as designed. This objective requires the receipt of ongoing feedback from participants and those in direct-line positions as to whether procedural guidelines are being followed as outlined. Outcome evaluation is used to assess the extent to which the groupwork achieved its desired effect. This is accomplished by taking measures of the identified problem(s) prior to and following the completion of the group. Impact evaluation is used to determine whether the outcome in the host setting really has any impact in the broader community. Impact evaluation requires additional data beyond that which is collected by the groupworker (that is, state or national survey data on specific issues).

> Process, outcome, and impact evaluation were integral aspects of the design of CHOICES. Standardised reporting by teachers, counselors, and the children have provided process evaluation data to help determine whether the CHOICES program was implemented as intended. Measures of targeted risk factors were administered to the children prior to and after their completion of the program. These measures provided outcome data used to determine whether the risk factors were moderated or eliminated as a result of the children's' participation in CHOICES. As the children become older and comparable state and national data drawn from the general population on substance abuse are available, an impact evaluation will be conducted. Currently, data from process and outcome evaluations are regularly provided to sponsors, host settings, and direct line staff (see Horn and Kolbo, 1997, for a review of the findings).

Conclusion

The best laid plans of groupwork innovators often go astray due to insufficient appreciation of the systemic complexities of implementing group models, once planned. Practitioners may spend considerable time and energy conceptually refining new groupwork models in order to meet the special needs of a particular target population. Yet those whose primary interests reside in the direct service arena may find their training and practice experience of limited value, as they attempt to negotiate for the variety of resources needed to deliver group services in accordance with the model they have laboured to develop. Needed resources may include, but are not limited to: space, time, staff, referrals, a funding or fee structure, recording forms, printed program materials, an evaluation plan, agency or community support, and backing from colleagues. The social context in which these resources are to be granted (or withheld) must be carefully considered at each step along the way.

The IDP which has emerged as an outgrowth of diffusion theory provides a framework to help guide groupwork innovators through these complexities as they seek to put their ideas into effect in the real world of practice. This paper has described an application of the IDP to the task of implementing CHOICES, a groupwork prevention program for school age children at risk for substance abuse. It has been our hope that other groupwork professionals will profit from this example as they try to translate their ideas into realities, where they stand to do the most good; in the lives of those who are in need.

References

Abramson, J. (1983) 'A non-client-centered approach to program development in a medical setting' in Weissman, H., Epstein, I. and Savage, A. (eds.) *Agency-based Social Work*. Philadelphia: Temple University Press, pp.178-187.

Corey, G., Corey, M. S., Calanan, P. and Russell, J. M. (1992) *Group Techniques*,. Second Edition. Pacific Grove, CA: Brooks/Cole.

Garland, J. A. (1992) 'Developing and sustaining group work services: A systemic and systematic view', *Social Work in Groups,* 15(4), pp.89-98.

Gilbert, M. C. (1990) 'Developing a group program in a health care setting', *Social Work in Groups,* 12(4), pp.27-44.

Glisson, C. A. (1981) 'A contingency model of social welfare administration', *Administration in Social Work,* 5(1), pp.15-29.

Horn, K. (1996) *CHOICES: A Structured Support Group Curriculum for Children at Risk for Alcohol and Other Drug Abuse*. Morgantown, WV: Pepper Press.

Horn, K. (1997a) *Academic Channels to Ensure Success (ACES): A Guide for Teachers Working With High Risk Children*. Morgantown, WV: Virginia Printing and Publishing.

Horn, K. (1997b) *Training Children At Risk for Drug Abuse as Healthy Lifestyle Peer Mentors: A Facilitators Guide*. Morgantown, WV: Virginia Printing and Publishing.

Horn, K. and Kolbo, J. R. (1995) 'Risk-based primary prevention strategies for elementary age children or alcoholics: A resource for social workers in the school environment', *School Social Work Journal,* 19(2), pp.1-14.

Horn, K., and Kolbo, J. R. (1997) *CHOICES: An Application of a Cumulative Strategies Model with Children at Risk for Drug Abuse*. Manuscript submitted for publication.

Rogers, E. M. (1983) *Diffusion of Innovations*. Third Edition. New York: Free Press.

Rogers, E. M. (1995). *Diffusion of Innovations*. Fourth Edition. New York: Free Press.

Turnbull, J. E., Galinsky, M. J., Wilner, M. E. and Meglin, D. E. (1994) 'Designing research to meet service needs: An evaluation of single-session groups for families of psychiatric inpatients', *Research on Social Work Practice,* 4(2), pp.192-207.

Applying a Strengths, Competence and Empowerment Model

Anna Nosko[1] and Margot Breton[2]

Introduction

In a recent paper, Breton and Nosko (1995) identify four principles which, they argue, should guide groupwork practice with women who have experienced abuse from their male partners. The principles reflect the belief that theories about violence and abuse should be subordinated to the reality of the women's situations as experienced and defined by the women and not vice versa, and therefore that it is imperative to stop looking at the women through the lenses of theories. Breton and Nosko insist that a change of theoretical lenses does not suffice, for these lenses always distort. Whether the theoretical perspective is 'clinical', 'political' or somewhere in between, and even though it may represent the best and the latest research, it cannot accommodate the vast range of experiences the women report (on this point, see for example, Nurius et al., 1992). This is not to say that theories are useless, or that they should not inform practice (which would be impossible anyway), but simply that they should not predominate and consequently warp the women's reality.

Over the past year, these principles were systematically tested in two groups in which one of the authors of the present paper was a co-leader. Four components of groupwork practice - planning, power, leadership, and use of resources - which were significantly affected by the application of the principles will be discussed herein. We

1. Family Services Association of Toronto.
2. Faculty of Social Work, University of Toronto.
Address for correspondence: Faculty of Social Work University of Toronto, 246 Bloor Street West, Toronto M5S 1A1, Canada.

begin by reviewing these principles and briefly describing the two groups, and we then report and discuss our findings.

Part one: four practice principles

The four principles are essentially the same as those which guide social work practice focused on strengths, competence, and empowerment (see for example, Breton, 1994; Cowger, 1994; Mullender and Ward, 1991; Saleebey, 1992). The first principle is that workers *demonstrate respect for the women.* This means that workers:

1. *let each woman tell her story* and use her new-found voice to 'name [her] world' (Freire, 1993, p.159);
2. *believe the women* and accept their representation of their situation as 'legitimate knowledge' (Weick, 1992, p.23);
3. *facilitate the process of consciousness-raising*:

   a. affirm the actual and potential competence and strengths of the women, emphasising 'how they have survived thus far' (Goldstein, 1992, p.32);
   b. confront the oppressor within (Freire, 1993), challenging negative self-images and self-evaluations;
   c. help the women to identify the common social, political, economic and cultural contexts of their situations: the workers should encourage diverse ways of dealing with these situations, including various forms of social action, but it is up to the women to choose what to do with the awareness they develop of the interconnection of issues.

The second principle flows from the first: it is that workers *base all interventions on member self-determination.* This requires that workers: first *trust the members*, stimulating the emergence of a mutual-aid system which acknowledges that the women are the experts at helping each other and mobilises their competence and strengths; second, *identify and affirm what the women want*, even when a member chooses to stay with an abusive partner, for it is *not* the workers' prerogative to dictate what another person should want. To challenge, discuss, and confront are in the workers' rightful domain; to pretend to know what is best for other people is not. Heeding choices and decisions that appear and may well be unsafe provokes anxiety in workers. However, the alternative is to disregard self-determination. It is the workers' responsibility to offer mutual-aid groups as part of 'a continuum of services specifically designed to enable [abused women] to choose whether or not to stay with their abusers' (Davis and Hagen, 1992, p.16), making sure that the women are informed about other possible choices and have the opportunity to weigh the consequences of their decisions. Beyond that, they have to recognise an individual's right to choose what to do. Even the notion of 'contracting,' as a mechanism to insure self-determination and to establish the conditions under which the group will operate may have to be jettisoned if the women interpret it as a constraint which locks them in a situation and once more makes them feel controlled.

The third principle is that of *individualisation*. For the principle to be congruent with a focus on strengths, competence and empowerment, workers must:

1. *Eschew pre-conceived plans and solutions*, 'generic' goals and all other forms of 'homogenisation of clients' (Rapp, 1992, pp.51-52) *and of groups*, as Breton and Nosko add. This involves a flexible approach to group structure: an open-ended or closed format, for example, will depend on the needs of the group at various points in its evolution, and termination will be individually-tailored, each member's coming about when she has achieved the goals she has set for herself and does not believe the group can be of further help;
2. *Reject labels* such as 'abused women' and 'abused women's group', seeing the women as whole persons, not just as 'victims'. This does not mean rejecting the fact of victimisation, but it puts the accent on the women as active subjects who can 'tak[e] responsibility for their lives' (Hartman, 1983, p.134). Seeing the women as whole persons demands that workers:
3. *Promote a group context and encourage group programs in which the women can demonstrate and share their specific strengths*: the group should enable the women to translate into action their changing ways of thinking and feeling about themselves.

Knowing that groups eventually end, post-group support which endures over time should be ensured. Therefore, the last principle is that workers *make maximum use of natural supports in the community*. This entails that workers:

1. *perceive the community as a resource* (Sullivan, 1992): identifying natural helpers as well as existing services such as recreation centers, libraries, and Ys, informing women about

these people and services, and connecting them to each other, if the women so wish;

2. *modify existing structures or create new structures to meet the members' needs* (Wood and Middleman, 1989): where personal natural support networks are non-existent, for example, workers would encourage group members to see themselves as the first 'links' in an on-going natural support system;
3. *create partnerships in the community* (Breton, 1994): by collaborating as partners with natural helpers and community services and institutions, workers can help the women to perceive themselves as members of a community, and to integrate and find supports in that community.

Part two: the groups

The groups are sponsored by the Family Services Association of Toronto, which has done this for over a decade. They meet in a multi-service center which has a health clinic, a legal clinic and a counselling unit. One group is led by two social workers, the other by one of these social workers (co-author of this paper) and a nurse. Working out of a multi-service center helps the leaders to maintain a broad perspective on the social context of the group as well as on the members' personal issues and needs - it serves as a reminder that violence against women is a social problem, and that interdisciplinary cooperation is essential to effective service (see, for example, Horton and Johnson, 1993).

The group led by the two social workers consisted of eleven members, of which an average of six or seven would show up on a regular basis. It was left to the group members to regulate their own attendance after the leaders explained that for the sake of having a group experience, it was important for them to attend as regularly as possible. The eleven members ranged between 20 and 60 years of age and were from various backgrounds: Aboriginal, Asian, Caribbean, European and Latin American. Three women were separated, four were living at home with a husband or a boyfriend, and the rest were presently single. When they were children, three had experienced physical abuse (such as severe beatings) and two had been abused sexually. Only two did not have children; those who had lived with them, except for one woman whose child was removed by the Child Protection Services due to the abuse the woman experienced in the home from her husband. Four were actively involved with other social agencies; half were on social assistance and the other half lived relatively well.

This group was open ended; when a few of the original members stopped attending, the leaders invited new members to join till a minimum of eight was reached. Admitting more women then became a group decision. Though the members were aware that the group would change and cohesion would have to be built up again, they decided that they wanted to help any woman who needed help. However, five weeks before the end of the program, which ran for sixteen weeks, the group leaders, judging that to admit anyone new would be too disruptive, perhaps also unfair to the new member, convinced the members that no one else should join at that point.

The group led by a social worker and a nurse had twelve members. Their children were simultaneously attending groups for children who had witnessed spousal abuse. Though one of the main *agency* program goals for these women was to help them address issues involving their children, more than half the meeting time was spent on issues related to their experience of abuse, which made it similar to the group described above. The background of the members resembled that of the first group. Three of the women were living with their partners, but in their case there had been no abuse since at least six months. Two women were separated and dating men, while three were separated but still being harassed by their former spouse, one very badly: he made regular hang-up phone calls, and threw garbage on her front lawn - she was convinced (though had no absolute proof) that he or a friend of his stalked her, and that he was responsible for the occasional broken window in her house. Of the remaining four who were on their own, one was a widow whose husband had died recently from a heart attack. Four women worked, two were on Unemployment Insurance, and six were on social assistance. All the women were searching to understand more clearly why they put up with so much abuse. The majority of the women wanted to learn how to express their anger differently as well as to 'get over' their anger, and all were interested in helping their children deal with the abuse. This group ran for twelve sessions and was a 'closed' group. Due to the short-term nature of the group and to the need for consistency in attendance for a group to form, members were advised that those who missed more than three consecutive meetings would be asked to leave the program (unless there were some exceptional circumstances). Only one woman left - the one whose husband died: 'He did me a favour - he died' she said at the last meeting she attended. The leaders surmised that with her husband dead, she was free of 'her' problems and did not need the group any longer.

Part three: applying and testing the principles

Three of the principles - demonstrating respect, self-determination, and individualisation - were tested and were found to significantly affect four components of group practice: planning, power, leadership, and use of resources.

Planning

In their past group practice, the co-leaders, following widely accepted practice in the field of group services offered to women who have been abused, felt it was necessary to have a 'grand plan' (though not an inflexible one) that outlined a complete agenda for the duration of their groups. That agenda was then presented to the members who were invited to add or subtract items, depending on what they felt was important. Now that they are systematically applying the principles presented above, there is no grand plan - which does not mean there is no careful preparation. The leaders make sure they are updated on the latest information in the area of violence against women by their male partners, and they also take responsibility to ensure that a group is established. However, they no longer consider that the foremost aspect of this responsibility involves taking the central and most active roles during the group formation stage. Instead, listening to and hearing members and being aware of what they bring to the group is what they consider to be most important. Following the principles has meant that the leaders no longer assume that the onus is on them to 'figure out' what is needed in the group; now they directly ask the group members.

Applying the principle of individualisation has meant that the group leaders have given up the belief that all groups and all members have the same 'learning curves', that they all need the same 'bundles' of information, and that they all need these at approximately the same time. For example, Walker's (1979) 'cycle of violence' used to be presented at the beginning of the group as a way of ensuring that members, over time, would increase their understanding of the pattern of violence in their lives. The leaders, who have always found the 'cycle' to be an excellent teaching tool, assumed that this teaching was applicable to all the women in their groups - that the cycle was universal - and that they should follow a fixed agenda or curriculum, in effect deciding and planning when the women would receive this teaching. Now, because they listen more closely to the women and because they reject all forms of homogenisation, the leaders have dropped these assumptions. They bring in 'cycle' theory if and when it is relevant to the discussion raised by the women whose exploration of their own concrete experiences of abuse and whose search for their own answers prompt the leaders to present the theory. In this way the agenda is determined by the women and the priorities they designate. So it is with any other information or knowledge the leaders possess. It is shared at the point when the women are struggling with a specific issue or when they ask for specific information.

Planning thus involves a state of preparedness consistent with the process of 'tuning-in' (Schwartz, 1971) which enables leaders to pick up on the clues and requests of group members. This state of enhanced readiness represents a 'leading by following' conceptualisation of group planning. The group leaders have their 'props' ready - the 'cycle of violence' teaching material, handouts, assertiveness skills training exercises, role-play scenarios, and so on - but they use them only in response to demands coming from the women. For example, when Mary stated she had trouble standing up to her husband because she got tongue-tied and overwhelmed by his tone of voice and strong words, other members, as if coaching her, jumped in with ideas of what they would have said. The leaders seized the moment and the opportunity in the 'here and now' to move into a role-play. Having got the approval of the group, they suggested that Mary take the role of her husband while the members who had ideas of how she could have responded take her role.

In previous groups, the leaders would have told the women that it would be useful for them to practice different responses through a role-play, and that therefore they, the leaders, would plan a whole group session around such a role-play. Much more than teaching moments were thus lost, for through this view of planning, the leaders clearly retained control of the group and its agenda, and the strengths and competence of the women got lost. The leaders have noticed that groups form even more cohesively when, as a result of leading by following, group content (issues and ideas to be discussed) is generated by the women. Preparing therefore also involves scheduling regular debriefing sessions to review this content, which helps the co-leaders to be 'tuned-in' and to keep these issues and ideas in the foreground when they next meet with the group. Finally, preparing involves ongoing evaluation as to the usefulness of the group content and process, which is achieved by asking the women, at the end of each session, what was useful *that day*, in *that session*. Previously, the leaders would not have asked this question, because they assumed, based on *their* analysis of the group process, that they already knew, or would determine later, what had been useful.

Power

From the moment of conceptualising the two groups, the leaders have put the issue of power up front. They openly acknowledge the power of each group *qua* group, and the power of each individual member - and through facilitating a process of consciousness-raising, they encourage the women to do the same. For example, they ask the group members how they have been able to manage thus far given their difficult situations. This question presumes that the women have strengths and competence and have coped with the adversities in their lives, without insinuating that they are to blame for the violence perpetrated by their partners. Assuming strengths and competence does not imply that the women need only be stronger and more competent (that is, need only modify their own behaviour) for the violence to stop. The leaders are well-aware of this particular brand of victim-blaming, one that Davis and Hagen (1992) argue is part of the anti-feminist backlash presently underlying many intervention models and services for women surviving violence.

The leaders also explicitly look to the women to learn about abuse rather than presenting themselves as the experts because they know the theories about abuse. For example, when the women discuss their abuse the leaders ask them how they explain the abuse to themselves. As a consequence of following the principle of demonstrating respect for the women, and therefore of believing in their strengths and competence, the leaders do not operate on the assumption, frequently made in the literature, that the women suffer from low self-esteem (for a good discussion of this issue, see Saunders, 1993).

Power is seen not only as the ability to influence the group process and each other, but as the readiness to take responsibility. Taking responsibility includes doing what is necessary to obtain what one believes one is entitled to: for example, the leaders acted as role models for the members when they stopped agency staff and various people from barging into the room where the group was meeting (the room contains the agency refrigerator). This type of modelling, in addition to the facilitation of consciousness-raising, has had a marked effect on the women. For example, when one group ended, three of its members insisted that they join the next (similar) group the agency would sponsor. They argued that not only would they benefit but that they would be an asset to the women in the new group. Each of these three women phoned the leaders several times to press her request. (This has never happened before in the leaders' ten years of practice with groups of women who have experienced abuse).

Taking responsibility also includes taking charge of one's own learning and of its application in one's life. For example, one woman talked about how much she was learning in the group about speaking up for what she believes in, and said she was teaching her 72-year-old mother to do the same - she believed that as a woman, her mother had taken too much abuse, and that it was never too late to change. In another example, a member pointed out to Laura that she must use the way she comes across in the group, clear and confident, in her every day life. In previous groups, the leaders did not pay much attention to the fact that every woman learns in a different way and applies that learning to her life as it makes sense to her. They might have questioned why a group member was trying to teach her mother the assertiveness skills she had learnt in the group instead of using the skills to get away from her abusive boyfriend, and they would have confronted the member about this. Similarly they would have checked up on Laura's behaviour outside the group at the very next meeting, and they would have asked her to identify instances where she might have been assertive, thus setting her up as accountable *to the group* for her actions. Now they work from the premise that each member is accountable *to herself* and that it is up to her to use the learning picked up in the group as she pleases and as best suits her life, which is far more complex than what is divulged in group meetings. In this way the leaders demonstrate their respect for each woman and their trust that each will take action as she sees fit.

As workers in a multi-service center, the group leaders face power issues that arise from the organisational structure. Some issues stem from policies which lag behind the latest knowledge; others stem from the ideological position adopted by the organisation. For example, the management of the center emphasises victims and safety. The leaders believe safety is a crucial issue, and it is a fundamental theme dealt with in the group. However, whereas previously they spent a great deal of time insisting that each woman develop a safety plan and that these plans be identified and discussed in the group, they no longer presume that the women have no such plans. They raise the issue of safety at the beginning of a group, but they wait for the women to respond in their own way and in their own time - which they do. The leaders also believe that a paradigm in which victimhood is the core construct is paternalistic, presumes fundamental weaknesses in the women, and fails to acknowledge their strengths, competence and power. This view appears to be shared by the group members: in one of the groups a woman commented that she was sick of being told directly or through implication by 'so-called helping agencies' that she should leave her abusive partner. She said she would not do so until she understood what kept her there, for she feared that she would end up with another abusive partner and she did not want this to happen.

In both groups, the women talk about their own anger and violence, which in their opinion are not necessarily associated with their partners' abuse. They have questioned why their violence is not recognised, and why only men are taught anger-management. Some of the members insist that they are violent persons, and that they want to stop being violent. This is another area in which the leaders have identified a lag in the provision of services to women because of ideological views, adopted by organisations, which focus on the women as victims and identify them as 'abused women', rather than seeing them as women who have experienced abuse but are whole persons, not just victims. When the leaders explain to the members why they refer to them as 'women who have experienced abuse' and not as 'abused women', the members are pleased, for they all agree that there is more to them and to their lives than abuse.

Leadership

Self-determination involves presenting group members with more rather than less choices: the co-leadership arrangement was seen as providing different role models. The co-leaders recognised the importance of feeling comfortable with each other and with the differences in their work styles. They knew that unless there was congruence in their combined efforts, their concerns would take precedence over the group's concerns. The need for congruence led them to identify a common baseline of knowledge that reflected the latest theories and research in the field, not to impose this knowledge, but to ascertain that neither was frozen in an ideological stance. They kept each other from usurping power from the group, and supported each other. In the group led by the social worker and the nurse, the co-leaders being very different in their approach agreed that one would focus on individuals while the other would focus on the group as a whole. In this way they integrated their differences and did not let them disrupt the work of the group.

The leaders, following the principle of demonstrating respect for the women, based their interventions in the reality of the members' experience. When members inquired about the state of theoretical knowledge on abuse, the leaders shared their information though they always underlined that the women were most knowledgeable of their own situations. For example, a member turned to one of the group leaders and said: 'Tell us what you know about why we are in these situations; are we nuts or what?' The leader responded in a way that reflected both the state of knowledge on abuse and the fact that theories could not explain why in the same group there was a woman who had suffered terrible abuse from early childhood and another who had been brought up in a very loving family in which there had been no violence of any kind, yet both were now in abusive relationships.

Basing all interventions on member self-determination - and therefore actively acknowledging that the women know best - the leaders no longer view themselves as responsible either for the women's learning or for their decisions, but firmly keep in mind that the women are responsible for what and how much they learn as well as for their decisions. Previously, the leaders worried that if members missed group sessions, they were losing out on much of the significant knowledge shared in the group and accumulated from session to session. Now the leaders realise that it is only when a member is open to new learning that she attends the group and participates. For example, one woman attended irregularly but she was very involved when she was present. She missed sessions more often than not because she slept in. Had she felt obliged to attend when she wanted or needed to sleep in, she would not have absorbed or contributed much to the group. The leaders' new approach assumes that this woman is the best judge of her own learning needs and abilities. Secondly, applying the principle of individualisation has meant that the leaders are comfortable with the idea that learning is not 'visible' in the same way for all members, and that each member learns at her own pace. For example, one woman was very aware of what she had learnt, and could list a number of interventions or topics that had helped her; another, perhaps not as aware, mentioned only one useful topic; while yet another could not mention anything that had been helpful. In the past this would have made the leaders anxious and they would have worked hard at convincing the women that they were learning. The anxiety would have activated the leaders' need to take charge of the provision of information in order to make sure the women were learning. Now the leaders do not rush to take charge but take the lead from the group, respect the members' control of their individual learning, and accept that different time frames are required by the members before they can integrate an idea or concept and operationalise it.

The application of the principles has helped the leaders to deal with the fact that not everyone is a 'group person', always at ease talking and sharing with more than one person at a time. Once the group stage of 'intimacy' (Garland et al., 1972) is reached, they trust that the women will monitor their participation, ensuring that everyone has their 'say' and that all contribute according to their own preferences, abilities and requirements. For example, one week the leaders noticed that Laura talked a lot in group while three women talked very little. Previously, they would have intervened as soon as they had become aware of this, limiting Laura's discourse and encouraging the silent members to speak up. On this occasion, they kept back. During their regular debriefing session, they decided that only in the event that the women would still be silent the following week would one of them intervene.

The use of resources

The use of resources, especially the sharing of information, is a critical aspect of group process. Traditional definitions of resources in Groupwork involved people or supplies external to the group. Group members are now seen as resources and everything they know and share is information which can be said to come from outside and inside the group simultaneously. Therefore it is now widely accepted that information finds its way into a group either via the group leader(s) or via the group members, and that it takes many forms (some of which serve as 'props', as discussed earlier): verbal presentation and discussion of ideas, distribution of printed material – newspaper clippings, scholarly articles, etc – presentation and discussion of films, and all types of audio-visual materials. Since the co-leaders have been working within an approach which stresses strengths, competence and empowerment, they focus on and give the greatest importance to the information that comes from the members, thus recognising the women as the experts - the ones more capable of helping themselves and each other.

The women's contributions include not only selecting topics or themes to be discussed, but leading the ensuing discussions. Once, when the members were examining good and bad episodes in their lives, one member suggested that it would help her, and all of them, to use a flip chart to map both their negative and positive experiences. She started with her own experiences, and acted as the recorder for those of the other women - in previous groups, a co-leader would have offered to act as the recorder. Contributions also include 'materials' individual members bring into the group to share with the other members, for example: a newspaper clipping from a *Dear Abby* column - 'Signals of Abuse' - which listed, in lay style and nonprofessional language, fifteen signs to look for in a person who is abusive; a poem entitled 'A Prayer', which asks God for help to be a stronger person and to do what one has to do; an outline of ten commandments for parents, which provoked a discussion of how important it is to be a good parent particularly when one's children have suffered from being exposed to violence.

When a member brought in such 'materials', it had the effect of intensely connecting the women, for they all recognised that in sharing an article or poem, that particular member was sharing a part of herself, a personal experience that she felt had been helpful to her and that she hoped would be helpful to the other women. When Barbara brought in the *Dear Abby* article, she told the women how she had sat down and read it carefully, analysing all the signals that in retrospect applied to her situation. She was very enthusiastic about how the article could benefit them also, particularly those who were interested in pursuing another relationship with a male partner. This type of information sharing makes clear to all the members that they are looking out for each others' interests as well as for their own. It also makes clear to the co-leaders that in order for the group to be a potent mutual aid system, it is crucial that they carefully listen to these 'materials' and appreciate their significance.

The leaders tested their traditional way of conceptualising and managing the imparting and sharing of information (in which they were the principal providers or sources of information/resources), against their new approach of giving preeminence to the information provided by the members. They observed, for example, that on numerous occasions, the handouts that they distributed were politely accepted but did not give rise to a discussion. On the other hand, anything brought in by a member would lead to an animated exchange, and the women would ask the leaders to photocopy the particular 'material'. The leaders also observed that when the members were given the choice to make use of theories when they felt it was appropriate, they did so selectively and very effectively. For example, over the years, the leaders have found that a brief summary of the Transactional Analysis concepts of the 'Parent' (the nurturing and critical - as in fault-finding - part of the ego), the 'Adult' (the logical and rational part), and the 'Child' (the emotional part), provided the women with a powerful and effective conceptual tool.

In previous groups, the leaders would explain the theory and immediately invite the members to react and apply it to their lives. In the two groups discussed in this paper, they explained the concepts in one of the early sessions, but left it up to the women to decide if and when to use them. The leaders observed that the members brought the 'parent/adult/child' concepts into many discussions. When they were talking about how they sometimes feel guilty, they listed some of the negative 'Parent' self-talk that perpetuates their feelings of guilt, and the converse positive 'Adult' self-talk. On another occasion, the members asked the leaders to type up a list of these 'self-talks', which they labelled 'Voices of', and to make enough copies so that each member could readily look at the list when she felt guilty. In other discussions, the members would refer either to the 'adult' who helped them to act in a rational way (for example, refraining to enter a circular debate with their spouse or ex-spouse) or to the 'nurturing parent' who helped them to feel positive about themselves (for example, when they needed support). This is a good example of what the leaders like to call the 'cross-fertilisation' of theories and ideas that is possible between leaders and members when the leaders trust that the members will know how and when to use various types of information or resources.

Conclusion

This paper has looked at groupwork with women who have experienced abuse, and has reported on the application in two such groups of practice principles which emphasise strengths, competence and empowerment. The effect of applying these principles was found to be significant in terms of planning, power, leadership, and use of resources. The two groups were potent support systems for the members, validating their personal strengths, confirming their abilities to cope, to make decisions and to take control, and drawing out their knowledge.

However, violence against women is a social problem, and the eradication of that problem will not be possible without addressing issues of justice for women. Those issues are lodged in the cultural, political and economic structures of society. The focus on interpersonal support systems and on personal change in this paper does not contradict that reality.

References

Breton, M. (1994) 'Relating competence-promotion and empowerment', *Journal of Progressive Human Services*, 5(1), pp.27-44.

Breton, M. and Nosko, A. (forthcoming) 'Group work with women who have experienced abuse' in Ephross, P.H. and Greif, G.L. (eds.) *Group Work with Populations at Risk*. New York: Oxford University Press.

Cowger, C.D. (1994) 'Assessing client strengths: clinical assessment for client empowerment', *Social Work*, 39(3), pp.262-268.

Davis, L.V. and Hagen, J.L. (1992) 'The problem of wife abuse: the interrelationship of social policy and social work practice', *Social Work*, 37(1), pp.15-20.

Freire, P. (1993) *Pedagogy of the Oppressed*. New York: Continuum. 20th Anniversary Edition.

Garland, J.A., Jones, H.E. and Kolodny, R.L. (1972) 'A model for stages of development in social work groups' in Bernstein, S. (ed.) *Explorations in Group Work*. Mass: Boston University School of Social Work.

Goldstein, H. (1992). 'Victors or victims: contrasting views of clients in social work practice' in Saleebey, D. (ed.) *The Strengths Perspective in Social Work Practice*. New York: Longman.

Hartman, S. (1983) 'A self-help group for women in abusive relationships', *Social Work with Groups*, 6(3/4), pp.133-146.

Horton, A.L. and Johnson, B.L. (1993). 'Profile and strategies of women who have ended abuse', *Families in Society: The Journal of Contemporary Human Services*, October, pp.481-492.

Mullender, A. and Ward, D. (1991) *Self-Directed Groupwork: Users Take Action for Empowerment*. London: Whiting and Birch.

Nurius, P.S., Furrey, J. and Berliner, L. (1992) 'Coping capacity among women with abusive partners', *Violence and Victims*, 7(3), pp.229-243.

Rapp, C.A. (1992) 'The strengths perspective of case management with persons suffering from severe mental illness' in Saleebey, D. (ed.) *The Strengths Perspective in Social Work Practice*. New York: Longman.

Saleebey, D. (ed.) (1992) *The Strengths Perspective in Social Work Practice*. New York: Longman.

Saunders, D.G. (1993) 'Woman battering' in Ammerman, R.T. and Hersen, M. (eds.) *Assessment of Family Violence. A Clinical and Legal Sourcebook*. New York: John Wiley and Sons.

Schwartz, W. (1971) 'On the use of groups in social work practice' in Schwartz, W. and Zalba, S. (eds.) *The Practice of Group Work*. New York: Columbia University Press.

Sullivan, W.P. (1992) 'Reconsidering the environment as a helping resource' in Saleebey, D. (ed.) *The Strengths Perspective in Social Work Practice*. New York: Longman.

Walker, L.E. (1979) *The Battered Woman*. New York: Harper and Row.

Weick, A. (1992). 'Building a strengths perspective for social work' in Saleebey, D. (ed.) *The Strengths Perspective in Social Work Practice*. New York: Longman.

Wood, G. and Middleman, R. (1989). *The Structural Approach to Direct Practice in Social Work*. New York: Columbia University Press.

Effective Groupwork Packages and the Importance of Process

David Henchman[1] and Susan Walton[2]

Introduction

The Probation Service in England and Wales has the statutory purpose to 'secure the rehabilitation of the offender, protect the public from harm from the offender or prevent the offender from committing further offences' (Criminal Justice Act 1991, Section8(1)).

Since the late 1980s, the development of successful groupwork with offenders in Britain has been informed by research and evaluation undertaken by the 'What Works' movement. The focus of What Works is effective work with offenders and the research, through meta analysis (for example, Andrews et al., 1990), identified the key components of successful programmes. These were:

- specific focus and consistency of intervention;
- intervention is specific to the offences committed;
- methods are matched to the characteristics of the offender;
- targeting people with the highest risk of custody and risk of re-offending;
- addressing the needs/problems of offenders and resolving them;
- clear goals and accountability;
- simple structure;
- committed leadership backed by necessary resources;
- optimistic, committed and enthusiastic staff who are valued by their organisation;

1. Freelance Trainer/Probation Officer.
2. Freelance Trainer/Probation Officer.
Address for correspondence: 143 Overndale Road, Downend, Bristol BS16 2RN.

Groupwork Vol. 10(1), 1997-98, pp.70-80

- a sense of ownership of the programme by practitioners who are suited to the methods;
- intervention is underpinned by a culture in which measuring outcomes is a natural component of good practice.

Clive Hollin (1994, p.4) also identified high treatment integrity as a crucial factor of effective work with offenders, i.e. the programme is put into practice as it was intended in theory and design. His research states that:

> Effective programmes with high treatment integrity are characterised by sound management, tight design and skilled practitioners

More recently Antonowicz and Ross (1994) conclude that:

> Few study reports describe their clients, their staff, their programmes, their results, or the analysis of their results in sufficient detail or with sufficient clarity to enable the reader to determine who did what to whom, why, how much, how often and with what results.

It is our contention that 'their staff' is a crucial dimension of overriding importance to the delivery of effective programmes, and common sense and experience suggest to us that no matter how tight the design or how sound the management, it is the skill of the practitioners in delivering the programme which determines the success or failure.

Furthermore we would contend that even with the assumption that the practitioners are skilled and that the programme that they deliver meets the 'What Works' criteria of effectiveness, it is *how* they deliver the programme—the energy and enthusiasm that they can generate in doing so—that has a determining effect on outcomes. Our client group exhibit entrenched behaviour patterns and are usually unmotivated. Therefore if staff have not got energy and enthusiasm there is little chance of them enabling change.

The original 'What Works' research, for example Andrews (1990), identified what was required of staff in terms of optimism and commitment and a sense of ownership. While more recent research did not support the findings that these were essential features of successful programmes, it concludes that not enough could be determined about their staff to arrive at such conclusions and does nothing in our opinion to detract from this 'common sense' view. The subject of this article is an account of one staff group's experience of achieving 'the sense of ownership' which we would contend is a precondition to 'the enthusiasm and commitment' which in turn are preconditions for the successful application of practitioner skills in delivering effective programmes.

The challenge that is before us in working with serious offenders is the selling of ideas, values and a lifestyle which are often totally new and alien to our client group and which often challenge their existing values and lifestyle at a fundamental level. Unless we believe whole-heartedly in what we deliver and are able to convey this belief we cannot hope to 'make a sale'. We would argue that the importance of a 'sense of ownership' (Andrews, 1990) lies also in the fact that it facilitates the expression of our belief and confidence in the product we are selling.

Therefore it is not sufficient to simply pick up a package created by another team of practitioners. How many bookshelves up and down the country are full of packages that fit 'What Works' criteria which were costly and time consuming to develop but now do little more than collect dust?

From our experience and involvement in the development of three groupwork teams within Avon Probation Service, we conclude that ownership by staff is fundamental to the success or failure of groupwork programmes, and the process by which a programme is developed and introduced is the determining factor of whether optimism, commitment and enthusiasm are achieved and sustained.

Background

For a number of years Bath Probation Office used groupwork as one of a range of methods of supervising its clients. However, in 1991 a decision was made that groupwork should become the primary way in which Probation clients would be supervised and therefore groups for offenders would become an integral part of all Probation Orders.

This move to a groupwork model was based on the belief that groupwork provides a more effective forum for clients to examine their own offending, to challenge and be challenged by group leaders and by their peers, and to take positive action to change. We also think that groups can provide an opportunity for the empowerment of clients and an invaluable sense of mutual support for offenders that is difficult to achieve in one-to-one contact. These elements are crucial if clients are to take responsibility for their offending and its consequences. Our evaluation of groupwork suggests that clients' experience of groups is that they are less oppressive because they enable the power difference inherent in our role, and exaggerated by one-to-one work, to be redressed.

The model ensured that within a month of a Probation Order being made, all clients attended a 'Tackling Offending' group which was originally based on broad aims and objectives formulated by a working party and adopted by the team. Beyond these aims no set programme was devised, rather group leaders employed a range of exercises and methods according to personal preference and experience. At this stage there was already a recognition of the importance of a cognitive-behavioural input informed by the 'What Works' research and studies such as those of Izzo and Ross (1990), Andrews et al. (1990). These had concluded that effective offender programmes need to include a multi-modal, skills oriented, cognitive behavioural focus. Group leaders were timetabled according to their availability and staff who found they worked well together were able to do so.

When the groupwork system was initiated, it was agreed that our work should be evaluated and that ideas and methods should be shared through the development of a resource bank. Neither materialised and whilst the system operated smoothly, the presentation and content of group sessions became staid and routine, and there was no shared commitment to development informed by practice.

Furthermore, new staff joined the team not knowing that groupwork was the prescribed method of work. They began to express their feelings of isolation and frustration at being required to take part in a programme for which they had no sense of ownership and it can be assumed limited commitment and enthusiasm. One consequence of this was that integration into the team was difficult, whilst there were explicit aims these were not meaningful to them and therefore they felt de-skilled and uncertain as to how they could be achieved.

The process

During 1992, there were major organisational changes within the Agency due to the introduction of the Criminal Justice Act 1991. An outcome of this was that the team decided to meet to focus exclusively on practice issues rather than the demands and restrictions of agendas dominated by management issues relating to the introduction of the Act. Within this forum the team agreed to review our groupwork system.

A three day event away from the office was arranged and outside, independent consultancy was employed to facilitate this review. Whilst it could be considered to be somewhat of a 'luxury' to have consultants, particularly at a time of economic restraints, we believe that this element was crucial for quality change and progress to be achieved. From our experience, it is not possible for a team colleague to act as an effective facilitator because of their involvement in the dynamics of that group of practitioners. To have two consultants, one male and one female, was especially helpful, particularly for a team in which questioning and positive challenge was not the norm. Like any team the dynamics were complex, and therefore assistance to change the culture was essential. Prior to the team event, the consultants spent some time with staff members as a group in order that we could clarify and agree on their purpose and role before deciding on the focus for the three days.

Statement of purpose and values

At the suggestion of the consultants the initial task was to agree a Statement of Purpose for the Bath team (Figure 1).

Fig. 1. Statement of Purpose

Within the framework of Avon Probation Service policy and objectives, to provide a non-discriminatory, quality service within the Criminal Justice System which:

- offers Courts appropriate and effective sentences;
- enables offenders to reflect upon their behaviour and its consequences in a way which assists them to reduce or stop the commission of offences;
- effectively supervises those on conditional release from custody.

This was arrived at by discussing and distilling the professional views of individual Probation Officers and the Team Manager, thereby agreeing a short but comprehensive Statement of Purpose that also encompassed the remit of the Agency and the Criminal Justice System.

The next task undertaken was to elicit the values which informed our practice and which underpinned our Statement of Purpose. This was achieved by paired discussion which was then developed and expanded by the whole group. By engaging in open discussion of these issues it became evident that by never engaging in open discussion about principles and values, we had been operating on the assumption that there were no differences in those that we held. All the staff at the Bath office were experienced Probation Officers, some of whom had participated in groupwork for many years. Consequently discussion about something as fundamental as our professional values had the potential to create feelings of vulnerability and defensiveness. For example individual beliefs which were not shared by colleagues might be seen to be politically incorrect. Our consultants enabled an open discussion and a culture began to develop where colleagues were candid and both gave and received constructive challenge and feedback. An example of this is that differences in leadership styles were discussed and it was openly acknowledged that variety could not only be tolerated but was a positive advantage to the team and its work. Having had the discussion about values, it became evident that we did in fact share core values and these formed the basis of a Statement of Values (Figure 2).

Figure 2. Statement of Values

- Treat individuals with value and respect
- Be open and honest
- Respect the principle of self-determination and the individual's right to informed choice
- Be empowering and anti-discriminatory in our practice
- Be open to giving and receiving constructive challenge and feedback
- Focus on offending behaviour within a framework of clear boundaries and expectations

This was a valuable team development exercise and also re-affirmed our commitment and belief in groupwork. Groupwork really was the obvious and best way for this team of professionals to achieve its overall purpose while remaining true to the principles and values which it upheld. The process took some considerable time but whilst it would have been tempting to have rushed it through, our experience has shown us that to do so is not a prudent move.

Values are fundamental and would determine both the content and delivery of our groupwork programme and it is our view that it was therefore crucial to be clear about what they were and to recognise explicitly how they would affect and guide decision making. If agreement had not been reached on a Statement of Core Values that was upheld by the whole team, tensions would surely have arisen which would jeopardise the consistency and effectiveness of the programme.

Our conclusion is that the process by which agreement of core values is achieved is equally important and must actively involve everyone in the team. Once achieved a statement of values provided a foundation that facilitated focused discussion of professional issues and enabled conflicts to be resolved without these becoming personalised.

Methods and material

As a means of promoting further team ownership while creating an open culture where effective working methods are shared and developed, the consultants facilitated a process in which each team member presented their favoured groupwork exercises, that is tools that they had used and found effective in achieving the original groupwork aims. Until this event, such an obvious means of exchanging ideas about good practice had not happened and in our view this was because it might have been misinterpreted as professional competitiveness. The process that the team had experienced over the three days had the effect of enabling all team members to talk to their colleagues confidently and enthusiastically about their own good practice. For example the authors demonstrated to the team the use of Critical Incident Analysis (Henchman and Walton, 1993) as an effective means of enabling offenders to give a detailed account of their behaviour, that it involves rational decision making and that there is an interplay between thoughts, actions and feelings. This was achieved by replicating a groupwork situation using team members as participants and modelling the use of the technique. A 'group member' volunteered to provide the incident to be analysed, and described a minor accident that she had been involved in that morning. This was an interactive process which involved the whole team in experiencing the benefits of this technique and as a consequence it became widely used by many of our colleagues.

Other team members presented their favoured tools and a sense of the value of the skills and experience that individuals brought to the team was thus preserved while promoting group ownership of the team's skills.

The groupwork programme

Having reached this point we recognised that the issue now was to improve our practice by striving to increase consistency. The previously quoted research by Hollin (1994) stresses the importance of programme integrity as a means of achieving programme continuity and enabling evaluation of this. To do this we decided to re-define the goals of our groupwork programme devised two years earlier. This was achieved through a team discussion that was informed by our Statement of Purpose and Values and based on our experience to date. Again our consultants played a crucial role in facilitating this and enabling us to condense the products of our discussion into a format that was agreed by everyone. All team members were actively involved in this process; enthusiasm and energy were growing, individual and team investment in what we were trying to achieve was escalating.

Having agreed these goals, the team now identified five key tasks that would need to be completed if the goals were to be achieved and an effective programme developed. These related to action plans for the development of:

- Programme structure
- Content
- Evaluation
- Procedures
- Delivery

These are all crucial features of successful programmes evidenced by 'What Works' research. Task groups were mutually agreed by the team to work on these five areas and the consultants facilitated these smaller groups.

The small groups were able to devote some time to their tasks over the three day period and a commitment was made to continue their work beyond the team event.

The work that was done in these small groups and the way the tasks were achieved was an important element of the overall process, ensuring equal investment and ownership by all practitioners.

Groupwork aims and objectives

In a small group, it was the authors' remit, with two colleagues, to address the programme content and to develop detailed Aims and Objectives for the 'Tackling Offending Groups', which would ensure integrity whilst allowing for professional autonomy and creativity in how they could be met. Our consultants had introduced us to the acronym SMARTA, as a means to promote aims and objectives that are Specific, Measurable, Achievable, Realistic, Time-limited, and Anti-discriminatory.

Once back at the office our task group continued to meet to complete our mandate. We collected all the exercises our colleagues had used in their previous Tackling Offending Groupwork. As part of this process we discussed with them in more detail what they had found effective. Our task group then compiled a draft of specific aims and objectives and furthermore identified relevant and effective exercises which were compiled to form a resource pack for our colleagues. These were shared with the whole team who after some amendments and fine tuning agreed the aims and objectives thereby providing the basis for an integrated and consistent groupwork programme. It was our experience that within these task groups, opinions were expressed strongly, there was lively debate and ideas flowed freely. As a consequence of having a clear reference point, that is an agreed purpose, values and aims, the work of the task groups was focused and its members were energised. Despite the autonomous nature of the work of these groups the shared process that preceded it ensured that group ownership was not jeopardised.

The other four task groups also continued to work and to feedback to the team. This process was further facilitated by a follow up day with our consultants, again away from the office. This was particularly helpful in maintaining an overview of the programme and ensuring that deadlines were met.

Evaluation

The major issue that subsequently emerged was that there was a need for a system of evaluation that was based on the groupwork Aims and Objectives; that ensured feedback from our clients and which required dialogue between group leaders. As a consequence, evaluation sheets were devised that would provide information that had the potential for the programme to evolve based on good practice and the team's experience of what is effective in achieving desired outcomes. This was done before the significance of programme integrity had been highlighted in research but Hollin (1995) confirms subsequently that we were progressing in the right direction. The lesson that we have more recently learned is that the process by which evaluation is achieved is also fundamental. If practitioners do not own the evaluation system and use it with enthusiasm and commitment then it will have no impact on subsequent practice because it probably won't be done. Who in their right mind wants to engage in what could easily be perceived as a tedious paperwork exercise at the end of a difficult and demanding group session?

Conclusion

'What Works' research has been and is crucial for the work of Probation Officers working effectively with offenders and undoubtedly the contribution it has made to the content of groupwork packages is proving to be very significant.

The more recent research (Antonowicz and Ross, 1994), while emphasising the significance of fewer programme characteristics also identifies the absence of information about the staff who deliver programmes. It is our contention that 'What Works' with reference to the content of programmes is only one facet of effective intervention and that equal attention must be paid to the skills, optimism and commitment of the practitioners who are to deliver programmes.

Our experience at Bath Probation Office has shown us that attention to the process by which the content of packages is devised, delivered and developed is the means by which the sense of ownership can be achieved and we would argue that this is the crucial ingredient of generating the energy, enthusiasm and commitment that practitioners require if they are going to be effective in enabling change in entrenched behaviour.

Postscript

In 1995, Avon Probation Service implemented a restructuring process, one purpose of which was to introduce groupwork County wide as the primary way of working with offenders. Consequently, Bath Probation Team was dissolved and with it the groupwork programme and the opportunity to use evaluation to develop the programme further or to demonstrate improved practice.

The authors joined a new groupwork team with a remit to develop a County wide groupwork programme. Our experience in Bath suggested that this new groupwork programme would be effective only if the groupwork team were able to participate in a process of programme development. It is our intention to record and comment on this process at a later date.

Acknowledgements

The Bath team were: The authors, Howard Hardman, John Harvey, Gareth John, Lawrie Keating, Di Love, Sue Pascoe, Jenny Rakoczi, Linda Sage, Steve Thompson. Special thanks are due to Jane Drewitt. The consultants were: Lin Thomas and Maurice Vanstone.

References

Andrew et al. (1990) 'Does correctional treatment work? A clinically relevant, psychologically informed meta analysis', *Criminology*, 28, pp.365-404.

Antonowicz, D.H. and Ross, R.R. (1994) 'Essential components of successful rehabilitation programmes for offenders', *International Journal of Offender Therapy and Comparative Criminology*, 38(2).

Henchman, D. and Walton, S. (1993) 'Critical incident analysis and its application', *Groupwork,* 6(3).

Hollin, C. (1994) 'The meaning and implications of programme integrity' in McGuire, J. (ed.) *What Works: Effective Methods to Reduce Re-offending*. Chichester: Wiley.

Izzo and Ross, R.R. (1989) 'Meta analysis of rehabilitation programmes for juvenile delinquents', *Criminal Justice Behaviour*.

Reviews

The Anti-Group
Morris Nitsum
London and New York, Routledge, £16.99 ISBN 0-415 10211 1

Wilfred Bion once wrote about the capacity to deal with the emotional bombardment in groups, comparing it to the experience of the soldier under fire in the first word war trenches. He wrote that the experienced officer is one who can think while under fire.

Morris Nitsun's book demonstrates as well as illustrates the capacity to think and to be articulate while under fire from the overt and covert forces that oppose constructive activity in groups. He is well placed to do this. He is an experienced senior psychologist with decades of experience in the health service whose tensions and problems of morale he is clearly aware of. He is also a trained and experienced group-analyst and has worked in the fields of applied groupwork with families and with teams and organisations.

For readers of *Groupwork* who want to update themselves of the latest book in the Routledge series coming from the Group-analytic world, I cannot imagine a better place to explore.

The thesis that runs like a current through the book is that there has been insufficient emphasis in group thinking on the nature, role and dynamic of the anti-group. This book comes from the second generation of group-analysts. Not those who trained with Foulkes who pioneered Group-analysis in this country, but from the generation who have seen the shortcomings in the idealisation of a charismatic pioneer, to sift through the wealth and the limited vision of Foulkes' bequest and legacy. This is the substance of chapter 2.

Nitsun describes in chapter 3, the anti-group as a feature of individual, sub-group and whole group dynamics. He identifies three areas that need exploration:

> 1) resistance to participation in groups linked to fear and dislike of groups, 2) hostility and anger arising in the group but directed destructively at the group itself, and 3) spiralling destructive processes in the group that could not be contained by usual clinical management.

While the main focus of this text is upon psychotherapy and clinical work, there is no doubt of its applicability to non-clinical settings such as social work or probation programmes of groupwork.

Nitsun's line is not just that there are issues and dynamics to be accounted for in the recruitment and management of the group setting. He argues that people's natural reluctance to groups needs to be taken seriously, It is not only because of potentially disruptive forces, but because the anti-group can provide the very seeds of the kind of transformative process that is necessary for a group to provide a creative experience for its members given the destructiveness they come from in their social and family group contexts:

> The underlying principle of transformation is that the group's capacity to survive the destructive threat of the anti-group is itself transformational in that it attests to the strength of the group and the greater power of constructive group tendencies (p.63).

For those looking for group material to illustrate theory - I am thinking of trainers, supervisors and students seeking to test their own experience - chapter 4 provides a rich seam to mine. There are examples from different stages of group development and illustrations from staff support and experiential groups as well as from therapy groups.

When it comes to theory, the author's opening line is to reap the rewards of the counter-point between Foulkes the idealiser of the positive aspects of groups (resonance, mirroring, exchange, translation from unconscious to conscious and the group matrix) and Bion with his focus on the destructive activities of groups designed to keep alive basic assumptions without which the group behaves as if it will not survive

(Dependency, pairing/expectation, fight/flight). In my view there has been too little attempt to bridge the great institutional divide in psycho-analytic approaches to groups between the Tavistock and the Institute for Group Analysis, despite that they are now housed a few doors away from each other. In this context I could add that it was disappointing not to have reference to the Tavistock's *The Unconscious at Work* (Obholzer and Roberts, 1994) or the Tavistock tradition of Miller and Rice with its focus on 'anti-task dynamics' in the caring professions. (It is easy for a reviewer to spot what might be missing in a work as encyclopaedic as this in its review of the writings of group analysts, when the main problem is how to do justice to the wealth that is there!).

For those who wish to take their understanding of group theory and group dynamics further, chapters 5 and 6 provide the heart of the book. Each chapter focuses on 'Determinants of the anti-group'. These include : Regression, survival anxiety, failures of communication, projective identification, envy (ch. 5); and Interpersonal disturbance, the primal scene, aggression and hatred, the death instinct (ch. 6) Each heading is explored from the perspectives of individual emotional experience, emerging group dynamic, and theory. Again examples and the capacity to think through the implication of recalcitrant group phenomena abound that make this a vital text for those wishing for a genuine encounter in groups that takes into account passionately felt and potentially destructive negative emotions.

This brings us to chapter 7 that addresses 'Technical considerations in dealing with the anti-group'. Groupworkers in many contexts will value the advice given about the setting, both physical and organisational, selection, drop-outs and preparation for the group. Here Nitsun introduces an original concept, 'the group-object relation' by which he means 'the internal representation of groups that is the product of the individual's group history and the way his attitudes towards groups have been externalised and enacted in the social milieu'.

Chapter 8 explores the role of the conductor. After responsiveness of the conductor to aggression and hatred of group experiences and techniques for dealing with them in the group, he turns to the inner resources of the leader, his personal experience of being a member of a therapy group, his professional training and current supervision and support. This attends to the inner resources the conductor has for dealing with the ongoing emotional demands to keep thinking and articulating the dynamics of individuals, sub-groups and the whole group as it develops.

This leads us to the next two chapters that describe 'The transformational potential of the anti-group' (ch.9) and provide a vivid illustration of such a transformation in describing one of the author's more destructive anti-groups (ch.10) Models of transformation are clearly described and widely referenced, complete with a critique of the limits of each.

Chapter 11, the longest in the book I thought one of the most exciting and readable. The author takes us on a tour of 'the anti-group in the wider sphere'. Here you can feel him drawing on his long commitment to work in the public services despite the experience of institutional undermining and in the fact of feelings in patient, colleague and political groups of despair that what is human will survive. There is family illustration and analysis, organisational and work group dynamics and cultural analysis. This is rounded off with a hypothesis linking the intra-psychic with the social in a way that is as sensitive to the difficulties as any I have read.

Chapter 12 searches for an 'Integrative theory of group analysis' looking for the possible role of the theory of the anti-group as a key and neglected element in forming the necessary dialogue between positive and negative aspects of group experience and group theory. He closes with a vision of three integrating perspectives that are dialectical, ecological and aesthetic in relation to the group.

As a practitioner of the group-analytic approach to psychotherapy groups as well as someone who has been involved over some years in organisational development and groupwork training, I can recommend this original book, as one that provides a vital inner resource for doing tough work sensitively.

Rick Morgan-Jones
Analytical Psychotherapist and Organisational Consultant

Capturing the Power of Diversity
Marvin Felt, John Ramey, John Wodarski and Aaron Mann (editors)
New York and London, Haworth Press Inc., 1995 ISBN 1-56024-971-4

This book is an edited collection of fifteen chapters, together with an introduction, which appear to have been presented at the 1991 conference on social work with groups, sponsored by the Association for the Advancement of Social Work with Groups in North America. There is no explanation for the delay in publication nor any indication of whether the published papers have been edited following presentation as papers at the conference. The opening four chapters are intended to address separate themes about diversity, themes which subsequent chapters are meant to explore. The themes are teaching and practice issues, macro systems and their consequences and the changing aspects of the environment in which groupworkers practise and the necessity to address inequality. It is not always clear, however, which chapters are addressing which themes, and the book is not organised in a way which clearly presents the themes it seeks to explore.

The book's objective, as stated in the introduction, is to illustrate the complexity, creativity and excitement of the concept of diversity. It falls short in this objective. To begin with, there is no analysis of the concept of diversity. There could have been a critical examination of this concept alongside that of difference, or of the relationship between inequality, disadvantage, oppression and diversity. The UK literature on anti-discriminatory and anti-oppressive practice, amongst other strengths, includes an analysis of assimilationism, multiculuralism and anti-racism, and draws attention to the meaning of concepts and the models of practice and relationships which they embody. The UK groupwork literature, including material published in this journal, has given expression to anti-oppressive practice. None of this material appears in this book. The meaning and scope of the power of diversity remains elusive.

Secondly, there are some surprising statements with which groupworkers might take issue. Social action is reported to be a dormant idea, and the concept of empowerment forgotten. The dominant location within which social work is practised in the UK might not generally provide a favourable climate for social action initiatives to flourish, and might constrain the potential of empowering practice. However, neither social action or empowerment are moribund. Whilst there is no room for complacency, the UK literature on anti-discriminatory and anti-oppressive practice has meant that social work education is better placed to present a curriculum relevant to the needs of minority groups that some contributors to this book believe.

Thirdly, those chapters which focus on education and training for social work and groupwork do not illustrate how groupwork practice can provide students with tools for empowering and anti-oppressive practice, or how the teaching and learning experience itself can build on the different, diverse experiences and perspectives which students bring to qualifying training. Additionally, the chapters frequently fail to turn their analysis of problems and challenges into strategies for action and practice. For example, the introduction to the book suggests that groupworkers may not have the necessary skills and knowledge to act in political arenas for social change, yet subsequent chapters do not define what these might be. In a passionately expressed chapter Bernard Wohl illustrates the importance of raising social issues of equality and justice in daily practice, and identifies transformative values for generating the strength to change macro issues. However, here too, there is little analysis of 'how'.

There are, however, some salient messages. Some contributors are clearly concerned that groupwork may be squeezed out of the curriculum because of what they perceive to be an impetus towards genericism. The same danger is present in the UK, with methods like groupwork and family therapy marginalised by constraints of a two year programme of qualifying study and of the emphasis on conformity to practice within local government. Several contributors warn of the dangers of a silence on dissent and dialogue and caution that social work will become irrelevant to many groups if its actions do not reflect concerns for social justice. They caution against falsely separating individual and collective empowerment, at a time when social work in the UK can be criticised for addressing social issues. They note that change strategies will be ineffective if they are not provided in the context in which difficulties for people arise and/or are not directed at the source of the problem. Once again, however, the exhortations are not translated clearly into practice skills.

Overall, then, this book is a disappointment. It fails to capture the power of diversity or to demonstrate new ideas on how groupwork practitioners and trainers can empower people to address the issues which lie behind personal experience.

Michael Preston-Shoot
Professor of Social Work and Social Care, Liverpool John Moores University

Mutual Aid Groups, Vulnerable Populations and the Life Cycle
Alex Gitterman and Laurence Shulman, L. (eds.)
New York and Chichester, Columbia Press,
ISBN: 0-231-08288, Pbk 0-231-08289-4

'Walking on Eggshells?'

This book runs to 448 pages yet leaves this reader wishing for more! In a world where books on groupwork are often worthy and informative, but hardly gripping, it is a pleasure to review a book that is not only practical and sensible, but also illuminating and enriching in both a professional and a personal sense. I do not recall being so moved by a book in groupwork since reading Gisela Konopka during student days. Konopka made full use of the actual speech and thoughts of group members, and this approach is reflected in most of the 21 chapters in this demonstration of 'the interactionist approach' put forward originally by Schwartz and practised by the many contributors to this volume. It is appropriate that the group member should 'speak' loudly in a book devoted to furthering the development of self-help groups.

This is the second edition of the book, published originally in 1986 as *Mutual Aid Groups and Life Cycle*. This edition contains several new chapters and a number of re-writes. In its present form, it opens with theoretically-orientated chapters by Laurence Shulman and Alex Gitterman. They write refreshingly straight language. They are the editors of the following seventeen chapters in which practitioners present examples of their mediating function in working with groups focusing on specific concerns facing specific persons at different stages in the life cycle. The book is rounded by an excellent concluding chapter by Judith Lee and Carol Swenson, re-presenting the concept of mutual aid that was at the heart of Schwartz's approach to working with people. For readers unfamiliar with his approach, reading the last chapter first would be helpful in creating a context for understanding and enjoying the myriad of group settings that make up the centre of this kaleidoscope of a book. It is not a book developing a sequential argument, and starting at the end will not spoil the middle, or the beginning.

In a largely jargon free book, Shulman argues for the need for groupworkers to avoid jargon (and includes facilitating and enabling in the embargoed words). Shulman draws strongly on Schwartz, urging the avoidance of an 'overly prescriptive approach' to groupwork, and supports 'leaving room for individual artistry'. The importance for workers' 'keeping alive...the belief in the ability of systems to change' is emphasised, along with the ability to 'tune in' to the fears and aspirations of group members.

Gitterman outlines the practical steps to be taken, and acknowledges that 'too often the group service is an anomaly added to workers existing caseloads;. He shows that organisational factors are 'crucial' in creating self-help opportunities, and in a memorable phrase writes that 'without vertical administrative approval the worker walks on eggshells'. Although all the work in the book is drawn from the United States and Canada, the above sentiments will ring a bell in the European groupwork scene.

The practitioner examples are provided in clusters reflecting the passage through life: two chapters with children; three with young people; ten with adults; two with the elderly. What the group members have in common is their vulnerability in the larger community. There is a real sense in which the members are 'in the same boat' - the 'boat' may be different, but they are in it together because some aspect of their lives (what an English novelist calls 'their bag of experience') has strong similarities and threatens to damage their future. What can be done about it to understand it, accept it, and deal with it in order to bring about change that will lessen the damage? Become part of a self-help group.

Allowing for the brevity of some chapters, and the unavoidable truncation of what in some situations was a long process, the descriptive/illustrative accounts in the central part of the book are a great testimony to the value of the approach. Critics will no doubt voice concerns about the permanence of changes in attitude and behaviour, but there can be less doubt about the importance of the experiences and feelings that group member share with each other (and through the skill of the writers, with the reader).

As a Mozart-lover, I know the answer to the question 'which of his works do you like best?' The answer is 'the one I'm listening to now'. I have a similar view about the chapters in this book, and find it impossible to rank them in order. If you work with children the chapters with bereaved children, and with that neglected group - the 'well siblings' of disabled children, will hold a high place. If your work is with young people, then the example of work in a school, and with a adolescents in a residential setting will demand attention. Groupwork with adults is fully represented - Work with Parent of Sexually Victimised Children; Men who Batter their wives; Women's groups for Sexual Abuse Survivors; Single Parents; Groups during the AIDS pandemic; Institutionalised Schizophrenic Women; Homeless Women; The 'Straight Ahead; Prison Group. I have listed them all, since one of them may be what you, the reader, relate to professionally and it will encourage you to get the book - and then read the rest. No, I have not listed them all: one picked out for special mention is work with Hispanic Parents of Children with Cancer. It makes the point that working in the language of the parents, and within the religious beliefs and cultural norms of the parents is a critical requirement. It is not difficult to see parallels in the European setting. Completing the age cycle, if your work is with the elderly, then the group dealing with the death of a member (and by extension their own deaths); and work in an institutionalised setting will have particular resonance.

Despite the varied agency contexts, all demonstrate the possibilities of self-help, and reflect the Schwartz tenet that change resides in the client, not in the helper. Apart from stating principles, the book is not a detailed 'how to' book. However, several writers and especially Shulman in his chapter on Single Parents, give indications of ways 'making the group work' and of the 'crucial skill of moving from the general to the specific' in assisting group members help themselves and each other through the interaction. Most of the groups rely on talk, but some workers also use activities (planting, cooking, rapping) in order to move to a position where verbal exchange is possible. Some groups focus more on understanding and managing their situation, others more on tasks associated with changing that situation. How the worker does the job is to be deduced from reflection on what the worker says and does. Each group also has a 'life' and the actions are related to beginnings, middles and ends of each group's span of existence. These spans range from a few consecutive hours, to some 31 meetings over seven months; the approach is shown to be applicable regardless of duration.

Groupwork comes in many forms and while the Schwartz approach so strongly demonstrated in this volume may not be appropriate in every situation the writers make a powerful argument for its usefulness to the social worker. The worker acts primarily as a mediator, helping the processes of communication and openness, and assisting group members in their interaction with each other and with the systems in which they are enmeshed. One the prisoners says 'You talk to each other like real people here' and the exchanges in the book come across as the talk of 'real people';: the workers concentrate on creating the opportunities for communication. Some may think this is not enough, but for many in the groups it has brought them to a new confidence in themselves and an awareness of their own ability to wrestle with the 'slings and arrows of outrageous fortune' and gain strength from sharing with others who are 'in the same boat'. It is a real accomplishment to capture this in print. It is to be hoped that many in Great Britain and elsewhere in Europe will take heart from this book, and gain inspiration from it. But first of all, get access to it!

Where are the practitioners on the European side of the Atlantic who can write of their work in a similar fashion? It is clear from the bibliographies that American groupworkers draw little from European writings. Yet there is much of relevance in the groupwork scene in Europe, and potential evidence to convince 'the vertical administration' of the need for self-help groupings. Perhaps what is needed are some self-help groups of groupwork practitioners, to enthuse and support each other in bringing about changes, and to deal with the blockages in the system, and in ourselves that prevent us from achieving our groupwork goals, and keeps us so often 'walking on eggshells'.

Harold Marchant, Independent Trainer and Consultant

Notes for Contributors

Articles are welcome from all who have an interest in work with groups (whether as practitioner, trainer, academic, researcher, user or consultant), and who wish to contribute to the development of groupwork theory and practice.

Types of articles

A wide range will be welcomed including:

* groupwork practice accounts which describe and reflect on group purpose, process, experience and outcomes;

* the significance of the context of groupwork (organisational, societal, policy);

* education and training in groupwork skills, methods and models (including consultation and supervision);

* group process and interventions in work groups and teams;

* issues of power and oppression in groups: the significance of race, gender, class, disability, sexual orientation and other factors in group process, and for anti-oppressive practice;

* research, monitoring and evaluation of groupwork;

* new developments: ideas for practice, ways of understanding group processes, concepts, models and approaches;

* international/European groupwork accounts/developments/comparisons/issues.

Structure and style

Please note the following points when preparing your article;

* the 'story' of groupwork practice which includes the members' own words and experiences can be very powerful;

* the use of anti-oppressive language and terminology is expected;

* please include a brief summary at the beginning, of not more than 150 words.

References

These should be quoted in the text by putting in brackets the author's name and year of publication. They should then be listed in alphabetical order at the end of the article as follows, please pay special attention to the punctuation and use of upper case letters in the examples below:

Books - authors surname, initials, date (in brackets), title of book (in italics), place of publication, publishers.

e.g. Barlow, D. and Lancing, D. (1994) *Groupwork Publications*. London: Daffodil Press.

Articles - authors surname, initials, date, title of article (within single quotes), title of journal (italics), volume, issue, page numbers.

e.g. Einstein, A. and Freud, S. (1920) 'The groupwork unconscious', *The Journal of the Future*, 24(2), pp.101-124.

Please note that it is the responsibility of the author/s to ensure that the referencing is done correctly before submitting the manuscript. Remember to double check that the date in brackets in the text corresponds to the date cited in the references list at the end.

Length of papers

The normal range is 2500-4000 words, but the editors will consider longer pieces on merit. There is also a place for briefer contributions on new developments, responses to previous articles, and other material of special interest.

Form of submission

Please supply 5 copies of your paper (3 for co-editors, 2 for assessors) initially, and keep your disk for the potential publication stage when it will be needed by the publishers. When you send your disk, please give full details of the w/p software package used, and include both the original file and an ASCII file copy. If your paper is accepted for publication, a further 3 copies of the final version will be required. Once accepted for publication, the author(s) will receive a paper indicating all the publishers' housestyle requirements, so that these can be incorporated into the final text/disc.

Please note: All papers should be sent in the first instance to Claire Wintram (address below).

Assessment for publication

When articles are first received the editors make a decision on potential suitability for the journal. Articles are sometimes rejected or returned to authors for major review at this stage. Otherwise, they are sent (anonymously) to two members of the journal's panel of assessors for their comments and views on publication. The editors make the final decision on publication, taking into account the views of the assessors. All authors receive personal feedback on decisions taken.

Book reviews

All books for review should be sent either to the publishers, or direct to Nuala Lordan (address below).

Enquiries to co-editors:

* Nuala Lordan, Department of Applied Social Studies, University College, Cork, Ireland. Tel: +353(0)21-902313/Fax: +353(0)21-275627.

* Tara Mistry, School for Policy Studies, University of Bristol, Block E, 8 Woodland Road, Bristol, BS8 1TN, England. Tel: +44(0)117-928 8492/Fax: +44(0)117-928 8586.

* Claire Wintram, Newington Services, 23 Braunstone Avenue, Leicester LE3 0JF, England. Tel/Fax: +44(0)116-255 5389.

GROUPWORK

Volume 10 Number 2 1997-98

SUBSCRIPTION, ADVERTISING AND BUSINESS ENQUIRIES
Should be addressed to the publishers, WHITING & BIRCH LTD, PO Box 872, Forest Hill, London SE23 3HL. TEL: 0181-244-2421 (Int'l +44181 244-2421).
FAX: 0181-244-2448 (Int'l. +44181-244-2448)

SUBSCRIPTION RATES
British Isles £37.50, North America US$85, Elsewhere £47.50
Special reduced rates apply as follows: Individuals to private address: £19.00 British Isles, North America, US$37.50 Elsewhere £25.00.
Special reductions for members of AASWG.
Groupwork is published three times a year.

PAYMENT
Should accompany order. Cheque or banker's draft (made payable to WHITING & BIRCH LTD) may be in any convertible currency to the relevant amount. Direct transfer can be made to our Girobank account (no. 5440564). The following credit cards are also accepted: Mastercard, Visa, Diners Club, American Express. Quote card number, expiry date and give cardholder's name and address if different from delivery address.

GROUPWORK is cited in: *Applied Social Sciences Index & Abstracts, Sociological Abstracts, Bibliographie Zeitscriftenliteratur aus allen Gebieten des Wissens, Social Care Update, Social Work Research & Abstracts, Special Educational Needs Abstracts*. and *Studies on Women Abstracts*.

PUBLISHED BY WHITING & BIRCH LTD, LONDON. ISSN 0951-824X
Printed in the UK by Watkiss Studios Ltd

Cultural Communication: Alliances or Boundaries?

A Personal Reflection on the 19th Annual Symposium on Social Work with Groups, Quebec City, Canada

I attended the 19th Annual Symposium on Social Work with Groups in Quebec City, Canada on October this year, an event hosted by Université Laval. I travelled with two colleagues from the Centre for Social Action based at De Montfort University, Leicester, though one is also a community social worker at the NSPCC. For Rhonda Wattley and myself it was our first Symposium; we considered Dave Ward an old hand as he had been four times before, until we got there and met people who had not missed a AASWG symposium for 5, even 10 years and a few people who had attended every one!

Perhaps this was one of the distinctive features of the symposium - a core of people who knew each other and each others' work well, surrounded by a larger group of people with less connection. However, established attenders made every effort to make newcomers feel welcome and would happily have breakfast with us as long as a 'real buddy' was not close by.

The venue was the Hilton Hotel - not a place I (nor I imagine many of the participants) were used to, but it served the purpose and the views from the 23rd floor, where some sessions were held, were magnificent.

For the three of us, the symposium started on Thursday afternoon when we ran a pre-symposium institute on 'Research for Empowerment'. However, the symposium formally started that evening with a reception, an opening banquet and after dinner speeches. The dinner over-ran, so Paul Taylor did not start his opening speech until after 9pm. He raised some interesting issues about cultural differences and how these differences affect communication between people of different

Groupwork Vol. 10(2), 1997-98, pp.91-94

nations. I am not sure I fully understood or agreed with his 'league tables' of different variables, but he did make many valid points about the need to consider and address the effects of culture-related communication. There followed four panellists, but I'm afraid I only managed to hear the speakers from Hong Kong and Cameroon before I was feeling the time difference from England too acutely and went to bed. Apparently, by the end of the speakers there were few people awake, many having travelled through time zones to get there.

The symposium was bilingual - French and English. Translation was provided for the large sessions, many of which were in English and some in French; while many of the French speakers managed to show the majority of us English speakers up by being able to comfortably speak both languages.

There were institutes, master classes, breakfast discussions groups, regional groupings and, of course, papers - literally hundreds of papers over the two days. The wealth and range of papers were incredible covering a huge range of topics from academics and practitioners – 'Support Groups for "Younger" Widows', 'Growing together: Horticultural Therapy with Children in a Community based Mental Health team', 'Narrative Therapy Approaches to Working in Groups', 'Program Activities: A Basic Group work Tool' – to name but a few. With some 200 presenters and over 400 participants, any imaginable theme or topic was covered, probably more than once, and if so, definitely from different perspectives.

The theme of this symposium was 'Crossing Boundaries and Developing Alliances through Groupwork'. Rhonda and I were presenting a paper on developing anti-racist practice, with the examples of working with black fathers and white women with black children, so we picked the presentations from the amazing range that had links with these themes - well you have to choose somehow! We went to papers that were discussing race and/or parenting.

The papers were paired - two presentations in one session. This meant it was possible to participate in a dynamic interactive paper for the first 45 minutes and then listen to a man reading a paper, while his colleague and wife silently read it behind him - their lips moving in synchrony, for the next 45!

Our groupwork at the Centre for Social Action is based on a clear and explicit value position. We believe in working with community members for their empowerment; we work in partnership with people and offer a process whereby they can identify their own issues and concerns and plan and create change for themselves. It was not easy to see much of this type of work on the menu, varied though it was. There was much clinical, therapeutic, behavioural and individualistic work. A completely new concept for me was people running groups that were attended by people paid for by health insurance. It was, therefore, the company that decided how many sessions took place, not the group, not need, not the individual - this seems to lead to the development of much programme-led work in groups.

In amongst this there were a few gems. For example, Tara Mistry talking about the process by which a book on groupwork within the ethnic minority communities was written in Britain. She likened the process to a groupwork process. Mace Delorme who suggests that , contrary to current social work literature, the first social work groups in North America originated among and were facilitated by Native Americans. He talked about the role of the Sweat Lodges and the Talking Circles in community decision making. Or John Hart talking about working with fathers in Norway and sharing with us the techniques he uses in the groups - this produced an emotional and thought provoking hour.

Other sessions got lost in the mass, like one on innovative practice working with adults with learning difficulties where there were more presenters than participants. Some papers had less attenders than that.

Sunday was breakfast by topic, but I found it impossible to find the group I was looking for and so just ate with friends. This was followed by the second musical interlude of the symposium, then the final plenary. The speakers were from Canada, America and England and they looked at the wider socio-political, economic and organisational changes that have impacted on social work and therefore groupwork practice. Dave Ward highlighted that there is a lot of difference between working *in* groups and groupwork. For me this encompassed the dilemma of the symposium - is *anything* that is done in groups OK? Should the AASWG welcome with open arms all people who work with a number of people in the same place at the same time? Or is *groupwork* actually something more than this? For me groupwork is about holding on to the centrality of the process and not bending to the market and instrumental pressures that are around. Groupwork should be based on clear values, incorporating notions of the power of sharing experience, of collective action and identifying group purpose. It should be about creating change in the lives of people who are discriminated against and oppressed. After all, the theme of the symposium was 'Crossing Boundaries and developing Alliances through Groupwork'. How can this be done by working with individuals only in the presence of their peers? Building alliances and crossing barriers is surely best achieved by groupwork which recognises the common experience of people, encourages the sharing of experience and knowledge and about actually changing the external world that creates the structural disadvantages that is the cause of people's problems.

For me, one of the biggest issues raised by the symposium, came not just from the papers but also conversations and by watching people. That issue is how differently it seems to me that race and difference are viewed and constructed in America, Canada and Britain. Being present at the symposium raised many questions about this for me and so far has provided very few answers. Something Paul Taylor said in his opening address has stayed with me. He made the point that when you move towards someone who is on the other side of a 'boundary', remember they are coming from another direction and everything will look completely different from where they are. It seems to me that we approach the building of alliances and crossing barriers in very different ways in the three countries and I will look for every opportunity to explore and discover this more.

As I hope I have managed to convey, the conference was more than the papers. Besides the swimming outdoors in the hotel's heated pool in the snow, and the beautiful old Quebec City, there were the meals in local restaurants with people from Ireland, Canada, America and England, the cups of tea and coffee and discussions. We came home with piles of cards from people in Detroit, Hong Kong, Bristol UK, Michigan, Quebec, Alabama and promises of keeping contact and continuing the debate and discussion. The e-mail is already buzzing.

Jennie Fleming
Centre for Social Action
De Montfort University
Leicester, England

Using the Sensory Orientation Group with a Frail Elderly Population

Norma D. Thomas[1] and Suzanne Coleman[2]

This research examined whether a sensory orientation group would stabilise or improve the cognitive functioning of frail elderly members. While all members benefited from participation, the outcome suggests that such a group is most beneficial to those who are functioning at higher cognitive levels upon entrance into the group.

Introduction

The elderly population will increase in significant numbers in the near future. In 1987, 12.2% of persons living in the United States were 65 years of age or older (US Bureau of the Census, 1989). By the year 2030, one in five people will fit into this category (US Senate, 1986). Population aging is occurring at a more rapid rate in the United Kingdom in that in 1988, 15% of the population was already 65 years of age or older (Kurian, 1991). It is estimated that at least 25% of persons age 65 and older will spend some portion of their life in a nursing home (Hooyman, & Kiyak, 1993). These demographic shifts and realities of population aging will call for service providers to

1. Assistant Professor, Center for Social Work Education, Widener University.
2. Social Worker, Bryn Mawr Terrace Nursing Home, Bryn Mawr.
Address for correspondence: Center for Social Work Education, Widener University, One University Place, Chester, PA 19013-5792, USA

Groupwork Vol. 10(2), 1997-98, pp.95-106

make drastic changes in their service delivery methods, especially in the provision of health and social assistance to the frail elderly.

There are discrepancies in the literature depicting the characteristics of the frail elderly. Some authors describe this group as the 'old-old' (persons over the age of 85), a group that Dorfman (1994) states has increased 232% over the last few years. Other authors offer that it is the vulnerability of the older person, be it physical, social, or otherwise, that characterises one as being frail (Lowy, 1983). In 1977, the Federal Council on Aging saw frailty as an 'accumulation of health, social, economic, and environmental problems which impede . . . independent living' (Mayer, 1983 p.11). For the purpose of this paper, the frail elderly will be defined as those vulnerable persons over the age of sixty-five who are afflicted with problems associated with their health/mental health and social environment. The frail elderly person can be vulnerable to a range of physical limitations, and emotional and psychological difficulties. They often rely on the care of others both within their own homes or within the homes of their families and loved ones, and need the help of a range of community health care and social welfare agencies.

The frail elderly population has a range of problems and service providers are searching for ways in which to meet their needs. Regulatory policies such as the Omnibus Budget Reconciliation Act (OBRA) of 1987 require long-term care agencies to offer 'supportive activities that provide stimulation and solace to residents who cannot generally benefit from other kinds of activities.' (Erikson and Leide, 1992 p.25).

Group process is one way of meeting the needs of this population. Schwartz and Weisman (1989) offer that a traditional group model cannot be used when working with populations such as the frail elderly because low motivation, high dependency, and unresponsiveness are often prevalent in such groups. The development of different models for group work with this population are needed.

Theoretical Framework

Group work with the elderly often necessitates an eclectic use of several theories. The most recognisable of these are reminiscence, activity, and environmental theories. The following is a brief explanation of each.

Reminiscence Theory

This type of group work uses cues to stimulate thoughts and images that lead to conversation. This conversation has a reminiscence quality, as the elderly person calls on those thoughts or remembrances most available to them from their long term memories. Reminiscence therapies have been associated with Robert Butler's research and development of life review therapy, in which older people return to an awareness of past experiences in order to reevaluate, resolve and ultimately integrate past difficulties (Butler, 1980-81). The use of reminiscence activities is seen as an outlet for socialisation, self expression, developing self esteem and companionship.

Activity Theory

Essentially this theory postulates that older people do not want to withdraw from society and that persons can and should stay involved with the world to the degree possible in order to promote well-being (Havinghurst, 1963; Rosow, 1967). The early theorists were describing people not hampered by physical or psychological problems. However, group process can provide even organically impaired persons some opportunity to use what capacities they have to the fullest (Corey, and Corey, 1997).

Environmental Theories

Environmental theories discuss the power that physical and social environments have on the individual.

Lawton (1983) developed a theory he called environmental docility, that states that an individual becomes increasingly dependent on and effected by the environment as his or her capacities decrease. Bowlby (1993) discusses the need for elderly persons in long term care settings to have supportive environments with familiar and stable settings because fixed schedules, and sensory isolation within a given environment can cause a decrease in cognitive functioning. Other environmental theories lend themselves to orientation therapies. Reality orientation was first developed by Folsom (1968) and was designed to improve behaviour and cognition in elderly patients living in institutional settings who suffered from confusion and disorientation by providing them with orienting information of person, time and place.

The reminiscence, activity and environmental theories along with reality orientation are central in setting up a framework for a method of group work called sensory orientation for the frail elderly who are cognitively impaired.

Sensory-Orientation Groups

There is evidence in the literature to substantiate the fact that those elderly suffering from cognitive deficiencies such as organic mental disorders, benefit from the introduction of sensory experiences within therapeutic group settings (Burnside and Schmidt, 1994; Ott, 1993; Bowlby, 1993, Corey & Corey 1997).

Bowlby (1993) discusses the need for an increased regimen of sensory activities, especially within those long-term settings where there is some sensory deprivation and it is difficult for residents to access needed stimulation from the environment. This type of deprivation is often found in institutional settings such as hospital wards and nursing homes. Along with the need for increased stimulation, those persons suffering from cognitive deficiencies like that of dementia, are in need of orienting experiences to person, place, and time. 'The goal of [reorientation groups] is to reduce confusion and help older persons remain as oriented as possible by providing them with basic information about their environment.' (Toseland, 1995 p. 167).

Corey and Corey (1997), stated that even when group members have high levels of organic impairment, they do benefit from brief periods of stimulation. In addition, they found it rewarding to see even minute changes, and found that three months after their group had ended, there was evidence that members remembered the group leaders.

Groups designed to reach persons who have an organic

brain syndrome can give members a chance to bolster peer relationships, gain emotional support, stimulate and encourage the functioning of whatever intellectual and social capacities remain, establish a sense of individual identity, and eliminate some degree of frustration by establishing social supports and group controls (Rice, 1997 p. 110).

The sensory orientation group serves the purpose of both stimulation and orientation for its members. The group's activities are designed to reach frail elderly persons through visual, auditory, touch, and olfactory cues that can offer validation and ego support. Sensory stimulation yields benefits to group members in that its cues promote discussion and lead to open forums for reminiscence and overall socialisation.

There are several factors that must be included when discussing the structure of a sensory orientation group, including the selection of appropriate clients, the setting in which the group takes place, the time of day, the group's size, and the format in which the group is held in order to cater to the needs of individuals. The following guidelines were adapted from Bowlby (1993), *Therapeutic Activities of Persons Disabled by Alzheimer's Disease and Related Disorders* in order to establish the Sensory/Orientation Group in this report.

Selecting the Appropriate Clients

If possible, it is beneficial to include participants at different cognitive functioning levels. Managing an entire group of individuals who are low functioning would be difficult. An individual who is in need of sensory stimulation, and responds to it particularly well, serves both as a role model for other participants and as a source of encouragement for the group leader(s).

Setting

The room should be quiet and comfortable and as homelike as possible. A table around which all participants can be seated is essential. The availability of a portable cassette, TV, and VCR is useful in providing a variety of visual and auditory stimulation methods to the group.

Time

It is essential to meet consistently at a set time and day. The recommended length of time for this type of group should be between 30 and 60 minutes. Depending on the nature of the physical or mental deficit, members may have difficulty enduring the group process and remaining attentive for longer periods of time.

Group Size

There is variability in terms of the suggested group size and its proportion to the number of therapists providing the interactions within the group. The recommended is one therapist to four to six cognitively impaired elders.

Group Format

In the first few minutes of the meeting, the leader should orient the members to the time, day, month, and season. Further information is given as to weather or current events. The group then turns it's attention to the sensory cue which occupies ten to twenty minutes of the session. The sensory cue can be visual, auditory, or olfactory, and take the form of a picture or video, music selection, or fragrance. Following the sensory cue, the group discusses the feelings and ideas the experience invokes. The group wraps up with a varied version of the orientation experience.

Following is a description of an application of the sensory orientation group processes to residents on a geriatric evaluation unit.

Group Intervention

A selected group of men, diagnosed with various organic mental diseases, between the ages of seventy-two and eighty years old, participated in this sensory orientation group in a geriatric evaluation unit of a Veteran's Hospital. Each member's mental status was measured before and after participation.

There were a total of twelve members who participated

within the sensory orientation group over a seven week period. These members were chosen for the study after a preliminary assessment identified them as having a desire to participate within the group. The staff on the unit was also instrumental in referring residents to the group. It should be noted that some participants were moved into and out of the group at different times during the seven week study. On the average, there were six to seven members participating within the group at a given session. The average age was 76. The members had a range of physical and cognitive limitations. It was found that the highest cognitive functioning member had a score of 25 on the Mini-Mental State (MMS) instrument. The most cognitively impaired member of the group scored a 6.

The Mini-Mental State Questionnaire (Folstein, Folstein, and Mchugh, 1975) was used to assess cognitive ability before members were initially admitted into the group, and again to re-assess members as they exited the group. The MMS has an optimum score of thirty points. The developers of the instrument present a continuum of cognitive ability based on a score ranging from alert (30 points) to coma (0 points). Questions on the instrument measure orientation to place and time, as well as overall cognitive functioning. Verbal participation on the member's part, either spontaneous or directed from the leaders, was noted on a tally sheet.

These measures were considered the most appropriate in terms of identifying the member's cognitive functioning before and after the group intervention was implemented. The number of times members verbally responded in the group was considered active participation, as well as showing their acceptance of the group intervention.

The presumption in running the sensory orientation group was that frail elderly persons on a geriatric ward can benefit from activities where sensory stimulating cues are used to enhance reminiscent communication. The assumptions that were tested were that participation of cognitively impaired residents on a geriatric ward in a sensory orientation group will stabilise mental status, and higher functioning members will participate more and experience the least cognitive decline.

Over the seven weeks, the sensory orientation group met twelve times. The choice of sensory cues that would eventually promote discussion was guided by an assessment of the client's observable and self-disclosed interests. There was an attempt to provide experiences that would be beneficial and enjoyed by all or most of the members within the group. Following are examples of some of the topics of the twelve sensory orientation sessions:

Sports

A video on the history of baseball was presented. Several pieces of sporting equipment were passed around for examination including baseballs, mitts, tennis balls, golf balls, and footballs.

Travel

Two excerpts of travel videos from Europe and America were shown. Several photographs were passed around depicting major landmarks in the United States. A globe was used to map areas where members had traveled throughout their lifetimes.

Nature

A wildlife video was displayed which included various aspects of nature and music selections depicting the sounds of birds and the rain forest.

Seashore

The group saw a video which portrayed the beaches of the island of Maui (Hawaii). A beach bag containing different objects used for the beach (sun-tan lotion, hats, snacks, sunglasses) was passed to each member. Music selections depicting the seashore played in the background.

Holidays

To recognise Valentine's Day, music selections reflecting romance were presented. Members were given Valentine's Day cards to make, with the assistance of the leader, for their families . At the end of the session, ice cream refreshments were provided.

Ethnicity

Photographs of international landmarks from several countries were represented. Individuals were asked about their own ethnic background. Additional photographs of foods from different countries were passed around for the inspection of the members. Music selections of varying cultures were provided in the background.

Gardening / Tools

Each member was given soil, seedlings, and a pot and were encouraged to garden. Small gardening tools were brought in and inspected by members.

Comedy

A segment from the show 'Honeymooners' video was shown. Cartoons were passed around to each member who was asked to reveal their favorite comedian, and to describe the use of comedy in their lives.

Results

For the purpose of reporting, the participants in the study were separated into two groups. Those members that scored 15 points and above on the MMS are Group A, and those who scored below 15 on the MMS are Group B. There were five members who were in Group A, the remaining seven were in Group B. The average attendance for Group A was seven sessions. The average attendance for Group B was 5 sessions. The average number of verbal participations per member was 15 for Group A, and 8 for Group B.

Table I
Sensory Orientation Group Results

Group	Average Attendance	Average Participation	MMS (+/-) In Points Per Group
A	7 Sessions	15 Verbalisations	+3
B	5 Sessions	8 Verbalisations	-2

In terms of the status of the MMS, neither group showed dramatic differences within their pre and post scores, but appeared to remain at or near their initial level of functioning as measured by the MMS. Three members who scored fifteen and above on the initial MMS (Group A) increased one point each on the post MMS test. No members in Group A declined in points. This is opposed to Group B where two members experienced a loss of one point on the post MMS.

Discussion

The results of this study were that most members who participated in the sensory orientation group remained relatively stable within their cognitive function as measured by the MMS. The number whose scores improved were offset by those whose scores decreased. The most cognitively intact members of the group were better able to participate and thus experienced less cognitive decline. Those members who represented the highest cognitive functioning levels (Group A), were able to participate the most within the group as measured by verbalisations, as opposed to those less functioning members in Group B.

Conclusion

This project set out to determine the effects of the sensory orientation group for frail elderly persons. The researchers were disappointed that there was not a more dramatic improvement of cognitive function in either of the two groups. In spite of this, the implications of the study do support the use of sensory stimulation and orientation education within geriatric facilities. There were other observed benefits produced by this group including enhanced self-esteem, socialisation, and the provision of recreational outlets.

Within the literature, there is a lack of available information concerning group work with the frail elderly. In order to support this segment of the population, practitioners must continue to focus on developing models of group work geared specifically to cognitively impaired older adults.

References

Atchely, R. C. (1991). *Social Forces and Aging,* 6th edition. California: Wadsworth Publishing.

Bowlby, C. (1993). *Therapeutic Activities with Persons Disabled with Alzheimer's Disease and Related Disorders.* California: Aspen Publishers

Burnside, I. and Schmdit, M. (1994). *Working with Older Adults: Group Processes and Techniques.* Boston: Jones and Bartlette Publishers

Butler, R. (1980-81). 'The life review: An unrecognized bonanza'. *International Journal of Aging and Human Development*, 12, pp. 35-38

Corey, M. & Corey, G. (1997). *Groups: Process and Practice.* Fifth Edition. Pacific Grove: Brooks/Cole Publishing Company

Dorfman, R. A. (1994). *Aging Into the 21st Century: The Exploration of Aspirations and Values.* New York: Brunner/ Mazel Publishers

Erickson, L.M. and Leide, K. (1992). 'Touch, taste, and smell the memories'. *Activities, Adaptation, and Aging*, 16(3)

Folsom, J.C. (1968). 'Reality orientation for the elderly mental patient'. *Journal of Geriatric Psychiatry*, 1, pp. 291-307

Folstein, M.F., Folstein, S.E. & McHugh, P.E. (1975). 'Mini-mental state: A practical method for grading the cognitive state of patients for the clinician.' *Journal of Psychiatric Research*, 12, pp. 189-198

Havinghurst, R. J. (1963). 'Successful aging'. In Williams, R.H., Tibbitts, C. and Donohue, W. (eds.). *Processes of Aging: Social and Psychological Perspectives.* New York: Atherton. pp.299-230.

Hooyman, N. R. & Kiyak, H.A. (1993). *Social Gerontology: A Muldisciplinary Perspective.* Third Edition. Boston: Allyn and Bacon.

Kurian, George Thomas. (1991). *The New Book of World Rankings* Third Edition. Oxford: Facts On File.

Lawton, M. (1983). 'Environment and other determinants of well being in older people.' *The Gerontologist*, Vol. 23, pp. 349-357

Lowy, L. (1983). 'Social group work with vulnerable older persons: A theoretical perspective'. In Saul, S. (ed) *Groupwork with the Frail Elderly*, New York: Haworth Press, pp. 21-32

Mayer, M. J. (1983). 'Demographic change and the elderly population'. in Saul, S. (ed) *Groupwork with the Frail Elderly*. New York: Haworth Press. pp. 7-12

Ott, R. L. (1993). 'Enhancing validation through milestoning with sensory reminiscence.' *Journal of Gerontological Social Work*, Vol. 20 (1/2), pp. 147-159

Rice, S. (1997). 'Group work with elderly persons'. In Greif, G.G. & Ephross, P.H. (eds.). *Group Work With Populations At Risk*. New York: Oxford University Press.

Roscow, I. (1967). *Social Integration of the Aged*. New York: Free Press

Schwartz, P. and Weisman, C. (1989). 'Worker expectations in group work with the elderly: Modifying the model for a better fit'. *Social Work With Groups*, Vol 12(3), pp. 45-55.

Toseland, R. W. (1995). *Group Work with the Elderly and Family Caregivers*. New York: Springer Publishing

US Bureau of the Census. (1989).*Statistical Abstract of the United States*: 109 edition. Washington D.C.: US Government Printing Office

US Senate. (1986). *Aging America: Trends and Projections*. Washington, D.C.: U. S. Government Printing Office.

Research into Practice Does Go: Integrating Research within Programme Development

Rob Harry,[1] Patricia Hegarty[2], Cathy Lisles[3], Richard Thurston[4] and Maurice Vanstone[5]

This paper is an account of the evolution of an integrated and continuous process of the practice and evaluation of groupwork with people who persistently offend, which underpins the work of the resource and policy unit in Mid Glamorgan Probation Service. It covers the historical context, the guiding principles, the evaluation structure and a delineation of the process of implementation which is illustrated by a description of a 'development day' involving researchers and practitioners. In a challenge to positivism, the authors advocate an honest and realistic approach to evaluation and research based on a self-reflexive learning model; and present their analyses and conclusions as an example of that model.

Introduction

This paper describes a model for integrating research and evaluation within the process of developing groupwork practice

1. Staff Development Manager, Mid Glamorgan Probation Service.
2. Probation Officer, Mid Glamorgan Probation Service. 3. Freelance Researcher. 4. Research Manager, Mid Glamorgan Probation Service.
5. Lecturer, University of Wales, Swansea.
Address for correspondence: Maurice Vanstone, Dept of Social Policy & Applied Social Studies, University of Wales, Singleton Park, Swansea, SA2 8PP

Groupwork Vol. 10(2), 1997-98, pp.107-125

in Mid Glamorgan Probation Service: inevitably, it is focused on a particular period in the life of a dynamic model, and does not reflect changes that have occurred since the end of 1995. To appreciate fully the value of the approach adopted, it is important to set this within the context of the history and function of the Resource and Policy Unit (RPU) within which the model evolved. The unit was established following the demise of the Schedule 1A Day Centre (see Vanstone, 1993), and during the early period of the STOP (Straight Thinking on Probation) experiment[1]. In different ways both had a significant influence on the shaping of the vision that informed the principles and purpose of the Unit; this influence requires explanation.

During the eighteen year history of the Day Centre (part of which included involvement in the original Day Training Centre Experiment – see, Mair, 1988)), there had been problems that are common to many specialist projects. Although it survived for a considerable number of years, changing staff groups achieved only intermittent success in maintaining a viable throughput of appropriate people. Moreover, the staff who had spent varying periods working in the Centre had experienced its positive and dynamic ethos but in a situation of relative detachment from the rest of the Service. Any explanation for this is unlikely to do justice to the complexity of its history: however, some aspects are of particular significance. Firstly, a situation in which a small group of people developed specialist practice led to an appearance of elitism; secondly, the gulf between the staff of the Centre and main stream staff created by the specialist nature of the project contributed to a disparate sense of ownership in the Service; and thirdly, the programmes which evolved owed more to the skills and interests of the current group of staff than to evidence of effectiveness. These factors, in particular, had a persuasive influence on the formulation of the concept of a field-based unit devoted to researching, resourcing and developing groupwork across the whole Service.

At a time when the Mid Glamorgan Service was embroiled in yet another discussion about the Day Centre's future, the STOP experiment was initiated. The concept of the experiment was premised on the notion that good practice should be informed by what is known about effectiveness from research findings. When the decision to close the Centre was made, the idea of creating offence specific group programmes shaped by the lessons of research, and located in the field teams rather than in a specialist unit followed a logical progression.

Accordingly, the Resource and Policy Unit was established with an explicit aim to develop, deliver and evaluate effective programmes for people being supervised by the Mid Glamorgan Probation Service. In turn, these programmes were designed to contribute to the strategy of helping people to deal with problems in ways which lessen the likelihood of re-offending and contribute towards 'protecting the public'. Its objectives are: firstly to work in close partnership with colleagues in the field teams, and to engage with relevant experts outside of the Probation Service; secondly, to ensure that all programmes are informed by what is known about best practice, and contain methods and exercises which research evidence shows are prerequisites of effectiveness; and finally to devise evaluation criteria which enable the assessment of the impact of the programmes not only on the participants but on the organisation itself.

The available knowledge base about 'What Works' in community sentences (for example: Lipsey, 1990; Andrews et al, 1990), and the STOP programme itself, has provided a template for each of the programmes as they have been developed. This incorporates: a method of ensuring the appropriateness of the target population for each group; structured programmes in manual format; a cognitive-behavioural theoretical model; the use of skilled group leaders; ownership by, and support from the field teams; mechanisms to ensure delivery of the intended programmes; on-going training and support for practitioners; and the integration of research and evaluation.

As indicated, the establishment of the RPU in 1992 augmented a policy that continues to develop focused groupwork programmes in conjunction with staff throughout the organisation. The RPU's role in developing such programmes is defined by three guiding principles: *Partnership, Effectiveness and Evaluation*. These principles have been, and continue to be, integral not only to programme development, but also to the values of the staff involved in such work. A policy document indicating the terms of reference for the RPU formalised these principles, thereby providing from the outset a sound framework upon which to develop and refine the programmes. This has proved to be particularly important in terms of ensuring the provision of resources by field teams, and the sustaining of a strategy that is shared across the Service.

The partnership principle rests upon an expectation that RPU staff work in close conjunction with colleagues in the field teams. On this basis, all the staff - development officers and researchers are involved in harnessing the knowledge and skills of field colleagues in order to develop, deliver and evaluate the groupwork programmes.

Programme development takes place within the structure of programme action groups (PAGs), the basis for which was established from the outset by a policy document which set out their terms of reference (see Appendix). Each PAG consists of at least one probation officer from each field team. They have volunteered to be involved for a variety of reasons: some for more experience in groupwork and cognitive behavioural methods, and others to contribute their ideas and experience from one-to-one work to the process of developing a groupwork package. The intention is that the groups act as a catalyst for ideas; provide continuing support for the delivery of the programmes; create a forum in which evaluation and research is discussed and programmes can be re-developed and refined; and, because of their 'democratic' structure, provide representation and links between colleagues and teams in the Service.

The co-operation of groups of practitioners in this way to develop programmes continues to access and build upon a broad range of knowledge and experience that has proved to be crucial to the effective delivery of the programmes. Although teams are expected to have one officer involved in the Programme Action Group for at least a period of 6 months there has been flexibility about this arrangement, and this has allowed local managers to utilise other interested staff in their teams to deliver the programmes. Also, officers have moved over time from one PAG to another, thereby facilitating 'cross-fertilisation' of ideas and creating further opportunities for staff development for themselves and for those who replace them. In addition Diploma in Social Work students have been encouraged to take an active role in the PAGs during their placements in the Service. To date, PAGs have focused on sex offenders, women offenders, drink driving, violence and aggression, auto-crime, and the Straight Thinking on Probation Programme (STOP). At any one time therefore, each team will have a number of its officers involved in the PAGs,

Fig.1 RPU Data Information System

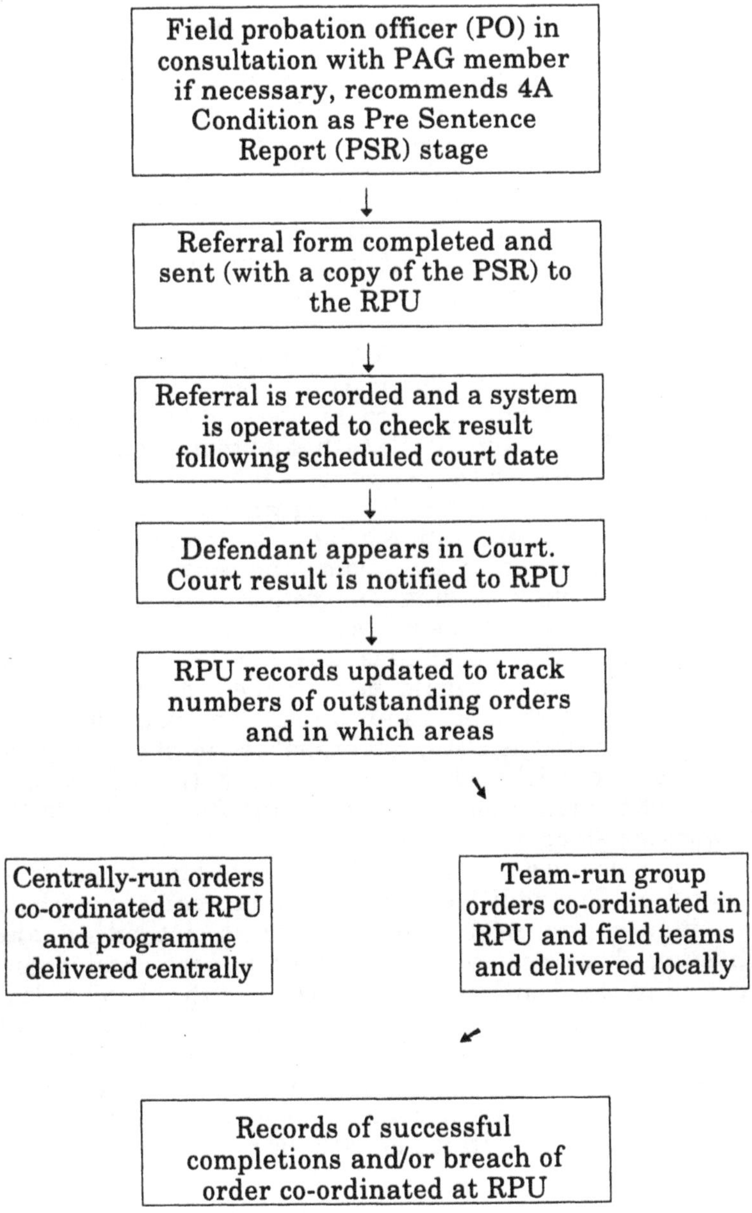

each being able to contribute to team discussions about current developments.

Administration and Organisation of the Programmes

In order for the programmes to be properly and efficiently organised, the Resource and Policy Unit operates an information system whereby all referrals and subsequent Orders to all the programmes are collated on a central data base (see Fig. 1 below). The system runs parallel to the Services' full data information system and serves a dual function, enabling RPU staff to monitor numbers and throughput regularly, and to evaluate programme process and outcomes (see Fig. 2).

Responsibility for the day-to-day running of all programmes lies with local managers. The PAG member in the field team keeps records of referrals and orders made, and when numbers allow reports back to the full PAG that a programme is viable. After consultation with the relevant local manager, staffing is arranged, following which the programme can go ahead. Throughout this process, administration staff play an essential role as information officers in teams and centrally, ensuring the comprehensive recording and collection of information needed for the process to be run successfully.

Staffing of the programmes has not proved to be as straightforward as we would have wished, as demands on officers' time are so many and varied. For example, when certain teams have been 'stuck' for numbers, joint working has been arranged with other areas. Every field team has contributed to programme delivery, with officers outside the PAG working alongside PAG members.

Programmes run centrally are delivered by staff from across the Service. The additional commitment required of both probationers and probation officers in attending and facilitating these centrally-run groups is considerable and evidenced in their enthusiasm. All areas of the Service have been represented in the programmes run in this way, although perhaps significantly, larger numbers of referrals have come from teams closer to the Unit's building. Whether programmes are run during the day or evening depends on information about the employment status of each participant.

An Integrated Model of Evaluation

The evaluation of community programmes run by probation services is most commonly undertaken on a short-term basis and by researchers employed as 'experts'. Where an individual agency might offer a range of programmes (groupwork or otherwise) usual practice and policy is to evaluate these separately as 'one-off' projects. Findings from research of this type, if communicated back to the organisation at all, are not always relevant to practitioners or managers within the organisational context, nor built-in to any developmental or implementation policy; and are thus often limited in the extent or meaningfulness of application. Where suggestions for improvement or change are proposed, this does not always take into account the realities of the working environment, in terms of barriers or conditions of service, which can result in the failure of unrealistic proposals to take hold. Furthermore, recommendations can be left on the shelf if they are not linked to a commitment by the organisation to implement them and a commitment to training, staff development, or further research and monitoring. Moreover, research into practice is rarely given the opportunity to become a continuous activity embedded within the culture of the organisation. The full impact of such a policy is rarely acknowledged, least of all evaluated (see Thurston, 1997).

With this in mind, along with the findings from the 'What Works' research that successful programmes tend to be those with integrated evaluation (Lipsey et al, 1990; Andrews, 1990; Raynor, Smith & Vanstone, 1994; and Raynor & Vanstone, 1996), we have developed a research model which attempts to contribute in a constructive and meaningful way to the development of effective programmes over a reasonable period of time. This is intended to enable practitioners and managers to build upon successes, mistakes and lessons learnt, but without allowing enthusiasm to lapse.

The research conducted in Mid Glamorgan Probation Service on groupwork has two broad aims: evaluative and explorative. The primary objective is to produce evaluations of programmes in order to inform the organisation at different levels about the efficacy of the programmes. This element of research work is mainly a descriptive and evaluative enterprise, and concentrates on programmes currently being run and developed within the Service. The RPU's role in this is to

Fig.2 Mid Glamorgan Probation Service Programme Evaluation Structure

Evaluative Method	Timing	By whom?
Probationers' profiles	Prior to programme start	Supervising Officers/ Admin Staff/RPU
Attendance and completions	During/After a programme	Admin Staff and Probation Officers
C.R.I.M.E.P.I.Cs (attitude change indicator)	At beginning and at end of programme	Trained Field Team Interviewer
Reconviction Data	During/After programme	RPU/Supervising Officers/Admin Staff
Session Evaluation	During programme	Officers facilitating programme
Consumer satisfaction questionnaires	After programme and at end of order (forthcoming)	Administered in private (organised by supervising officers)
Group interview (sample)	Near end of programme	Researcher (or facilitating officers)
In-Depth interviews with a sample of probationers	After programme and at end of order	Researcher and Practitioner-Researchers
Life history work	As part of content of some programmes	Practitioners and Researcher
Interviews with Probation Officers (group facilitators and supervising officers)	At various periods during the development of programmes	Research and Practitioners Researchers

facilitate and co-ordinate so that evaluative work is integrated within practice rather than 'an added extra' or 'an added burden'. One of the aims of this work is to encourage various actors in the process to produce evaluations from their own perspective in the organisation; either as employees or service users. Another is to generate insight and analyses from existing information systems (for example, see that described above). The findings from all these activities can then be fed back into practice development and policy formulation. The work is intended to contribute constructively to debates in the Service, such as those which take place in PAGs, concerning current and future practice through highlighting key issues emerging from evaluations.

It is also intended that research might contribute to more explorative initiatives by providing overviews involving more detailed and theoretically informed critiques on particular themes between and across programmes. Indeed, the information system described above is designed for this purpose of aggregation and comparison. For instance, it is possible to collate comparable data, such as: consumer satisfaction of completers; attitude change; reconvictions; consumer satisfaction of non-completers; and organisational and cultural contexts for groupwork. In order to carry-out the necessary evaluations of groupwork programmes within such a remit, the following research model (see Fig.2, below) has been developed alongside and integral to groupwork in the Service.

The application of this model is aimed at encouraging the comprehensive gathering and analysis of a range of information, both qualitative and quantitative, relating to the content, process, development, contexts (social and organisational) and impact of groupwork programmes. The aim is to have a structure which is eclectic, flexible, accessible, and durable.

The diversity of methods and subsequent diversity of insight cover a whole range of factors considered valuable for understanding the effectiveness of programmes, including: referrals from courts, attendance, profile information about participants (e.g. previous offending, age, gender, etc), completions, reconvictions, attitude change, satisfaction (on a number of measures), and insight into the experiences of programme participation from both probationers' and practitioners' perspectives. This diversity is built-in to try to ensure that no single 'measure' is allowed to stand alone as an index of the programme's efficacy or value; this is particularly important given the current over-reliance upon measures such as reconviction which are difficult to verify and encourage simplistic and often misleading analyses of programmes and participant change at a local level.

The model has a firm basis in the information system described above (Fig. 1), but adds other research methods and approaches. The intention is to allow for: continuous and regular monitoring of programmes (referrals, attendance, completions, etc); the involvement of field team staff; analyses involving the comparison and aggregation of data from and across all programmes, so that longer-term and broader patterns relating to the effectiveness of programmes can be analysed (for example, in relation to reconviction data, attitude change, targeting of appropriate participants, etc); and the inclusion of current and future programmes as and when they come 'on line'.

Our approach to research acknowledges the added benefits of encouraging a 'culture of curiosity' within an organisational context, and the research model reflects our desire to develop this. Simply put, this approach is characterised by being 'inclusive' rather than 'exclusive'[2]. Indeed, a large proportion of people who are supervised by the Service, and practitioners running and developing programmes, have participated in, and/or facilitated evaluation. For example, research interviews and focus groups have been carried-out extensively with groupwork participants.

It is acknowledged that a research process of this sort, which is grounded in the views and experiences of participants, can have considerable benefits. It can encourage participants to actively take part in decision making in the organisation, and allow for their views and experiences to be acknowledged and acted upon in the process of developing programmes. In this sense, the research work is seen as modelling skills and values which are an underlying part of the programme's approach. For example, cognitive programmes value and encourage participants' skills of critical self-reflection, and research interviews can further reinforce that. As such, the elements of the research model which directly involve probationers in this way are understood as part of the intervention and not separate to it. It is hoped that they provide a further opportunity for participants to review their order, whilst reinforcing a self-reflexive learning model.

This may seem to contravene the 'sacred laws' of social science - especially in respect of 'objectivity'. However, this relates to important criticisms of positivist approaches to the application of research methods. In relation to interviewing techniques, for example, Christine Griffin (1991) argues against a 'nodding dog' approach which involves implicit collusion with everything being said by the interviewee; with the 'justification' that this is necessary to remain neutral yet at the same time elicit information. Not reacting in any way (theoretically possible, practically impossible) might give the impression of passive approval. This can be questionable on ethical, personal, political, and effectiveness grounds. Clearly all this has to be balanced with the goal of producing 'valid' research, and so is a process that needs to be dealt with honestly and realistically; certain tensions and contradictions remain and clearly define the research process as a complex one influenced by a range of factors. This contradicts those who view research as necessarily clear-cut, objective, rational, and immune from social processes or organisational and cultural contexts.

Similar concerns and values are associated with our approach to involving practitioners in research. For the large part practitioner-evaluation of programmes is on-gong and routine, and facilitated via Programme Action Groups. This contributes to a dialogue between practice and development, and is recorded in minutes of the meetings. For example, shortly after the production of an interim evaluation report on the Steering Clear programme, a development day was held with ten staff who had contributed to the programme's development and delivery as members of the PAG. Clear aims were outlined for the day as follows: to discuss and analyse the main findings from the research; and to generate ideas and strategies for developing the programme based upon the findings. The day started with a summary of statistical feedback concerning attendance levels, completion rates and profile information on participants (age, previous convictions, etc). PAG members discussed issues arising. For example, they were particularly interested in how age and previous conviction was a factor in differential completion rates and this prompted a discussion of appropriate targeting and assessment. Participants also made proposals relating to the direction of future research and analysis; a number of PAG members, for example, requested a breakdown of feedback and outcomes group-by-group in subsequent reports.

Prior to the development day, a selection of the more qualitative material from the research had been prepared in an accessible form. Participants were asked to analyse feedback from probationers and the probation officers who had run the programme. The aim of this was to engage practitioners in considering in-depth the meanings attached to the programme as experienced by a sample of those who had run or participated in it. This was intended to frame the rest of the day by formally grounding subsequent discussions and developments in the research and the experience of both staff and probationers. The discussion was wide-ranging and prompted discussion of various avenues for consideration in future development work.

A number of issues in particular were identified in the PAG members' analysis of the research, which together generated the identification of one key area for further development work. It became clear from a detailed reading of the qualitative feedback that some probationers were ill prepared for the intensive engagement required of the groupwork. This had caused problems in the initial stages of the group, and was manifested in terms of resistance to the material and group processes, and in some cases was linked to absence and suspension from the programme. Alternately, some excellent work was identified as being undertaken by supervising staff in teams prior to the start of the group. A proportion of both probationers and officers expressed the view that not enough could be done in the time limits of the groupwork programme, and that it was unrealistic to expect the changes in behaviours and attitudes necessary to make a difference to offending to accrue from groupwork alone. Members of the PAG also highlighted that some of the officers interviewed for the research had felt frustrated because it was not possible to go into as much depth on certain issues as they felt was necessary; this was echoed by those present who had run the programme themselves.

A further issue identified by PAG members involved a sophisticated analysis of the data presented to the officers in the morning of the development day. A brief profile of the probationers who had been interviewed had been provided noting a number of relevant details including the length of time which had lapsed from their participation in the group to the date on which they were interviewed. PAG officers were impressed by the 'freshness' and detailed knowledge expressed in a number of comments probationers had made in the research interviews over a year after the group had ended. On further examination and discussion it was revealed that these probationers had been supervised by officers who had a detailed knowledge and some experience or interest in the Steering Clear Programme and the methods and focus of its content. This had been used to instigate further focus on themes from the programme in subsequent one-to-one supervision, thus acting as reinforcement to the groupwork element.

More generally, concern was expressed by PAG members that the programme was seen by some staff as separate to other aspects of probation in the culture of the organisation. One danger identified in discussion was the potential for probationers to experience contradictions between the groupwork and post programme supervision elements of a probation order. This was associated with concerns that programme integrity needed to be ensured across the whole order in order to avoid different messages, methods or focus being employed which might counteract the work done in the group. Consequently, the development group felt that it might be more helpful to talk about a 'Steering Clear Order' rather than single out the groupwork as 'the place for doing interesting and challenging work". It was suggested that future research might be devised to emphasise such a focus on enhancing both the integrity of offence focused work and to increase the effectiveness of the whole order.

Whilst this insight generated by PAG members may seem to be anecdotal and commonsense, the process of engaging officers in analysing research findings in this way did prompt a fresh, critical and explicit focus on issues which can all too easily be passed over in pragmatic and sometimes short-sighted attempts to simply get programmes up and running. In this respect, we agree with Richard Johnson's (1996) assertion that:

> The first and still most important form of cultural studies is to make explicit what we know already implicitly as participants in a culture. (Johnson, 1986)

Furthermore, the solutions which followed were grounded in, and built upon, the discussion of the research findings.

Indeed, the morning's debate shaped the focus of the afternoon into a developmental forum. The group decided that a focus on pre- and post-programme material was needed as the next stage in the development of the Steering Clear Programme. The research discussion of the morning prompted and informed a further debate relating to the pros and cons of such work, and strategies needed to implement the necessary changes in practice.

The fact that such a process was undertaken with a group of staff who represented their field teams across the whole Service is crucial. Members of the PAG were able to return to their offices and discuss with their team colleagues the renewed enthusiasm for their work and a greater insight into the effectiveness of that particular area of practice. A further and more profound knock-on effect of the approach is to start to demystify groupwork and research as exclusive specialisms. Indeed, the development day described here should be viewed as part of a process of opening-up practice development and research. The benefits of doing this are wide-ranging. One central aspiration of our approach, however, is that any subsequent proposals for change generated via the processes outlined in this paper are more likely to be met with informed, positive and critical engagement rather than hostility or suspicion. Two years on, we're now reaping benefits of this kind from the work undertaken and initiated on this development day. The proposals made by the Steering Clear PAG in relation to developing pre- and post-programme material were later taken up by the other PAGs for the Drink/ Drive Programme, the Anger Management and Men's Violence Programmes and the STOP Programme.

Having a unified and managed system for research and practice development across all these programmes and across the whole Service has meant that research findings and consequent practice developments, such as those described here, are shared, co-ordinated and applied throughout the Service. Moreover, these changes have had an effect on the culture and direction of the organisation. The Service's initial investment and focus on effectiveness - as described in this paper - has been on groupwork. Yet the developments outlined above have shifted that focus properly into other areas of the Service's provision, most importantly one-to-one supervision. It is possible to show how the work described in this paper has acted as a catalyst for this process along with other research and developments which have occurred during the same period (see for example: Deering, Thurston & Vanstone, 1996).

Thus, with practitioners firmly involved in the process of evaluating the programmes they run, it is hoped that this has a number of effects, not least in terms of the following:

- Practitioner-ownership of programmes and research and evaluation;
- Research findings and recommendations for improvements are more quickly and enthusiastically taken up by practitioners.
- Accessibility of findings for practitioners when research is informed by their own concerns and by those of probationers.
- Greater appreciation and knowledge of approaches to evaluation and research.
- Opportunities for improving communication between practitioners, managers and researchers.
- Promoting a 'culture of curiosity' through routine discussion, reflection and learning.

Conclusion

Our aim to co-ordinate an integrated model of development and evaluation within practice is not as yet fully realised. The process of engaging an organisation in change of this type, which impacts upon the whole professional culture, is a task constrained and shaped by a large number of factors, relating, for example, to the local management of resources, changes in legislation and Home Office policy, as well as local management priorities.

Furthermore, it would be hypocritical for us to advocate a system based upon on-going critical reflection and learning, and not to realise the need to reflect on our own practices as development and research workers. As an integral element of the research conducted over the last four years, staff perspectives concerning the role and function of the RPU have been sought. Our belief that such self-reflexivity is essential is justified on two grounds. Firstly, we think it acts as a model reinforcing the importance of being self-critical and responsive; secondly, because as researchers we are always as much a part of the organisational culture as those who we designate as 'research subjects'; and thirdly, because it provides an important perspective on the implementation process so often neglected in research into groupwork programmes in probation and elsewhere.

As a result of this self-reflection we have been made aware of many areas in need of further consideration and improvement. For example, we have found difficulties in obtaining large enough samples to satisfy rigorous research criteria. Moreover, it has proved unrealistic to believe that it is possible to apply a complex research strategy equally and as intensively across a range of Service provision. We have been forced to consider very carefully often subtle distinctions between the different functions fulfilled by monitoring, evaluation and research. In this respect, we have had to vary the intensity of research scrutiny according to the different stages of development that a programme goes through. We have also learnt abut the need for (both senior and middle) management support and ownership in the processes examined above - including inclusion within Service policy and planning. Significantly, we have learnt that when in place, evaluation can provide a basis for consistency in service provision even (or rather especially) during a time of cuts and changes in legislation and working practices.

Nevertheless, what we hope to have communicated here is a system which can create the conditions within which development of practice is grounded upon continuous critical appraisal and reflection, and empirical knowledge of what works best, via an approach which values the inclusion of people within that process.

Acknowledgement

The authors would like to thank all the staff of Mid Glamorgan Probation Service upon whose work this paper is based.

Notes

1. The STOP programme is based on the Reasoning and

Rehabilitation model developed by Robert Ross and is essentially a cognitive-behavioural groupwork programme. See Raynor, Smith & Vanstone (1994) and Raynor & Vanstone (1996) for descriptions and subsequent evaluation of the STOP programme in Mid Glamorgan.
2. See David Faulkner (1996) for further development of these concepts in relation to public service provision in the criminal justice system.

References

Andrews, D.A., Zinger, I., Hope, R.D., Bonta, J., Gendreau, P. and Cullen, F.T. (1990) 'Does correctional treatment work? A clinically relevant and psychologically informed meta-analysis', Criminology, 28, pp369-404.

Deering, J., Thurston, R., & Vanstone, M. (1996) 'Individual Supervision and Reconviction: An experimental programme in Pontypridd', *Probation Journal*, Vol.43, No.2, June.

Harry, R., Hegarty, P., Thurston, R., Vanstone, M. & Young, C. (1995) *'It gives you a different perspective on life": Interim Report on the Steering Clear Programme*. Bridgend: Mid Glamorgan Probation Service.

Faulkner, D. (1996) *Darkness and Light: Justice, Crime and management for Today*. London: The Howard League.

Griffin, C. (1991) 'The researcher talks back', in W.B. Shaffer and R.A. Stebbins (eds) *Experiencing Fieldwork: An Inside View of Qualitative Research*. Newbury Park CA: Sage.

Johnson, R. (1986) 'The story so far: and further transformations', in David Punter (ed), *Introduction to Contemporary Cultural Studies*.

Lipsey, M.W. (1990) 'Juvenile delinquency treatment: a meta-analytic inquiry into the variability of effects'. Paper presented to the 2nd European Conference on Law and Psychology, University of Erlangen, Nuremberg.

Mair, G. (1988) *Probation Day Centres. London: HMSO.*

Raynor, P., and Vanstone, M. (1996) "Reasoning and rehabilitation in Britain: The results of the STOP Programme', *International Journal of Offender Therapy and Comparative Criminology,* 40(4), pp272-284.

Raynor, P., Smith, D. & Vanstone, M. (1994) *Effective Probation Practice*. Basingstoke: Macmillan.

Thurston, R. (forthcoming) *The Influence of Organisational Factors upon the Implementation of Effective Programmes*. Oxford:

Probation Studies Unit.

Vanstone, M. (1993) 'A Missed Opportunity Reassessed: the Influence of the Day Training Centre Experiment on the Criminal Justice System and Probation Practice', *British Journal of Social Work*, 23, 3, pp213-29.

Vanstone, M. (1995) 'Managerialism and the Ethics of Management', in R. Hugman & D. Smith (eds) *Ethical Issues in Social Work*. London: Routledge.

Appendix 1

Programme Action Groups
Terms of Reference

These Terms of Reference are particular to the following Programme Action Groups; Drink/Drive; Anger Management; Women Offenders; Violence; Steering Clear; Sex Offenders.

1. They monitor and evaluate programme development including research aspects, in conjunction with staff of the RPU. To use the information collated to consider the adaptation and refinement of programmes when appropriate.
2. To act as a Support Group which will facilitate shared learning for staff involved in running programmes. Any training needs identified must be referred to the RPU Senior Probation officer (SPO) for consultation with the field SPOs and the Training SPO.
3. PAG members will be expected to be involved in the delivery of programmes. (It is acknowledged that this will not be possible on all occasions, but the final decision on all group leadership issues will be made following discussion between the relevant field Senior Probation Officer and the RPU Senior Probation Officer).
4. PAG members, with support of the group to act as reference point within the team for all issues relating to the programme. This will include discussion of referrals, collation of referrals, dissemination of information and maintaining the profile of the programme.
5. Under normal circumstances, to maintain consistency within the PAG, membership should be for a minimum of six months.
6. These Terms of Reference will be reviewed annually.

Brief Group Therapy and the Use of Metaphor

Christian C. Sunderland[1]

This article examines the use of metaphor in brief groupwork, beginning with a selective historical overview of brief psychotherapy. The author introduces a brief group named Strategic Group which runs for ten weeks with ten themes. The use of metaphor in Strategic Group is explained. Metaphors can include activities, stories, film clips and pictures. It seems that the metaphors cause a response leading to group discussion, as well as achieve a cohesive group in a faster period of time and resolve standstills when 'cohesive' becomes 'stuck'. Metaphor as a tool in groupwork may have promise as it serves as instrument to help clients reframe their thinking and address psychodynamic issues.

Brief Therapy: A selective historical overview

Traditional psychotherapeutic groups using a psychodynamic model operate for long periods of time. It is not uncommon to see these traditional groups run for months, even years. In these groups the therapist has minimal participation in directing the group. The notion is that the group belongs to its members and moves forward at their pace, the major role of the therapist being to facilitate interaction between group members (Yalom, 1995).

Brief group therapy has a long history. Even in the early days of psychoanalysis therapy was brief (Budman & Gurman,

1. Clinical Social Worker.
Address for correspondence: Cardston Clinic, Provincial bldg, 576 Main Street, Cardston, Alberta T0K 0K0, Canada

1988). As the goals of therapy became more complex focusing more on the client's personality than 'symptom relief', the course became more and more prolonged (Malan, as cited in Koss et al, 1986). However, it wasn't until the late 1960s, and particularly during the 1980s that the sociopolitical climate continued to favour the development of short-term therapy models (Budman & Gurman, 1988).

This emphasis on brief methods (including group work) in current clinical practice has been attributed to three major factors. First, clients entering therapy are seeking specific problem resolution. Second, studies show brief therapy to be as effective as long-term therapy. Finally, economic restraints have placed limits on the number of sessions that health care systems pay for (Levenson et al, 1995). 'Long term therapy of unlimited duration is quickly becoming a relic of the past ... the therapist of today is beginning to bear little resemblance to yesterday's practitioner of long term psychoanalytically oriented treatment' (Dast, 1995).

In addition, an informed public are no longer ready to accept clinical recommendations unquestioningly. The Zeitgeist is to seek faster, less costly and more efficient therapies. It is these contributing factors that give brief treatment its increasing prominence (Budman & Gurman, 1988).

The therapist's techniques are modified in brief group therapy. The groups are generally more structured and have a specific plan. The therapist undertaking short-term therapy in groups must attempt to develop as much cohesiveness as possible to enable members to derive as much as possible from the experience (Sadock, 1989).

The distinguishing features of brief psychotherapy are outlined by Koss et al (1986):

1. Limited time
2. Limited goals
3. Maintenance of focus
4. High therapist activity
5. Prompt intervention

The brief group work that I am involved with incorporates the above principles of brief psychotherapy. The name of our brief group is Strategic Group. It was thus called because it is a group whose goal is to find strategies for increased coping.

Strategic Group

Strategic Group is a structured group, meaning that each session has a theme, i.e.—family, feelings, stress, relaxation management, grief work, etc. The major assumption is that the clients understand the definition of the theme but have trouble incorporating the theme into their lives. Strategic group focuses on strategic plans, new choices clients may have, discusses how different behaviours work to accomplish desired goals. This is done through role play, therapeutic metaphor and group discussion. For example, if the theme was self-esteem, little time would be spent in defining self-esteem. Most of the discussion would focus on how to incorporate self-esteem into our lives, what the barriers are and how they are overcome.

Strategic Group is a closed-ended group. The group lasts for 70 minutes twice a week. One theme will be presented per week for two groups, for a period of 10 weeks. The major focus of this group is that change can be accomplished by planning and structuring the group. To this end, 10 themes are presented. These themes are:

1. Self-talk, Reframing
2. Feeling and Communication
3. Self-esteem
4. Family
5. Relationships Closure
6. Relaxation
7. Stress Management
8. Addictive Behaviour
9. Grief Work
10. Overview/Closure

Selection Criteria

There are two other therapists that work in the same clinic as I. As we review clients' files potential names for strategic group are discussed from each of our case loads. Priority is given to clients who may benefit from the instillation of hope and the universality that comes with group process (Yalom, 1995). Clients considered for group are those who are having difficulty coping with any of the theme areas discussed in strategic group, and who might benefit from group interaction that they don't receive in individual counselling.

Pre-Group Orientation Interview

Once names have been selected, appointment times are scheduled to meet with each potential group client. Together, all three therapists conduct the interviews. In the January to April 1997 group, twelve people were interviewed. The results were that two people were not interested and that two other people were considered less appropriate at this time. By the end of this process eight individuals completed a consent form for admission to strategic group.

The group consisted of both male and female participants. It was hoped that shared perceptions from both sexes would encourage maximum interaction. In this group client problems were not sex specific so a mixed group seemed appropriate. The group included a wide range of ages—the youngest 32, and the most senior, 73. There was diversity in education and socio-economic status. All group members were heterosexual caucasians, whose ethnicity included living in a rural farming community. Metaphors that were selected for group were done so trying to be sensitive to the above demographics.

These clients were told during the interview that there would be 20 time-limited group sessions and they were given an itinerary that schedules the 10 themes discussed in group. Group members were instructed that the group is named strategic group because the focus of the group is to explore new strategies for coping in the theme areas. The emphasis is on reframing current problems, changing perception and strategising new alternatives in the '*here and now*' (Yalom, 1995).

Introduction Group

The purpose of the introduction group is for the members to meet one another, and to determine in the clients' minds if the 20 sessions group experience might have potential. Many of the points explained in the pre-group orientation interview are again reiterated here, though this time with the use of a therapeutic metaphor. As clients came into the session, for example, there is a game of chess set up on a small round table in the centre of group. Group members are told that strategic group is like playing chess. We then proceed into a discussion on the game of chess having the group explain the purpose that strategic thinking plays in the game. In this particular group all the members knew about the game of chess and seemed to understand the link between the game and strategic thinking. One male client used his own metaphor of army officers planning war manoeuvres to accomplish desired goals. However, some games like chess, are culturally defined and perhaps not accessible to everyone. Chess maybe more familiar with one sex than another, and presume a degree of intellectual understanding and ability that is not always shared. It is vital if metaphors are to be effective that they can be generalized to incorporate the differences that may exist within the group members. Again, the objective with this metaphor was to have clients consider what the next few moves will or could be in dealing with their present problems. Then the clients are encouraged to disclose their personal goals for group and how they might strategise and accomplish the same.

Change and Metaphor

Nicholas (1984) states in her book *Change in the Context of Group Therapy* that 'most psychological and emotional disturbances are related to inadequate frames of reference'. A frame of reference or paradigm is how one sees the world. A paradigm shift is a change in how one sees the world. Covey (1992) gives an example:

> Two battleships assigned to the training squadron had been at sea on manoeuvres in heavy weather for several days. I was serving on the lead battleship and was on watch on the bridge as night fell. The visibility was poor with patchy fog, so the captain remained on the bridge keeping an eye on all activities. Shortly after dark, the lookout on the wing of the bridge reported, 'Light, bearing on the starboard bow.'
> 'Is it steady, or moving astern?' the captain called out.

> Lookout replied, 'Steady, captain,' which meant we were on a dangerous collision course with that ship.
> The captain then called to the signalman, 'Signal that ship: We are on a collision course, advise you change course 20 degrees.'
> Back came a signal, 'Advisable for you to change course 20 degrees.'
> The captain said, 'Send, I'm a captain, change course 20 degrees.'
> 'I'm a seaman second class,' came the reply. 'You had better change course 20 degrees.'
> By that time, the captain was furious. He spat out, 'Send, I'm a battleship. Change course 20 degrees.'
> Back came the flashing light, 'I'm a lighthouse.'
> We changed course.

The paradigm shift experienced by the captain and by us as we read this account puts the situation in a totally different light. It is these shifts in perspective, causing us to view something differently because of the aid of the metaphor, that is of interest in strategic group. It is the aim of Strategic Group to assist individuals to change their frames of reference. When we can learn to see things differently, powerful change can happen in the individual (Covey, 1992).

Metaphor has been referred to as the 'language of change' (Watzlawick, 1978).

> As long as recorded history has been around, and in myths that date back into the farthest and dimmest memories of human existence, metaphor has been used as a mechanism of teaching and of changing ideas. Shamans, philosophers, and prophets alike have intuitively known and used the power of the metaphor. From Plato's allegory of the cave right through to Voltaire's Zadig, from the teachings of Jesus and Buddha to the teachings of Don Juan, metaphor is ever present as a tool for changing ideas and affecting behavior. (Bandler, as cited in Gordon, 1978).

Robbins (1992) states:

> Whenever we explain or communicate a concept by likening it to something else, we are using a metaphor.

Whenever we 'liken' something to something else with the

intention of instructing or advising the listener, or if the listener implies for himself such an advisory relationship, then that comparison becomes for that person a metaphor. (Gordon 1978)

In his book, *Guru: Metaphors from a Psychotherapist*, Sheldon Kopp defines metaphor as follows:

> Generally, a metaphor is defined as a way of speaking in which one thing is expressed in terms of another, whereby this bringing together throws new light on the character of what is being described. (Kopp, as cited in Gordon, 1978)

Kopp's conception of metaphor as a wide-ranging source of 'new light' on old concerns is one which we can profitably use in the context of therapeutic metaphors (Gordon, 1978). Again, it is the comparison and symbolism (ie, life and lemons), and the imagery, (ie, make lemonade), that give metaphor its power. Metaphor knits ideas together in memorable ways, it also stimulates new associations, offering alternative choices (Rempel et al, 1993). By reframing clients' problems, metaphors challenge constraining beliefs, thereby opening new ways of thinking, perceiving and believing (Rosen, as cited in Rempel et al, 1993).

Some common sentence examples of metaphor are:

> 'I'm as happy as a lark.'
> 'I'm at the end of my tether.'
> 'I've got the whole world on my shoulders.'
> 'When life gives you lemons, make lemonade.'

Metaphor informs by ways of likeness or resemblance between two ideas that are not literally alike. Metaphor is like seeing with new eyes as metaphorical imagery reveals new possibilities for consideration (Garcia, 1995).

Metaphorical Intervention in Strategic Group

On one level, Strategic Group acts as a metaphor in and of itself. Nicholas (1984) comments on this phenomenon while speaking of group work in general:

> Group therapy provides a plethora of new metaphors for the client in the form of stories, analogies and actual events. In addition, at any given moment, for each individual, the group can 'be' a number of different things, each existing on a different logical or metaphorical level. The group can function as a support group, a collection of friends, and a source of objective feedback, while simultaneously (paradoxically) having a metaphorical existence as a surrogate family, microcosm of society, a slate of transferences, or a representation of the different parts of self. Any or all of these can occur for any one person singly or in combination.

This is an interesting line of thought. However, I am more concerned with actual metaphorical techniques used within the group and as part of the therapy plan.

The types of metaphor used in Strategic Group include activity, story, film clips and pictures. The metaphors are chosen, based on their ability to encourage discussion on the theme that is being presented.

Activity Example

Heap (1985) states that activities in groups 'bring up issues which strongly invite discussion. Indeed, they often thrust important material into the discussion whose fervour reflects the intensity and relevance of the experience.' In Theme One, Self-Talk and Reframing, a metaphorical activity is used. The objective of this theme is to show that two people can see the same thing, see it two different ways and both be right.

I show the group two pairs of sunglasses, one with dark brown lenses, the other with yellow lenses. Each group member is invited to look through both pairs of sunglasses in turn. The clients are told that the dark lenses represent a reactive, pessimistic, rigid lifestyle. The yellow glasses represent a proactive, optimistic and flexible lifestyle.

As each client looks through both pairs of glasses they see the same visual field but in a different light. The clients are then reminded that they have the choice to see the world through either pair of sunglasses. Just as changing the lenses shows they have the power to change aspects of their vision, so they also have the power to choose their own direction.

Reframing occurs as they articulate a transference of the metaphor illustration to their own life situation.

Story Example

Stories can produce a safe emotional parallel to real life experience that are non-threatening. Group therapists should be aware of the need to familiarize themselves with a culturally rich cross section of stories to potentially touch the differing experiences of group members. In Western and European cultures, for example, Cinderella and Show White are well known stories. Initially, it may be easier for a client to discuss Cinderella's and Snow White's abuse than it is to discuss their own abuse. Once the door is open to a discussion about abuse, clients can discuss their own abuse, if relevant, as they feel comfortable.

Bettelheim as cited in Gordon (1978) states that:

> the fairy tale is therapeutic because the patient finds his own solutions, through contemplating what the story seems to imply about him and his inner conflicts at this moment in his life. The content of the chosen tale usually has nothing to do with the patient's external life, but much to do with his inner problems, which seem incomprehensible and hence unsolvable. The fairy tale clearly does not refer to the outer world, although it may begin realistically enough and have everyday features woven into it. The unrealistic nature of these tales (which narrow-minded rationalists object to) is an important device, because it makes it obvious that the fairy tales' concern is not useful information about the external world, but the inner processes taking place in an individual.

Love You Forever is a children's story by Robert Munsch (1986). The story is about a mother and son. In the book, the mother expresses an enduring love for the son in each stage of his development. In each stage, the mother is shown holding and rocking the son. Finally, the son becomes an adult and has a child of his own. The mother becomes old and frail and the book ends with the son holding and rocking the mother and expressing that he would 'love her forever'. This story metaphor was helpful to one client in Strategic Group whom I shall call Jim.

Jim came to the Strategic Group having attempted suicide and feeling deeply depressed. Jim idealized his father whom he described as being strong and independent with an 'old country' mentality. Lately, the father's health was deteriorating, making it difficult for him to work. There was an expectation in Jim's mind that he would eventually need to take over the family business. The prospect of this frightened Jim.

With the father's declining health and Jim's growing depression, great worry and stress developed in Jim's traditional European family. There was little evidence to suggest that the family supported one another or expressed their fears to one another. Jim's suicide attempt was impulsive and appeared to be a cry for help in a worried and psychologically defended environment.

Jim entered Strategic Group appearing shy, wanting to please and stating that he was 'happy, with no problems'. He was difficult to engage in group work; his comments were shallow and suggested he lacked insight and depth. At times, Jim looked puzzled, as though he did not understand the group around him.

In Theme Four, Family, the story *Love you Forever* (Munsch, 1986) was presented. This emotionally charged story usually produces a significant response; it certainly produced a response in Jim. He became animated, his affect was brighter and he began to fidget in his seat.

Jim stated that he could 'Identify with the son in the story'. Where he was seeing his own situation as pessimistic, the story comparison instilled hope, offered a new perspective, provided a new frame of reference. Perhaps, said Jim, he could care for his ageing parents, particularly his father. The story seemed to release in Jim a flood of emotion. It was the first time that Jim had been able to speak of his family in Strategic Group. He stated that he wanted a family similar to the one in the story.

Whether Jim could really take care of his family and run the family business was not important at that moment. What was important was that he felt empowered by the comparison and was open to consider new alternatives. Through the medium of metaphor, Jim was able to discuss his feelings and see some organisation of a possible plan for the future. The metaphor seemed to help him change his frame of reference.

Film Clip Example

Film clips seem to be a very powerful metaphorical tool. Television and films have a role in modern story-telling. The combination of sound, colour and moving picture is both enjoyable and memorable. Whittock (1990) in his book Metaphor and Film, states: 'The greatest metaphors, cinematic and literary alike, encapsulate the most telling truths'.

Movie clips used in Strategic Group are brief, averaging five minutes in length. A number of clips have been used, each chosen for its ability to relate to the theme being discussed.

'Steel Magnolias' (Tri-Star, 1989) has a powerful scene that deals with the theme of grief. In the film, Sally Field weeps and wails over the death of her daughter, played by Julia Roberts.

After showing this clip, a client asked fellow group members 'Is it OK to be angry like that?'. The client apparently interpreted what she saw in the clip as a healthy display of anger. Usually reserved, her unspoken question seemed to be: 'If I got angry like Sally Field (if I incorporated this new social skill), would I still be accepted by the group?'. With resounding support, the group reassured this client that she belonged, whether angry or not and encouraged her to be open about her anger and abolish her old `keep a stiff upper lip' paradigm.

The emotional intensity in the scene from 'Steel Magnolias' seemed to have paradigm shifting potential. Other movie clips I have used include a clip from 'Gandhi' (Columbia, 1982) that demonstrates listening, understanding and conflict resolution; a clip from the movie 'Beaches' (Touchstone, 1988) which shows how two characters work through an angry confrontation to a successful resolution and a clip from 'Fried Green Tomatoes' (Universal, 1991) which shows empowerment when Kathy Bates breaks down a wall with a sledge hammer, symbolically taking emotional control of her life. This latter clip can serve as a metaphor for clients who need to break free of the walls that surround them.

There are socio-cultural differences in the ways men and women are given permission to express anger or grieve loss. For this reason other film clips have been selected that model male emotional reactions. 'Shadowlands' (Savoy, 1993), for example, shows a father and son together grieving the loss of their wife and mother. 'Dead Poet's Society' (Touchstone, 1989) shows several ways of dealing with anger, authority figures and resolution.

Dramatic metaphors seem to compel attention and consideration. They can both model alternative behaviour and cause group members to consider other alternatives.

Picture Example

A simple picture may be the catalyst to start change when used in a brief group setting. The following case example shows how a picture might be used.

Irene, in her mid-forties, was suffering from depression and suicide ideation. She was grossly overweight and presented herself as a pleasant, yet tired and worried individual.

Irene's husband was a truck driver and this meant that he was often away from home. Her daughter lived out of town with her partner and their child. Irene's other child, a son, had just left home. Irene was struggling with the 'empty nest syndrome'. Her life was centred around her family which she now saw as being gone.

Irene's family described her as loving but so much so that it bordered on 'smothering'. Both her son and daughter described a need to get on with their own lives. Both felt controlled and guilty about their mother's illness. She would frequently remind them that she had sacrificed the 'best years of her life'.

Irene was recommended for group therapy. To participate in group therapy, a large chair was brought in to accommodate her size. There was a picture on the group therapy room wall. It was a picture of a large, derelict barn in the middle of a barren field. During one group session in which Irene participated, the group was asked to look at the picture of the barn and respond to what they saw. Irene, upon studying the picture responded by saying she 'felt like the barn'. She was asked to explain what that feeling was. She described the feeling of being big, empty and lonely.

The picture metaphor was the beginning of her exploration of her feelings about herself. The picture was the catalyst, it started a catharsis and process which led to insight into her situation. As group therapy progressed, she became an active group participant. Irene's depression gradually lifted, she lost a significant amount of weight and appeared to be motivated to lose more.

Her family relationships improved as her own mental state improved. She was willing to grant her children their independence as she found meaningful activities to occupy her own time.

Finding and Discussion

It would appear that metaphors work in group psychotherapy because of the rich imagery associated with the comparison. Metaphor seems helpful in four different areas:

1. Metaphor causes a response that leads to discussion.
2. Achieve a cohesive group in a faster period of time.
3. Resolve standstills when a cohesive group becomes stuck
4. Metaphor may stimulate memory.

Often the best group work is achieved at a cohesive stage. (Yalom, 1995) Cohesive groups take time to evolve and don't just happen. However, in brief group work there isn't always the time that traditional norms would dictate. How do you help a group during its initial stage of orientation and hesitancy move toward a cohesive working group? One can answer: maybe with the introduction of metaphors.

I have observed that metaphor helps produce a language that only the group seems to understand. Over the course of strategic group clients would make reference to stories, clips, etc. that were discussed in past groups. For example, some clients stated, 'I've got to overcome my own 'dragons', or 'I'm coming out of 'the cave'. Outsiders observing such comments would not understand their significance. But the group understand the metaphor and becomes part of the group identity and that mutual understanding potentially binds the group, reinforcing a feeling of cohesiveness.

Another observation is that metaphor can stimulate discussion when a cohesive group becomes stuck. For example, a client wanted desperately to reconnect with her father, but because of her intellectual approach, failed to gain the emotional support and feedback that the group was capable of giving. Stuck, a clip from the movie 'On Golden Pond' (1981) was shown. The clip modelled a father and daughter resolving years of conflict. The experience was extremely powerful and the group moved quickly from an intellectual experience to an emotional one (Sunderland, 1995).

It also seems that metaphor may stimulate memory. When group members were asked to review what happened in past groups, very often the thing first recalled were the metaphors used from previous groups. When the group was asked to recall the sessions on self-esteem, for example, their first comments were about 'cows and dragons' (metaphors from the stories told in those groups). It seemed that the discussion of cows and dragons helped them to remember what was said about self-esteem. Just as children seem to learn the alphabet more quickly when the letters are set to music, clients seem to recall group themes when metaphors are applied to them.

I also observed that giving potential group members an itinerary of group themes seemed beneficial. Not only was it a schedule, providing structure and a time frame, it also gave clients something to think about beforehand. Often clients were ready to get right to work when group began because of the internal processing that was done even before group. Comments such as, 'I knew this was coming up...' or 'I'm looking forward to...' or 'I'm anxious about an upcoming theme', were common.

Concluding Comments

Metaphor is a therapeutic tool that acts as a catalyst in encouraging change. Metaphor, according to Falkenheim (1993), 'is another way of prying ourselves loose from the narrowness and repetitiveness of our singular experience'. I have found that metaphor, in our brief strategic group, is one way of presenting a stimulus in the hope of expanding clients' experiences, thereby creating an atmosphere of change.

I have observed that metaphor can illustrate a point, suggest possible solutions and other alternatives and models of behaviour. Where language is often inadequate, metaphor seems to speak to the inner life where feelings, affections and beliefs exist (Ember, 1966). It also seems that metaphor has the power to bypass resistance, particularly in relation to feedback, by the therapist or other members (Yalom, 1996). Zeig (1985) states, 'Metaphors create an atmosphere where patients feel less threatened; where suggestions can be interspersed in a way that bypasses defences'.

Metaphor, then, is a technique to further the process of exploration and emotional understanding within a brief strategic therapy group setting. The purpose of metaphor is to elicit a response in the group member, whether their interpretation of the metaphor is positive or negative. Such responsiveness can 'jumpstart' the group into a working mode encouraging group process, cohesiveness and reframing. With the use of activities, stories, film clips and pictures clients may interpret these metaphors from their own unique perspectives. Their own personal interpretation can be fertile ground where insight and growth may occur.

I am aware, however, that more research and follow-up need to be done. The suitability and effectiveness of different modes of metaphor needs exploration and the dangers or disadvantages of metaphors also require rigorous attention. Currently, I am in the process of evaluating differing measurement instruments so that I am able to better assess our data. But my experience so far is that metaphor as an instrument to reframe thinking and address psychodynamic issues has promise.

References

Budman, S. and Gurman, A. (1988) *Theory and Practice of Brief Therapy,* New York: The Guilford Press

Covey, S. (1992) *The Seven Habits of Highly Effective People*. London: Simon/Schuster.

Dast, B. (1995) 'Creative short term group therapy in a managed care environment', *Groupwork*, *8(3)*, pp302-312.

Ember, W. (1966) *Metaphor and Meaning*. Deland, Florida: Everett Edwards.

Falkenheim, J. (1993) 'The education of a clinical social worker: Finding a place for the humanities'. *Clinical Social Work Journal,* 21, pp85-96.

Garcia, J. (1995) "Freud's psychosexual stage conception: A developmental metaphor for counsellors',. *Journal of Counselling and Development*, *73*, pp498-502.

Gordon, D. (1978) *Therapeutic Metaphors: Helping Others Through the Looking Glass*, Cupertina, CA: Meta.

Heap, K. (1985) *The Practice of Social Work With Groups: A*

Systematic Approach London: George Allen & Unwin.
Koss, M. P.; Strupp, H. H. and Butcher, J. N. (1986) 'Brief psychotherapy methods in clinical research', *Journal of Consulting and Clinical Psychology 54,* (1), 60-67.
Levenson, H., Speed, J. and Budman, S. (1995) 'Therapist's experience, training, and skill in brief therapy: A bi-coastal survey', *American Journal of Psychotherapy, 49,* pp95-117.
Munsch, R. (1986) *Love You Forever.* Willowdale, Ontario. Firefly Books.
Nicholas, M. (1984) *Change In The Context of Group Therapy.* New York: Brunner/Mazel.
Rempel, K. Hazelwood, E. and McElheran, N. (1993) 'Brief therapy group for mothers of troubled children', *Journal of Systemic Therapies, 12,* 32-48.
Robbins, A. (1992) *Awaken The Giant Within.* London: Simon & Schuster.
Sunderland, C. (1995) 'Right brain metaphors: A catalyst to group work', *The Canadian Group Psychotherapy Association Chronicle,10,* pp6-8.
Watzlawick, P. (1978) *The Language of Change.* New York: Basic Books.
Whittock, T. (1990) *Metaphor and Film.* Cambridge: Cambridge University Press.
Yalom, I. (1995) *The Theory and Practice of Group Psychotherapy.* Fourth Edition. New York: Basic Books.
Zeig, J. (1985) *Ericksonian Psychotherapy. Volume II: Clinical Applications.* New York: Brunner/Mazel.

Videos

Attenborough, Richard (1982) Gandhi.
Attenborough, Richard (1993) Shadowlands.
Aunet, John (1990) Fried Green Tomatoes at the Whistle Stop Cafe.
Marshall, Garry (1988) Beaches.
Ross, Herbert (1989) Steel Magnolias.
Rydell, Mark (1981) On Golden Pond.
Weir, Peter (1989) Dead Poet's Society.

We'd Like You to Come Back

Hilary Hopkin[1]

This article is an account of the setting up and running of a group for people newly registered blind or partially sighted. There is emphasis throughout on access of all kinds and on multidisciplinary working. I have discussed the groupwork methods used, the grieving process involved in sight loss and the social implications of sight loss.

Introduction

Soon after I started work in the St Paul's Eye Unit of the Royal Liverpool University Hospital, I attended a meeting of a consumer group campaigning for better services and improved environment for visually impaired people. At that meeting a young woman described her feelings on being registered blind some years before.

> I walked out of that clinic and I could have gone straight under a bus for all my life was worth. I was the only person this had ever happened to. I was completely alone. There was no-one there for me. I cried for weeks after that.

Of course there was someone there for her, but the link had not been made effectively, and there were services available, but after a long delay. However the same sense of desolation

1. Social Worker.
Address for correspondence: Social Work Dept, Royal Liverpool University Hospital, Prescot Street, Liverpool L7 8XP.

and desperation has often been expressed by visually impaired people who have been registered. It was with the idea of helping at this point of crisis that the Registration Group was set up.

Three Agencies

The Eye Unit had long wanted to re-establish a social group for registered blind and partially sighted people that had met monthly in the evenings some time before. The staff were motivated to renew discussions when a minibus was donated to the Unit which could be used to provide transport to such a group, as well as for the community diabetic eye screening which was its main purpose. At the same time Liverpool Voluntary Society for the Blind (LVSB) was planning a rehabilitation group for visually impaired people and their carers with a fixed programme. They were also trying to develop closer links with the Eye Unit. As the social worker covering the unit I was aware of both plans and the need to deliver the specialised service more quickly to newly registered people, who often waited several months for their initial visit, so I proposed meeting to discuss running a group jointly. The result was a series of six meetings, which, it was intended, would provide helpful information, establish contact with local specialist services and give an opportunity for mutual support among visually impaired people and their carers. We met fortnightly in the Eye Unit, with each agency taking responsibility for the meetings most appropriate for it. The sessions were repeated and are now an accepted part of the clinic's life, taking place three times a year.

Planning

Planning for the group was largely practical and was done at one meeting between the three members of staff directly involved and managers from two of the agencies. We had all participated in groups and sometimes led them, but I was the only one with any formal knowledge of groupwork or training in it. I have to say I did not feel particularly expert, having boned up on notes from my social work course a decade previously and given some thought to the processes before the planning meeting.

Times and dates were agreed without difficulty, as was the programme already largely prepared by LVSB. The format of the sessions was not controversial, nor the need for transport, which was offered by both LVSB and St Paul's.

Michael Preston-Shoot lists eight kinds of groups in *Effective Groupwork* (1987): psycho-therapeutic; counselling; educational; social treatment; discussion; self-help; social action; and self-directional. This one was clearly to be educational or information-giving in nature, with elements of helping people to help themselves. One of the aims was to 'reduce the powerlessness, isolation ... attached to members as individuals' and to 'narrow the gap between potential and actual functioning ' (ibid).

We thought it might have a therapeutic function as well, but this was not the motivation for the group. It was never to be a social action group as a local group of visually impaired people exists to campaign for the removal of environmental barriers. We tell our members about this so they can if they wish take a hand in shaping their own environment and making the wider public aware of their needs.

The group did not replace work with individuals: I had assessed and given a certain amount of information to all members previously and they had individual home assessments by a rehabilitation officer while the group was running or soon afterwards.

The planning group discussed whether we should have an open or a closed group. The clinic and LVSB representatives wanted to include new members as we went along, so that newly registered people would be offered information and support quickly. I favoured a closed group because the literature seemed to suggest that the dynamics were better and I had had practical experience of groups where people had disclosed quite personal material at an early stage. The majority decision turned out to be a good one: we have been able to integrate new members very well as we went along because each meeting had a separate topic and was self-contained. The timetable meant that it was time limited.

We did not discuss confidentiality as an issue, yet in practice our professional ethics ensured that confidentiality was maintained when people brought individual problems to us and there was frequent mention of the confidentiality of all our services throughout the sessions.

There is a lot of healthy debate around models of disability and definitions of terms such as impairment, handicap and disability (see Swain et al, 1993). People vary in the degree that they are handicapped by their sight loss, especially in later life. They need to make a personal adjustment to this as well as seeing that the environment and public policy and attitudes disadvantage them. Sally French insists that not all disability is a social construct, and I believe that many of our group members feel disabled by their acquired inability to scan their world as they did when their sight was good. This disability lies within them as much as the use of printed matter for the dissemination of information and for pleasure lies outside them and needs to be compensated for by our literate society. One aim of the group is to make a start in addressing both issues.

The Members

Fifty people who had been registered in the previous six months were invited to the first series and encouraged to come with a friend or relative (25 attended the first meeting). Subsequently people were invited as and when they registered. The age range reflected the visually impaired population i.e. 90% were over pension age (Bruce et al, 1991). Two of the groups we have now run had one or two members from ethnic minorities. A number of people had other health problems and it was noticeable in the first group particularly that some of the carers were very frail or had disabilities themselves. Hearing impairment was common in all groups.

Basic Principles

We were keen to make the meetings as accessible as possible, so invitations were issued personally, a handout in large print was provided by the clinic staff and a letter together with the programme in large print was sent out by post. An RNIB survey has shown that three out of four people with a visual impairment can read large print (Bruce, et al, 1991). Some people, with whom the first contact was by telephone, were invited over the 'phone as well as by letter.

We used a portable loop system for the first meeting, but it was not very successful, so we borrowed an amplifier and microphone for several meetings until we got a grant from the hospital League of Friends to buy a Minivox portable amplifier with microphone. This has worked extremely well, as long as it was only used in the main group, and its use has been extended to announcements for waiting patients in all the eye clinics. A service user poignantly expressed the need for this to Rayner (1995): 'When you go blind you go deaf somehow or another'.

In spite of the use of the Minivox, background noise and a suitably sized meeting place continued to be a problem in the running of the group. The first area we met in was a large open space which echoed and which was closed off to the public by a grille rather than a solid door. Even though we met in one corner of it, we felt exposed on two sides. We tried an area which was almost an alcove and screened it off, but noise was still a problem and late-comers could not see us from the entrance. Unfortunately we have not been able to find a room with good acoustics which has easy public access.

We have used the Unit's minibus, which has no special facilities, and LVSB's old and new minibuses as time has gone on. The new one has special features for visually impaired people (contrasting markings at the entrance and on steps, for example) as well as a low step. A tail-lift for physically disabled people and wheelchair users is to be fitted shortly. If a suitable vehicle was not available for a particular member, the Unit ordered a hospital taxi. Only a small proportion of people took up the offer of transport, most of them making their own way by public transport, private car or taxi, with or without an escort.

Most written material has been provided in large print, with a little on tape if available from public bodies like the Benefits Agency. We booked an interpreter from the local Interpretation Service for several meetings in our first series, for the benefit of one member. This was paid for by the Social Services Department.

In these ways we tried to emphasize not the disability of the individual, but the removal of barriers so that the group members could participate fully and with dignity.

Multidisciplinary working was another priority, so we gave

all the agencies involved an equal say in organising and managing the meetings. Where one agency had special skills or knowledge, for instance when LVSB were running a session on mobility and guiding, we made sure someone from the clinic welcomed people and introduced the session. The Out-patient Manager organized the talk on medical aspects of registration and provided the meeting place and refreshments most weeks. I organized the meeting on benefits.

The Programme

The first session is an introduction to the group with a talk about the registration process and how people might be feeling, followed by a talk on eye conditions by a doctor. The reason for this was that people long registered had often expressed their confusion about the meaning of registration to LVSB and each other in consumer groups. LVSB also reported that people often seemed not to know what was wrong with their eyes or what the name of their eye condition signified. One member asked in an early meeting, 'What exactly is glaucoma?'. It was very important to the clinic staff as well as the members to be able to deal with questions like this authoritatively. Registration is often seen as the end of the road, and doctors as well as patients can focus on eyesight and eye health rather than on a future living with a disability and adjusting to it.

The second meeting has always been on benefits, because questions on benefits and concessions have been the among the most frequent to all the agencies. Liverpool is economically deprived by any measure, and maximising benefits is of great importance to many pensioners, as well as younger people, particularly when their disability incurs extra costs, for instance in transport, or getting help in the house or garden. Rayner (1995) recorded two comments which expressed the need for help in negotiating the benefits system: 'I think they should have said it's not that easy, none of the benefits are very easy' (service user) and 'I played [the benefits information tape] in the car and I just couldn't understand it ... It was just so complicated' (doctor).

This session gave us some of our biggest problems in getting competent and visually aware speakers and in managing a lot of queries about personal finances which needed to be dealt with in private. Our first outside speaker was a local Benefits Agency trainer who had little experience of speaking to visually impaired people. In subsequent programmes we used a Benefits Agency worker who had been seconded to a blind welfare organisation some distance away. Because we had large numbers at the first series, we arranged for a local Welfare Rights adviser with experience of disability to back her up in the 'surgery' which formed the second part of the session. This left us with the problem of what to do with people when they were not seeing the benefits advisers.

The third meeting is usually on Mobility. We take carers in a separate group to work on their awareness with the use of simulation spectacles before giving some training in guiding. Simulation techniques are now a controversial subject. The local Social Services Disabled Workers' Group has lobbied successfully to prohibit the use of these techniques in the department's training on the grounds that it serves no useful purpose and that 'pretending to be disabled' is demeaning to disabled people (a controversial term in itself). There is a range of opinions among visually impaired people themselves and the Forum of Organizations providing Services to Visually Impaired People on Merseyside, which has a respectable representation of visually impaired people in its management and service provision, supports the use of these techniques.

The visually impaired members have their own session on the use of various canes and methods for mobilising safely indoors and out, but both groups are led by trained rehabilitation officers. Help with mobility is not always a perceived need. People may have given up trying to go out. RNIB research shows that an even higher proportion of visually impaired people are housebound and isolated than disabled people as a whole (Bruce et al, 1991). The public perception of mobility training is about white sticks and guide dogs. There are two problems with this: people do not perceive themselves as blind because they have some residual vision, and they may not want to use either a dog or a white stick. The question of using residual vision to move about safely or learning how to guide and make the environment safe usually needs to be raised by trained people. This session gives carers an opportunity to relate their own experiences and express their feelings in relative privacy. These are often similar to the patients'. They say that they have denied that things were so bad, or that they didn't understand that sight loss was so disabling. They express feelings of guilt, sadness and anger, as documented in classic writing on bereavement, such as Kubler-Ross (1972) and Parkes (1975).

We hold the fourth session off-site, visiting a resource centre which has a display of aids to daily living. Sometimes we have been at the resource centre as a group of holiday-makers has arrived back. Members have shown a lot of interest, and have occasionally signed up there and then for the next holiday. Perhaps for the first time they acknowledge the reality of their sight loss. They may also be resuming an activity they had given up. We see this as movement through the grieving process as well as a way of overcoming practical difficulties in pursuing normal social activities by the provision of appropriate resources.

The fifth session is usually on communication skills, a technical term covering reading and writing, the use of tape recorders, VDUs etc. The fact that people with visual impairments know little about these alternatives shows how unaware our literate society is in general of the need to provide not only the tools themselves but the information about them in accessible formats for visually impaired people.

The final session in each series has been an open session to recap on the programme, help people decide what aids, services and activities they would like to take up and to evaluate the programme with all concerned.

The Group in Practice

The full session lasts two hours with a longish break for tea, chat and individual consultations with the staff in the middle. One of us has always introduced the sessions and encouraged questions. The use of a Minivox with its roving microphone has been invaluable in this. We have not excluded any subjects if they were of interest or concern to the group members. Quite often the difficulties they expressed have been offered to the group for solutions. We have tried to make announcements about local events of interest, such as meetings of other organisations, and have fitted in other bits of information such as the procedure for getting a Disabled Person's Car Badge, or tax and VAT concessions, as part of the announcements.

As always in groups, some members contribute more than

others. Early contributions are almost always tentative, stimulated by a reference perhaps to a difficulty in distinguishing coins, or to the frustration of not being able to tell the time even by a large clock or watch. We feel it is much more effective and informative to ask the group if anyone else experiences such a problem or has found a solution to it. Quite shy people seem to enjoy demonstrating their talking watch and telling the others where they got it and how much it cost, or they will talk to their neighbour in the interval about how they organise their coins and banknotes so that they can distinguish between them.

Few of the common problems, such as silence, dominant members or conflicts were evident, though occasionally two members would talk together rather than participating in the whole group. The main problem with this was one of hearing, as otherwise we encouraged members to help each other and form relationships.

When it came to the last meeting of a series there were always one or two people who did not want to stop meeting even though it had been made clear that the programme was fixed and new people would be starting at the beginning of the next programme. We had a modest celebration tea with cakes at the end of a series to acknowledge the importance of the group for the members and ourselves, a rite of passage or 'symbol of non-rejecting endings', as Preston-Shoot puts it (ibid). LVSB provide other group activities which members may move on to.

Evaluation

Formal evaluation by means of a simple questionnaire in large print prepared by the clinic manager is carried out at the final meeting. Many attenders, including the carers, complete their own questionnaires or help each other. Staff are available to read or write for other members. The results have been almost totally positive. We clearly meet our objectives of providing information, professional help and mutual support soon after registration. The few negative remarks have enabled us to address difficulties such as the use of the amplifier in small groups, which did not work. We have had one very positive suggestion for improvement, which was that we should provide hand-outs at the end of the session, so that people could remember the information better. We failed to do this for the following group, but have now produced the majority of them and will give them out at future meetings. We will also include a previous attender to give the service user view.

After the third group I surveyed the non-attenders by completing a questionnaire on home visits. This was designed to establish whether the non-attenders had access to the same information as attenders. The group was never intended to give its members an advantage over those who did not attend. We were pleased to find that on the whole non-attenders had received a visit or visits from a rehabilitation officer or support worker during the time the group was running and had, one way or another, had access to similar information. The big gain for the group members was in meeting other visually impaired people and, for the carers, getting some training in guiding techniques and visual awareness.

A largely unforeseen result for the attenders, established by interview with the Senior Rehabilitation Officer and the manager of a day rehabilitation centre, was that the attenders were much more focused on their needs when they had their individual assessments and they were much more accepting of their sight limitation at that stage than the non-attenders (Rayner, 1995). It seems that the group had served to take the members further in the grieving process for their sight loss than would otherwise have been the case. This enabled them to benefit more quickly from formal rehabilitation programmes and other services available to them. We had been aware of the inhibiting effect of loss on visually impaired people's ability to benefit from rehabilitation from research commissioned by Christopher Grange Day Rehabilitation Centre, but were somewhat surprised by the therapeutic effect the group seemed to have.

Our success has been due to very good planning at the beginning. As time goes on problems are creeping in, partly because we are a bit complacent about the programme and our past success and do not plan as meticulously as before, partly because we do not have any joint supervision. We three professionals have supervision within our own agencies, the purpose and styles of which may be different, but we do not have help in coping with the practical problems of the group, difficulties in the group process or difficulties between ourselves which may lie below the surface. We have a lot of communication before and after the group meetings and relationships are good, but I think we must now address the need for supervision and training. I suspect the three agencies will come with different expectations and agendas and that addressing them may be quite painful.

Keys to Success

Certain key measures seem to have ensured the success of the Registration Group. Firstly we were responding to service users expressed needs. Then the warm personal invitations backed up by a letter in a format accessible to most visually impaired people (large print). Thirdly, the use of amplification, which followed the example of meetings run by 'experienced' visually impaired people themselves (The Merseyside Action Group and the local branch of the Partially Sighted Society). Next, help with suitable transport where necessary. Also, the use of expert speakers who are sensitive in their communication with this user group and the use of qualified interpreters. There is a strong feeling that, because patients see the St Paul's Eye Unit as a helpful place with caring staff, it is easier to come back here than to go to a new place in the community, which might have an off-putting or emotive name such as 'Social Services' or 'The Blind Society'. Encouraging friends or relatives to attend increased people's ability to take in information and gave both carers and visually impaired people their own space to express frustrations and other feelings.

Our multidisciplinary working enabled people to make the transition from hospital-based services to community-based services and support, and from perceived health problems which prevented normality in everyday life to a more informed position where they could cope on a practical and social level. This is in keeping with the recommendations in Hill et al (1988) that 'links between hospital and community services should be explored in order to enable a swift and appropriate response to be provided to people needing a rehabilitation service'.

Applications for Other Groups

I found virtually no literature on the kind of group we are running at St Paul's, which is more an information group with a therapeutic spin-off than a long-term support group or a therapeutic group, yet I know that our group bears some similarities to a carers' group for dementia sufferers and a stroke group that are run in local hospitals. There are support groups of all kinds throughout the country. I believe there is a place for hospital based groups for people whose crisis is identified in a hospital setting - diagnosis of cancer, amputation, head injury, neurological disorders. All the key measures noted above could be relevant for the success of such groups.

In the field of visual impairment we have shown that a group for newly registered people can have benefits. In situations where there is a shortage of rehabilitation staff, it can actually bring the services to the people more quickly and provide them with an informal support network, which they might otherwise not have been able to create.

References

Bruce, I. McKennell, A. and Walker, E. (1991) *Blind and Partially Sighted Adults in Britain. The RNIB Survey*. Volume 1. London: HMSO.

Davidsen-Neilsen, M. and Leick, N. (1989-90) 'Open grief groups: The resolution of complicated loss', *Groupwork*, 2(3).

Hill, R., Horan, T., Jobbins, M. et al. (1988) *A Wider Vision*. London: DHSS.

Kubler-Ross, E. (1972) *Death and Dying*. London: Tavistock Publications.

Parkes, C. M. (1975) *Bereavement: Studies of Grief in Adult Life*. Harmondsworth: Penguin.

Preston-Shoot, M. (1987) *Effective Groupwork*. Basingstoke: Macmillan

Rayner, R. (1995) *The Role of St Paul's New Registration Group as an Information Provider: A Multi-Disciplinary View*. Unpublished research Liverpool University

Swain, J, Finkelstein, V., French, S. and Oliver, M. (1993) *Disabling Barriers - Enabling Environments*. London: Sage

Further Reading

Hull, J. (1990) *Touching the Rock*. London: SPCK.
Lomas, G. (1993) *A New Deal for Blind and Partially Sighted People*. London: RNIB.
Moore, N. (1993) *Information Enables: Improving Access to Information for Disabled People* . London: Policy Studies Institute.
Oliver, M. (1996) *Understanding Disability*. Basingstoke: Macmillan.
Stevens (ed) (1993) *Back from the Wellhouse.* CCETSW Paper 32.1.

The Use of Music in Group Work with Out-patient Alcoholic Couples: A Pilot Investigation

Wilfred A. Gallant[1], Melanie D. Gallant[2], Kevin M. Gorey[3], Michael J. Holosko[4] and Sammi Siegel[5]

Although much practice-related research exists on social work with groups or music therapy with alcoholics, not a single study to date has combined the two intervention strategies. Previous practice experience had suggested that the use of music may facilitate generalist social work practice in small group or family formats with alcoholics; this study begins to explore this possibility. A qualitative assessment of the use of music in brief (four two-hour sessions) group work was conducted with three couples, one of each of whom was an identified alcoholic by virtue of their past completion of a residential programme for alcoholics. The couples concurrently participated in an aftercare programme and were also engaged in work with a mental health professional outside of this study's preview. This qualitative study made the following tentative inferences: (1) that such combined music-group work intervention will facilitate generalist problem-solving across psycho-social domains (e.g., alleviation of depression, fewer problems with personal relationships at home or at work); (2) an estimated nine of every ten clients are expected to experience such problem alleviation

1. Associate Professor of Social Work, University of Windsor. 2. Research Assistant, Human Services Research Unit, University of Windsor. 3. Associate Professor of Social Work, University of Windsor. 4. Professor of Social Work, University of Windsor. 5. Assistant Professor and Director of Music Therapy, School of Music, University of Windsor.
Address for correspondence: Social Work Program, University of Windsor, Lambton Hall, 401 Sunset Avenue, Windsor, Ontario, N9B 3P4, Canada.

Groupwork Vol. 10(2), 1997-98, pp.155-174

> *or amelioration (Cohen's [1988] U3 of 88%, a 'very large' interventive effect); and (3) that, not surprisingly, the effectiveness of this intervention is specific to those clients (an estimated 80%) who reported that they enjoyed music. This study laid the theoretical groundwork for the coherent design of a music-group work intervention, the more methodologically rigourous evaluation of which is currently underway with a large quasi-experiment for out-patient clients.*

Historically, the use of groups with alcoholics preceded their endorsement as the therapeutic modus operandi of Alcoholics Anonymous (AA) (Chalken, 1979; Tournier, 1979). The relative cost effectiveness of groups, their mass appeal plus their natural 'goodness-of-fit' with alcoholism rehabilitation and recovery caused them to become a cornerstone principle of AA In turn, it is well established that AA philosophy laid the foundation of contemporary alcoholism rehabilitation in North America be it in-patient, out-patient, or self-help (Armor, Polich, and Stambul, 1976).

In reviewing the past 30-40 years of clinical and empirical literature in this area, there have been consistent pleas for: 1) more studies of group effectiveness in out-patient community settings (Bloch, Reibstein & Crouch, 1985; Butler and Fuhriman, 1980; Miller and Hester, 1986); 2) more studies defining effectiveness criteria and outcomes for alcoholic groups (Brandsma and Pattison, 1984; Colson and Horowitz, 1983; Dwoskin, Gordis and Dorph, 1979; Heather, Edwards and Hore, 1975; Parloff and Dies, 1977); and, 3) more studies exploring the differences between group effectiveness and other forms of alcoholism treatment (O'Farrell, 1992; Sobell, Brocre, Sobell, Roy, & Stevens, 1987).

Brandsma and Pattison, two leading and respected investigators [in the alcoholism field] who conducted a major review of group literature with alcoholics a decade ago concluded:

> ... despite the scientific problems, we would like to state that considering the state of the art of empirical research, there seems to be decent clinical fact and some empirical validity to group therapy being a valuable addition to treatment or as part of a programme. The preponderance of evidence in this area is in a positive direction and supports clinical and anecdotal conclusions, but lacks as yet robust and substantive validation. (1985; p.160)

The past ten years of research in this area has done nothing to change this contention, in particular as it relates to the effectiveness of alcoholic groups in out-patient settings (Kinney, 1996) .

Certain requisites of out-patient alcoholic groups whether they are: orientation or alcohol education groups, groups of unrelated married or unmarried alcoholics, spousal groups, couples' groups, family groups, or groups of alcoholics and unrelated spouses of other alcoholics (Anderson, 1983), increase the likelihood of their effectiveness. These include: 1) a trained group leader [preferably experienced] whose orientation is clear, (e.g., Rogerian, insight-orientated, problem-solving); 2) structured time parameters around the group process (e.g., short-term [3 sessions] to long term [1-2 years]); 3) therapeutic goal-oriented sessions (e.g., communications skills training, marital, family or feminist therapy); and, 4) relatively homogeneous groups of alcoholics at the same stage of recovery. Not surprisingly, as a cohort, these criteria for alcoholic groups present as success criteria generalisable across a variety of client groups (Yalom, 1985).

Alcoholic clients who have volunteered for group generally respond positively to music therapy in addiction treatment (Dougherty, 1984; James 1988a, 1988b, Murphy, 1983; Tredor-Wolff, 1990b). Specifically, the role of music is to facilitate therapeutic goals, enhance one's insights, develop group cohesion and support, and break through typical addiction problems such as denial, resistance to therapy, disclosure and self-discovery (Beasley, 1987; Broucek, 1987; Gallant, 1995; Gallant & Siegel, 1995, Gladding & Heape, 1987; James, 1988c; Rosellini & Worden, 1989). Indeed, with such group approaches, it has been shown that 'music seems to be able to influence clients non-verbally in ways not open to the human therapist, who is limited to words' (Halpern & Savary, 1985, p.103). Conspicuously absent in this body of literature is any study of the use of music in alcoholic groups in out-patient settings, as all of the published accounts of such group effectiveness are limited to in-patient samples (Treder-Wolff, 1990a).

The purpose of this exploratory study was to conduct a pilot investigation assessing the use of music in social work with alcoholic couples in an out-patient setting. Two main rationales for the study were: 1) there is a distinct void in the literature in this field; and 2) that since this was deemed a 'level 1' exploratory study in the classic sense (Tripodi, Fellin & Meyer, 1983; Grinnell Jr., 1994), it would assist in question generation and hypotheses formulation for subsequent investigations involving more rigourous methods. The main assumption put forward was that social group work [using a social work problem-solving approach with groups] and music are effective in working with this population and this study sought to explore more about this variable relationship.

Method

Client Participant Sample

A convenience sample of three heterosexual married couples (*N*=6) agreed to participate in this qualitative study by giving their signed consent. The sample was predominantly white, middle class and Canadian and they ranged in age from 31 to 51 (M*d* = 43) and had been married to each other on an average of seven years. They were all concurrently participants of an evening aftercare programme for couples at the Brentwood Recovery Home for Alcoholics in Windsor, Ontario where one member of each couple had completed a three-month residential programme during the past two years. This programme is essentially based on the a '12 Step' recovery model with a spiritual underpinning (Gallant, 1994). Moreover, the couples each had an established and ongoing relationship with a mental health professional (e.g., social worker, psychologist or certified alcoholism counsellor). This was important because the approach to interest them in this study reportedly appealed to their altruism, rather than to any expected personal benefits, that is, they were being asked to help build an interventive strategy which may be expected to benefit other clients in the future. The purpose of the study, that is, its proposed exploration of the use of music in working with alcoholics and their families, was didactically presented to them before they volunteered in June, 1995. This outline as well as the study design had been approved by both the University of Windsor's and Brentwood's institutional or 'human subjects' review boards.

Group Intervention Format

In a brief small group format' four two-hour sessions over two weeks' the participants were asked on a structured open-coded questionnaire about their perceptions of 12 folk songs (all with three or four stanzas and a refrain, and acoustic guitar accompaniment) and 2 poems during the structured group sessions. Working within the context of Brentwoods's Model of Recovery and its treatment philosophy, the topical-song/poem selections that were used distinctively connected to pertinent spiritual and rehabilitation issues brought up by clients during the four two-hour sessions over two weeks and consistently parallelled the major themes or talks covered overall in the daily programme. These songs and poems included: (1) 'Ruffled Waters', (2) 'Danielle Danielle', (3) 'In You I Take Refuge', [Poem], (4) 'Where Teardrops Fall', (5) 'Ode To Song', (6) 'Father and Daughter' [Poem], (7) 'Hand in Hand', (8) 'In The Stillness of My Journey', (9) A Precious Love, (10) 'Among The Wildwood Trees', (11) 'Sharing The Love That Frees Us', (12) 'Will You Pardon Me?', (13) 'A Healing Hand', and (14) 'Candle In The Night' . These topical songs and poems respectively paralleled the following major Brentwood themes of: (1) Pain and Guilt, (2) Being Influenced, (3) Insecurity-Security, (4) Chaos and Confusion vs. Balance and Enthusiasm, (5) Conformity, Submission, Surrender, Cooperation and Contribution, (6) Respect, (7) Involvement, Love and Maturity, (8) Decisions, (9) Decisions-Direction, (10) Sharing, Friendships and Relationships, (11) The Now Talk, The Missing Link, Interest in Others, and (12) Caring, and Forgiveness, (13) Healing, and (14) Freedom. Both the songs/ poems and topics were systematically related to issues of recovery, recognition of marriage problems and provided 'food for thought' in dealing constructively with such issues. Although the music was predominantly folk in nature, the songs were reflective of a universal combination of Celtic, classical, country, blues, and contemporary styles. All of the songs had lyric refrains with engaging 'sing-along' melodies. Such music has a non-threatening appeal to both young and older people as well as to a variety of cultural groups.

The intervention was structured the same way during each group session. It involved five to ten minutes of relaxation/ orientation, the playing of the previously mentioned topical/ theme songs, followed by instrument administration, and finally, the members of the group sharing their written responses to the music. In the group process which ensued, the group leader, a social worker and certified addictions counsellor with twenty years of practice experience, engaged the clients with active listening responses (ie clarification, paraphrasing, reflection, summarisation, probing, confrontation, interpretation, and the giving of information) to facilitate the collection of as much conceptually relevant music-specific content as possible during the brief group work period (Cormier & Cormier, 1991).

Procedure

A brief, predominantly qualitative questionnaire about their general enjoyment of music and its potential therapeutic uses was administered immediately before and after the sessions. It included a standardised 20 item psychosocial screening inventory (Hudson, 1982) which identified potential client problems across a range of affective, cognitive-behavioural and social-familial domains. This assessment was included to provide at least some tentative notions about the specificity of such music-social work-small group interventions.

Content analyses of the resultant anonymous verbatim transcript was then conducted. The unit of analysis was each individual client's response, be it a short phrase, a sentence, or a paragraph or more of content. As such, 1,023 such client responses were gathered. Overall, client insights about the use of music tended to be metaphorical, related to generalist problem-solving notions (Johnson, 1995), or related to existing theories about overall group work benefits (Yalom, 1985). Also, client responses were sometimes also applicable to more than one category. For example, the following client comment was conceptually related to the generalist process of problem-definition, and also to the group work therapeutic factor of universality: 'The candle burning [in the recorded song] is like our love ... That is something I have to work on with my daughter, getting back the closeness.' In such instances, a client's response was coded in both relevant categories; thus, a total of 1,423 client responses were analysed.

Results

Group Work Effects

Although this exploratory study was designed as one which would simply identify the therapeutically relevant concepts about the use of music in group work with alcoholics and their families, the process itself seems to have benefited the client participants. For instance, on a global rating scale, 5 of them expressed that the use of music in the group was indeed 'very helpful' to them; and one woman thought it was 'not at all helpful.' Furthermore, these same five clients rated their enjoyment of music as 4 on a similar four-point scale ('very much'). Perhaps not so surprisingly, the clients generally found their participation in this basically altruistic pursuit itself to be helpful, and the expressed degree of its helpfulness seemed related to their enjoyment of music. Indeed, it appears that the use of music in generalist group work practice with alcoholics may be most effective among a significant sub-population of them who also enjoy music.

Selected items on the Hudson Psychosocial Screening (HPS) instrument (Hudson, 1982) systematically replicated the above qualitative inferences (see Table 1). Even though the group of six clients worked together only very briefly, they consistently expressed less problems after their group experience than before. For example, Table 1 shows a consistent pattern of improvement as values of $p < .5$ were deemed as the benchmark for depicting this change. For example, Table 1 shows that after the sessions, on average they were less depressed and less anxious, and also seemed to have fewer problems with personal relationships at home or at work. In fact, their average HPS score, computed across all 20 items, was significantly lower (indicative of fewer psychosocial problems) at post-intervention (M = 32.3, SD = 12.7) than at intake (M = 42.3, SD = 8.5), t (4) = 2.75, $p < .05$ (one-tailed t-test). One client improved by 25 points on the 100-point scale, three by 10 or more points, one by less than 5, and one client's score did not change at all. Again, evidence suggestive of an effect specific to musical enjoyment was found; as the same client who had a lower music enjoyment rating than the others was the one whose overall HPS problem score remained the same.

Table 1
Client's Expressed Problems: Comparison of Intake and Post-Intervention Responses on Selected Items of the Hudson Psychosocial Screening Inventory (Hudson, 1982)[1]

	Median of the Inventory Score Distribution	
Problem	Intake	Post-Intervention
Feel depressed	2.0	1.5
Have low self-esteem	3.0	2.0
Feel unhappy	2.0	1.5
Feel afraid	2.5	2.0
Feel anxious	3.0	2.0
Have problems with anger	2.0	1.5
Have problems at work	1.5	1.0
Have problems with our sexual relationship	2.0	1.0
Have problems with my children	3.0	2.5
Have problems with other family relationships	3.0	2.0

1. A 20 item inventory of problems self-rated on a frequency scale from 1 ('rarely or none of the time') to 5 ('most or all of the time'), with a total theoretical score range from 20 to 100.

The corresponding Cohen's (1988) U3 statistic of 88% is, by definition, indicative of a very large effect. The magnitude of this interventive effect may be interpreted as follows; over a hypothetically large [and similar] client population, nine of every ten of them may be expected to score lower on the problem inventory after they have experienced the group work intervention than they did on average before it.

Content Analyses of Sessions

An overview of the session's content analysis suggests that music and accompanying lyrics may provide a useful backdrop for effective social work practice with small groups. The summarisation of client responses displayed in Table 2 seems to indicate that the songs were perceived as most facilitative of the problem-defining process, perhaps also enhancing or activating the work through the instillation of hope, which came about during group members' process of discovering that they are not alone. Through their identification with the songs, as well as their sharing of experiences with each other, it

Table 2
Music-Specific Content Analysis of Client Responses During Eight Hours (Four Sessions) of Group Work: Percentage Distributions (N=1023 responses)

Concepts	No. responses	%
The Use of Metaphor		
Problem definition	149	55.8
Problem-solving[1]	118	44.2
Generalist Problem-Solving Process		
Motivation-activation	186	38.0
Problem definition	179	36.6
Assessment	64	13.1
Goal setting	43	8.8
Action plan development	17	3.5

1. In reference to past efforts, whether they were successful or not, or present plans.

Table 3
Therapeutic Factors Used in Group Sessions (N=1023 responses)

Therapeutic Factors[1]	No. responses	%
Instillation of hope	195	36.6
Universality	161	30.2
Catharsis	66	12.4
Existential Factors[2]	49	9.2
Altruism	38	7.1
Interpersonal learning	24	4.5

1. Adapted from Yalom (1985).
2. Predominantly in reference to one's own responsibility to act and the freedom which results from such a stance.

appears that a universal-cathartic group problem-solving process seemed to be developing well as indicated in Table 3. One could envision the process continuing very effectively for 10 to 15 problem-solving sessions.

Anecdotally, approximately two-thirds (696, 68%) of the client responses referred specifically to cognitions, and 327 (32%) of them were expressed in an affective or emotive manner reiterating the findings of Table 3. Furthermore, the mode of client expression was strongly associated with their reference to either the song's lyrics or musical elements; the vast majority of the 'thinking' responses referred to the lyrics (78%), while 'feeling' responses referred more often to the music or the song in general (55%); X2 (1) = 110.91, $p < .001$. Also, when the participants made specific statements about the effectiveness of a song, 66.4% of such responses cited the lyrics, while the remaining 33.6% mentioned other elements of the song. It appears that both aspects of the folk songs used in this study, the moods imparted by the musical compositions themselves along with their lyrical story-lines, were important facilitators of the group process, and in this case, the lyrics more so. As such, one could envision group workers using specific songs, or even specifically composing them, to meet specific client needs or to facilitate specific group processes.

Discussion

The use of music therapy as a specific intervention has been empirically documented since about World War II, and the use of music as a therapeutic intervention in social work is expanding (Mazza, 1986; Slivka, 1986). It appears that the profession may benefit from the combined interventions of both social work and music as impacting on client systems (Bruscia, 1989; DuBois and Miley, 1992; Ho and Settles, 1984; Mazza, 1986; Slivka, 1986; Unkefer, 1990). Further, the ability to predict the effectiveness of the combined use of both social work with groups and music intervention with alcoholics and their spouses within the context of generalist social work practice has important implications for social work. In this regard, this exploratory study provides empirical support for beginning to understand how group work, social work and music intervention are related.

The sample consisted of white, middle class couples in the age range of 31 to 51 and married on average for seven years. This convenience sample although small, appeared generally typical of individuals in alcoholism outpatient programmes in this community as well as the province (Brentwood Annual Report, 1995; Personal communication, Addiction Research Foundation, September, 13, 1995). Further, they had all volunteered for the study, had expectations of being helped and generally enjoyed music, which we acknowledge may have influenced the overall positive results of the study. Although the literature argues in favour of having homogeneous groups of volunteers for such samples (Brown & Peterson, 1991; Hepworth & Larsen, 1993; Levine, 1965; Toseland & Rivas, 1995), the extent to which these people were in the same level of recovery was not empirically determined. As has been recommended before, (e.g., Van Wormer, 1987), future research of this nature, therefore, should screen such study participants. Based on the preceding, there is really no strong argument for not making a case for the generalisability of this out-patient sample. Thus, this study contributes to a distinct literature void, as the vast majority of investigations about the group effectiveness of alcoholics use exclusively in-patient populations (Addleman & Castericone, 1986; Murphy, 1983; Anderson & Gilbert, 1989; Cooper & McCormick, 1992; Lovett & Lovett, 1991). It should also be noted, that although this pilot investigation sampled heterosexual couples, nothing about the accumulated evidence would lead us to believe that its findings are not generalisable to work with gay or lesbian couples. Such extensions of the work ought to be incorporated in this field's future research agenda.

Turning to the results of the study, Table 1 indicated that individuals on selected items (10 of 20) on the Hudson (1982) Psycho-Social Inventory (HPS) did better (a score change of + .5) after they received the group intervention combined with the music. Among the other 10 items, the majority stayed the same or showed no change. An inspection of the items on Table 1 revealed that these are very typical issues confronting alcoholics in out-patient rehabilitation (Gallant, 1992; Gallant and Charbonneau, 1994; Landry, 1994). Further, all of the items in Table 1 reflected content areas covered in the structured group sessions before the music was played (i.e. resistance, anxiety, disclosure, etc.). More importantly, these same issues were further emphasised in the songs that were played for the groups as part of the overall intervention. Thus, the songs reiterated the same issues which in turn, produced a 'double barrel' effect of both dealing with them first therapeutically in group and then amplifying, echoing and/or reframing these very themes through music. Therefore, we were not surprised by the findings of Table 1, as they reflected the overall intended therapeutic effects of the group's content and music intervention. Indeed, the t and U3 statistics showing a statistically and practically significant differences between the pre- and post-test items noted in Table 1 were deemed as one indicator of group effectiveness of this particular approach. Future research should attempt to further delineate effectiveness criteria of such approaches.

Table 2 reflects the generalist method of social work used in the group sessions. This orientation used the generic problem-solving approach which has seven steps to it, namely:

1. preliminary statement of the problem or need for change;
2. statement of preliminary assumptions about the nature of the problem and of the change relationship;
3. selection and collection of information available and classification of diagnosis;
4. analysis of information available;
5. development of a plan or examining alternative routes and goals;
6. implementation of a plan into actual change; and
7. evaluation of the plan or achieving a terminal relationship (Johnson, 1995; O'Neil, 1995).

A content analysis of 1,023 verbatim responses as reported in Table 2, revealed that these couples were still in the problem-solving mode of this model (ie stages 1-3). Specifically, few responses if any, reflected any mention of an action plan development, and intervention strategy, and/or a termination plan. This finding was not expected as all phases of the generalist model were not used in the structured sessions. Thus, it appeared that even after such clients go through in-patient programmes (which all did) and evolve into out-patient settings, they are still confronting issues perceived of as 'problems' on which they need to work. There was, therefore, a degree of congruence between Tables 1 and 2 in that the former highlighted specific types of problems and the latter reiterated this through the social work approach model used. Further, as indicated in Table 2, when clients were asked what stage of recovery they perceived themselves in: 55% indicated the problem-definition phase and 42% said the problem-solving phase. This finding corroborated the fact that such clients appear stuck on very real problems which they need to address therapeutically (Jacobs, 1981).

In an effort to further understand the way in which such clients dealt with such problems, a list of therapeutic factors adopted from Yalom (1985) were used as criteria to categorise the qualitative responses. These 11 empirically based factors are as follows: 1) instillation of hope (the client has a high expectation for treatment effectiveness); 2) universality (the clients are aware that others have similar types of problems); 3) imparting of information (the group relies on direction or instruction); 4) altruism (there is a reaching out and being helpful to each other); 5) developing of socialising techniques (social skills are learned and enhanced); 6) imitative behaviour (clients can model the behaviour of successful group members); 7) catharsis (clients ventilate and share their deep emotional experiences); 8) corrective recapitulation of the primary family group (clients learn to repair damage done from past familial experiences and to take on the challenge of newly learned behaviour); 9) existential factors (sensitivity to life issues such as freedom and responsibility, isolation, death, and meaninglessness are relevant concerns within the group context); 10) group cohesiveness (clients can be supportive of each other to enhance therapeutic outcomes); and 11) interpersonal learning (clients learn corrective ways to engage their manner of thinking, feeling and doing in the group) (Yalom, 1985). Table 3 lists these factors and reveals that 'instillation of hope' and 'universality' account for over 66% of the responses. Yalom (1985) indicated that the former refers to the group aspect where the client has a high expectation for treatment effectiveness and the latter conveys that the clients are aware that others have similar types of problems (Vinogradov & Yalom, 1989). In tying Table 3's findings to the music intervention, all of the songs played in these sessions had lyrics about hope (e.g,. 'a new beginning', 'a better tomorrow', 'seek happiness within and go forward', 'go to the light', 'reclaim the soul', 'take charge of your life', 'seek happiness and peace') and universality (e.g., ' you are not alone', 'we are all addicted', 'love and support are here', 'everyone will begin again', etc.). Thus, once again, the music intervention seemed to enhance the overall therapeutic structure of these sessions for these couples.

Concluding Remarks

To our knowledge, this is the first study attempting to understand the relationship between group effectiveness using a social work practice model and music intervention with out-patient alcoholic couples. It is not however, without its limitations. Specifically, these include a small sample size, instrumentation lacking reliability and validity norms, rigourous controls for external or rival hypotheses impacting on the findings, and the lack of a control group. We fully acknowledge these as very real methodological issues which need addressing in subsequent research of this nature. We present this investigation however, as a 'level 1' qualitative study which sought to explore the combined effects of group work, social work and music intervention with such clients.

The data in this study pointed clearly to the fact that: 1) the structured groups were effective, 2) the social work generalist model had application for such use and; 3) music intervention impacted significantly on these couples. In regard to the latter, it was deemed that the music intervention seemed to serve as a catalyst or embellishment to the overall group process, that is, reiterating, amplifying, echoing, reflecting, what was actually transpiring in these sessions. These data plus other anecdotal information not reported here supported this contention. Less well known was the precise nature of this phenomenon namely: Was it the client's willingness to embrace this approach? Was it their state of 'recovery'? Was it the combination of the structured sessions plus the music? Was it other dynamics in the group process itself (i.e., group support, group expectations, the influence of the leader)? Was it the tempo, lyrics, content, or the overall universal appeal of the music itself? or Was it some other variable, (i.e., spousal support/expectations) which contributed to this main finding? Future research, therefore, should attempt to address such concerns.

Further, any study of group effectiveness by its very nature is delimiting as to how one defines effectiveness. Researchers must fully acknowledge the complexities involved in defining such a value laden and nebulous term as we struggled with it immensely. In short, we found empirical support for group effectiveness on the criteria which we ascribed as effectiveness criteria. In short, criteria which could be used to define effectiveness were not considered. We recommend, therefore, that more studies of group effectiveness with any client group take place, as they can only serve to enhance knowledge in this area.

Considering this was an exploratory study whose purpose was to learn to ask some questions in order to formulate hypotheses for subsequent studies (Tripodi, Fellin & Meyer, 1983), the authors wish to present a series of questions directly emanating from this study, as follows: 1) How should group effectiveness be measured? 2) How can music intervention be used in groups with alcoholics? 3) To what extent does one's enjoyment of music enhance its likelihood of being helpful in a therapeutic context? 4) Can music intervention and social work practice be extended for use with diverse populations such as youth, non-traditional, same-sex couples, the elderly, the dying and so on? 5) What is the role and responsibility of the social group work leader in facilitating the music intervention as well as the group experience? 6) Should music intervention be considered as an important aspect of social work curriculum building and as an adjunct to social work education as a preparation for practice?

Finally, all of this study's findings are probably best thought of as tentative hypotheses for future research testing; as its procedures did not control for a number of possible alternative or confound explanations. The most potent alternative explanation for the observed interventive effects among only six clients is sampling bias. The consistency of this study's positive findings though, bodes against the potential reactivity of small samples as a salient alternative explanation. It remains for more extended music-group work (12 sessions) with more clients (50), which is currently being evaluated with a quasi-experimental research design (with a non-music comparison group), to more confidently answer this and other questions which, in a sense, have merely been uncovered or posed by the present exploratory study.

Acknowledgements

This work was supported by a grant from the University of Windsor's Social Sciences Research Group. We sincerely thank the six clients who participated in this study; their willingness to serve will surely benefit future clients. We also gratefully acknowledge the helpful administrative assistance provided by staff members of the Brentwood Recovery Home for Alcoholics of Windsor, Ontario. The musical and lyrical compositions of the songs used in this study are available upon request from the first author.

References

Adelman, E., and Castricone, L. (1986) 'An expressive arts model for substance abuse group training and treatment'. *The Arts in Psychotherapy*, 13, pp53-59.

Anderson, J., and Gilbert, F. (1989) 'Communication skills training with alcoholics for improving performance of two of the Alcoholics Anonymous recovery steps' *Journal of Studies on Alcohol,* Vol. 50, (4), pp361-367.

Anderson, S. C. (1983) 'Group therapy with alcoholic clients: A review',. *Advances in Alcohol and Substance Abuse,* 2, pp23-40.

Armor, D., Polich, M, and Stambul, H. (1976) *Alcoholism and Treatment*. New York: Oxford University Press.

Beasley, J. (1987) *Wrong Diagnosis, Wrong Treatment.* Dallas: Creative Informatics.

Bloch, S., Reibstein, J., and Crouch, E. (1985) *Therapeutic Factors in Group Psychotherapy*. Oxford: Oxford University Press.

Brandsma, J. M., and Pattison, E. M. (1985) 'The outcome of group psychotherapy with alcoholics: An empirical review',. *American Journal of Drug and Alcohol Abuse,* 11, pp151-162.

Brandsma, J. M., and Pattison E. M. (1984) 'Group treatment methods with alcoholics' in Halanter, M. and Pattison, E.M. (eds) *Advances in the Psychosocial Treatment of Alcoholism*. Washington: The American Psychiatric Association.

Brentwood Annual Report, (1995) Brentwood Recovery Home. Windsor, ON.

Broucek, M. (1987) 'Beyond healing to "whole-ing": A voice for the deinstitutionalization of music therapy'. *Music Therapy,* 6, pp50-58.

Brown, H., and Peterson, J. (1991) 'Assessing spirituality in addiction treatment and follow-up: Development of the Brown-Peterson Recovery Progress Inventory (B-P RPI)' *Alcoholism Treatment Quarterly,* 8(2)

Bruscia, K. (1989) *Defining Music Therapy*. Philadelphia: Temple University.

Butler, T., and Fuhriman, A. (1980) 'Patient perspective on the curative process: A comparison of day treatment and out-patient psychotherapy groups'. *Small Group Behaviour,* 111, pp371-388.

Chalken, M. R. (1979) *Alcoholics Anonymous: A Sociological Study*. Unpublished doctoral dissertation, UCLA: CA.

Cohen, J. (1988) *Statistical Power Analysis for the Behavioral Sciences* (2nd ed.) Hillsdale, NJ: Lawrence Erlbaum.

Colson, D.B., and Horrowitz, L. (1983) ' Research in group psychotherapy', in Kaplan, H. I. and Sadock, B.J. (eds.) *Comprehensive Group Psychotherapy*. Baltimore: Williams and Wilkins.

Cooper, A., and McCormack, W. (1992) 'Short-term group treatment for adult children of alcoholics',. *Journal of Counseling Psychology,* 39,(3), pp350-355.

Cormier, W. H., and Cormier, L. S. (1991) *Interviewing Strategies for Helpers: Fundamental Skills and Cognitive Behavioral Interventions* (3rd ed.) Pacific Grove, CA: Brooks / Cole.

Dougherty, K. M. (1984) 'Music therapy in the treatment of the alcoholic client',. *Music Therapy,* 4, pp47-54.

DuBois, B., Miley L., and Krogsrud, K. (1992) *Social Work: An Empowering Profession*. Needham Heights, MA: Allyn and Bacon.

Dwoskin, J., Gordis, E, and Dorph, D. (1979) 'Life-table analysis of treatment outcome following 185 consecutive alcoholism halfway house discharge', *Alcoholism and Clinical Research,* 3, pp334-340.

Gallant, W. A. (1992) *Sharing the Love that Frees Us: A Spiritual Awakening from the Struggles of Addiction and Abuse*. Toronto: Captus Press.

Gallant, W. A. (July, 1994) engaging the troubled family: Toward effective models of treatment. Paper presented at the 35th Annual Institute on Addiction Studies, Hamilton, ON.

Gallant, W. A. (1995) *Can Music be a Valid Form of Intervention in Social Work Practice?* Unpublished Paper. Windsor, ON: School of Social Work, University of Windsor

Gallant, W. A. , and Charbonneau, P. (1994) *Alcoholism and Brentwood: A Spiritual Model of Recovery*. Toronto: Captus Press.

Gallant, W. A., and Siegel, S. (1995) *The Healing Sound of Music: Guiding the Process of Anguish and Affliction toward an Inner*

Resolution. Paper Presented at the National Music Therapy Conference of the Canadian Association for Music Therapists, Waterloo, ON.

Gladding, S. T. (1985) 'Family poems: A way of modifying family dynamics',. *The Arts in Psychotherapy*, 12, pp239-243.

Gladding, S. T. (1985) 'History and systems of counseling: A course whose time has come', *Counselor Education and Supervision*, 24, pp325-331.

Gladding, S. T., and Heape, S. E. (1987) 'Popular music as a poetic metaphor in family therapy', *American Journal of Social Psychiatry*, 7, pp109-111.

Grinnell Jr. R. M. S. (1983) *Social Work Research and Evaluation*, (4th ed.) Itasca IL: F. E. Peacock.

Halpern, S. and L. Savary (1985) *Sound Health*. New York: Halpse and Row.

Heather, N., Edwards, S and Hore, B.D. (1975) 'Changes in constraining and outcome of group therapy for alcoholism', *Journal of Studies on Alcohol*, 36, pp1238-1253.

Hepworth, D. H., and Larsen, J. A. (1993) *Direct Social Work Practice: Theory and Skills*. (4th ed.) Pacific Grove, CA: Brooks Cole Publishing Co.

Ho, M-K., and Settles, A. (1984) 'The use of popular music in family therapy', *Social Work*, 29, pp65-67.

Hudson, W. (1982) *The Clinical Measurement Package*. Homewood, IL: Dorsey Press.

Jacobs, M. R. (1981) *Problems Presented by Alcoholic Clients*. Toronto: Addiction Research Foundation.

James. M. R. (1988a) 'Music therapy and alcoholism: I. An overview of the addiction', *Music Therapy Perspectives*, 5, pp60-64.

James. M. R. (1988b) 'Music therapy and alcoholism: II. Treatment services', *Music Therapy Perspectives*, 5, pp65-68.

James, M. R. (1988c) 'Music therapy values clarification: A positive influence on perceived locus of control', *Journal of Music Therapy*, 25, pp206-215.

James, M. R., and Townsley, R. K. (1989) 'Activity therapy services and chemical dependency rehabilitation', *Journal of Alcohol and Drug Education*, 34, pp48-53.

Johnson, L. C. (1995) *Social Work Practice: A Generalist Perspective*. (5th ed.) Boston: Allyn and Bacon.

Kinney, J. (1996. *Clinical Manual of Substance Abuse*. (2nd ed.) Toronto: Mosby Year Book Inc.

Landry,. J. (1994) *Understanding Drugs of Abuse*. Washington: American Psychiatric Press Inc.

Levine, B. (1965) 'Principles for developing an ego supportive group treatment service', *Journal of Social Service Review,* 39.

Malekoff, A. (1994) 'A guideline for group work with adolescents', *Social Work With Groups,* 17, pp5-19.

Mazza, N. (1986) 'Poetry and popular music in social work education: The liberal arts perspective', *The Arts in Psychotherapy,* 13, pp293-299.

Mazza, N., and Price, B. D. (1985) 'When time counts: Poetry and music in short-term group treatment', *Social Work With Groups,* 8, pp53-66.

Miller W. R., and Hester, R. K. (1986) 'Inpatient Alcoholism Treatment: Who Benefits?' *American Psychologist,* 41, pp794-805.

Murphy, M. (1983) 'Music therapy: A self-help group experience for substance abuse patients', *Music Therapy,* 3, pp52-62.

O'Farrell, T. J. (1989) 'Marital and family therapy in alcoholism treatment', *Journal of Substance Abuse Treatment,* 6, pp23-29.

O'Farrell, T. J. (1992) 'Families and alcohol problems: An overview of treatment research', *Journal of Family Psychology,* 5, pp339-359.

Parloff, D. B., and Dies, R. R. (1977) 'Group therapy outcome research, 1966-1975', *International Journal of Group Psychotherapy,* 27, pp281-319.

Pearson, D., and Anderson, S. A. (1985) 'Treating alcoholic family systems: Intervening in the marital subsystem', *Family Therapy,* 12, pp211-220.

Ritzman, T. A. (1982) 'Depression and the nature of God', *Medical Hypnoanalysis,* 3, pp129-139.

Rosellini, G., and Worden, M. (1989) *Barriers To Intimacy: for People Torn By Addiction*. Minneapolis: The Hazelton Foundation.

Rotunda, R. J., Scherer, D. G., and Imm, P. S. (1995) 'Family systems and alcohol misuse: Research on the effects of alcoholism on family functioning and effective family interventions', *Professional Psychology: Research and Practice,* 26, pp95-104.

Segal, R. M. (1984) 'Helping children express grief through symbolic communication', *Social Casework,* 65, pp590-599.

Slivka, H. H., and Magill, L. (1989) 'The conjoint use of social work and music in working with children of cancer patients', *Music Therapy,* 6A, pp30-40.

Sobell, M. B., Brocre, S., Sobell, L. C. , Roy, J., and Stevens, J. (1987) 'Alcohol treatment outcome evaluation methodology: State of the art 1980-1984',. *Addictive Behaviors,* 12, pp113-128.

Sonne, J. C. (1984) 'Music and Marriage', *International Journal of Family Psychiatry, 5,* 95-119.

Toseland, R., and Rivas, R. (1995) *An Introduction to Group Work Practice.* (2nd ed.) Boston: Allyn and Bacon.

Tournier, R. E. (1979) 'Alcoholics Anonymous as treatment and as ideology', *Journal of Studies on Alcohol,* 40, pp230-239.

Tripodi, T., Fellin, P. A., and Meyer, H. J. (1983) *The Assessment of Social Research: Guidelines for the Use of Research in Social Work and Social Service* (2nd ed.) Itasca, IL: F. E. Peacock Inc.

Treder-Wolff, J. (1990a) 'Affecting attitudes: Music therapy in addictions treatment', *Music Therapy Perspectives,* 8, pp67-71.

Treder-Wolff, J. (1990b) 'Music therapy as a facilitator of creative process in addictions treatment', *The Arts in Psychotherapy,* 17, pp319-324.

Unkefer, R. (ed.) (1990) *Music Therapy in the Treatment of Adults with Mental Disorders: Theoretical Bases and Clinical Interventions.* New York: Schirmer Book.

Valliant, G. E. (1983) *The Natural History of Alcoholism: Causes, Patterns and Paths to Recovery.* Cambridge, MA: Harvard University Press.

Van Wormer, K. (1987) 'Alcohol abuse interventions: A review of the literature', *Small Group Behavior,* 18, pp254-268.

Vinogradov, S., and Yalom, R. D. (1989) *A Concise Guide to Group Psychotherapy.* Washington, DC: American Psychiatric Press Inc.

Yalom, I. D. (1985) *The Theory and Practice of Group Psychotherapy* (3rd. ed.) New York: Basic Books.

Zimpfer, D. G. (1992) 'Group work with juvenile delinquents', *Journal for Specialists in Group Work,* 17, pp116-126.

Reviews

Race and Groupwork
Tara Mistry and Allan Brown (eds)
London, Whiting & Birch, 1997
ISBN 186177 010 3 (hbk) £35.00 / 1 86177 011 1 (pbk) £16.95

This book undoubtedly fills a gap in the groupwork literature, as the editors themselves prove in their survey of books and articles. It is only in recent years that writers have been including the dimension of racism and racial discrimination into their thinking about group dynamics. Practitioners, especially black workers, may well have been doing so for much longer, but unfortunately their experiences have not been committed to print. This book offers a rich collection of practice experience and reflections, alongside some theoretical perspectives.

The editors aimed originally to cover theory, practice and the role of organisations as groups. Material for the latter proved elusive and has therefore not been included. However, the first two aims are amply fulfilled, and the lack of the third perspective is not missed amidst the wealth of other material.

Seeing a title like this raises questions about the use of 'race' as a term. What is a term socially constructed to demonstrate white superiority doing in this context? The introduction to the book explains the approach taken. 'We hope that the use of the term in the title makes clear to readers the general territory with which we are concerned, which also includes racism, oppression, ethnicity, and culture' (page 4).

The title may also lead readers to expect a book which focuses on issues which relate to black people in groups. However, this is not the case. A broad interpretation has been taken so that, for instance, a chapter on groups with Travellers and Gypsies is included. The editors have not imposed any particular definition of 'black', 'to reflect the complexities of that definition in the 1990s' (page 4). There is some discussion of the meaning of 'black' in the chapter, written by Juliet Amoa, which describes a group for black people with learning difficulties. Here it is more about how the group members explored, adopted and explained the concept to others. The process described seemed to me to be very similar to how many black people of whatever ability, background and ethnicity arrive at this self-definition. The use of the term 'Asian' in several chapters is not clarified, although the point is made in once chapter 'Communities in Struggle', written by Gita Patel, that the cultural differences between communities, such as those who are Bengali or Gujerati speaking, need to be acknowledged and explored. Patel also discusses the relevance of the use of 'black' and the gender issues which have arisen in her work with three very different groups.

There is a noticeable dearth of black men both amongst the writers and as members and leaders of groups. This draws comment from the editors, and indicates the need for further work in this area. Other gaps include the groupwork issues for older black people, for black gay and lesbian people, and for black people with physical disabilities. The fact that these gaps exist reflects the general picture in terms of groupwork writing.

One group for refugees and asylum seekers comprised a group of black African women with a white male therapist and white woman co-worker. 'Working across gender and across culture' is how Jeremy Woodcock perceives and explores the situation. Racism was an experience for the women in the outer world, which appears to have been discussed only as such, rather than as a power dynamic of the group.

Issues of black/white co-working and of 'mixed membership' are discussed in two chapters previously written by the editors and reprinted. Both provide a useful reminder of practice and research outcomes, and offer an appropriate start to the book. The two chapters on groups in prisons provide some practice examples of a varied membership, including the dynamic of a variety of languages. The issue of a white woman facilitating a group for black men is mentioned but not reflected upon in depth. The urgency of other issues predominated within the group sessions.

Readers may want to dip into this book and read those chapters which most interest them. There is a wide scope in terms of subject and approach. A few chapters verge on either too much theory or too much description of events. Both feel less useful than those chapters which reflect on practice experience and make links to relevant theory. In that respect I was particularly interested in the chapter written by Aileen Alleyne: 'Black and White Issues in Training Groups: A Psychodynamic Approach'. Here the avoidance strategies often adopted by white groups working on racism are revealed for what they are, together with analysis and approaches for dealing with them. I recognised everything described from my own experiences as a trainer, and found the theoretical perspective helpful.

Overall I found this an excellent and stimulating book. All groupworkers, whoever their group members and whatever their setting, should refer to it. I hope that the book will lead the way in encouraging more writing on the subject.

Raya Tibawi, Consultant, trainer and group facilitator, with a particular interest in equalities issues

Creative Relaxation in Groupwork
Irene Tubbs
Oxford, Winslow, 1996
ISBN 086388 143 2 (spiral bound) £23.95

As the title suggests, this is a text which aims to provide the groupwork practitioner with a comprehensive range of creative techniques for inducing relaxation. It is divided into four discrete sections. Section 1 provides an introduction to the theory of relaxation, drawing on research evidence which supports its benefits, with particular reference to health and medical settings where the author has experience as a physical education specialist and as a founder-contributor to rehabilitation programmes for patients with health conditions.

In Section 2, the author goes on to discuss in some detail a comprehensive range of techniques which include focused breathing, creative imagery, dance, music, exercise and alternative therapies. This section is difficult to read because it is so densely packed with information. Ms. Tubbs does break up the text by having a section on teaching and learning aids for each technique covered. It is best used as a resource pack for dipping into when particular information is needed. It is structured and set out in clear, well-referenced style which facilitates this kind of usage.

The real strength of the text, or manual as the publishers term it, is in the very extensive Section 4 which provides one hundred pages of practical workshop ideas for groupwork practitioners. These range from warm-up exercises through main theme techniques of stress management to relaxing-down exercises for the specific aims. Suitable age group, time span, equipment needed and step-by-step instructions clearly set out. This Section would be invaluable for groupwork practitioners of all kinds, particularly those who work in healthcare or hospital settings, but not at all exclusively so. The music, art and imagery techniques are suitable for a wide range of ages and settings and there are a number of activities earmarked as of particular reference to elderly group members.

The author provides all the necessary cautions and guidelines to readers about the use of these techniques in Section 3, where she makes the very important point about the necessity for practitioners to have themselves experienced the use of a technique prior to facilitating its use in a group.

The manual is compact in design and the ring-binder cover facilitates ease of access and photocopying for personal use - an important feature of a manual of this type.

Given the author's interest in creativity, I was disappointed in the dearth of illustrations throughout the book. I would consider that even simple line drawings would enhance and clarify many of the exercises. I would also suggest that for the price of £23.95, an audio tape would have been a useful accompaniment.

Overall, however, this manual brings together in a clear and coherent way, a wide range of useful creative and relaxation techniques which would prove an addition to the repertoire of most groupworkers.

Group Psychotherapy with Addicted Populations:
An Integration of Twelve-Step and Psychodynamic Theory
Philip J. Flores
Binghampton, NY, Haworth Press, 1997 (2nd edition)
ISBN 0 7890 6001 9 (paperback) £19.99

This book, carrying the sub-title 'an integration of twelve-step and psychodynamic theory', was first published in 1988. At that time it was widely recommended and claimed as a classic in its field. In this new edition there are additional chapters on object relations theory and other developments in modern analytical approaches as well as detailed discussion of treatment issues for group leaders, such as stages in groups, diagnosis, counter-transference and special considerations of resistance to addiction etc. It is underpinned throughout by the most recent research.

This is, then, an ambitious and comprehensive text clearly intended to appeal on a number of levels. It can be assumed that the readership of this journal does not need convincing of the usefulness of groups although even here Flores can be recommended for his wide ranging introduction to various group work theories, some of which may be more familiar to the American than the British or European audience. His most favoured approach is Yalom's interactive model and the strength of this text is Flores' detailed application of Yalom's model, with many examples from practice, emphasising the core issues of client selection and retention, effecting change and group leadership.

The Yalom model is not offered uncritically, however. Flores sees it as most helpful in the early stages of work and viewing object-relations and self-psychology as more appropriate for treating the characterological features that, he argues, almost always accompanies addiction. Flores welcomes the increasing influence within psychoanalysis of the work of Kohut and Mahler whose ideas are discussed very fully. At every point Flores provides references for further reading.

Apart from this detailed discussion what interested me is the general theme and Flores' commitment to working therapeutically with people who are addicted, mainly but not exclusively to alcohol. This is a client group that is routinely disregarded within social work in the UK and any systematic input is associated with AA, a movement whose members I have drawn upon in my teaching social work students and who have won my grudging respect for the sheer enormity of their effort. I have, however, hitherto been wary of their evangelical, anti-theoretical fervour (Flores quotes several times the AA advice to new members, 'Don't analyse. Go to ninety meetings in ninety days') and the emphasis on the disease model, which I have seen as the antithesis of therapeutic work. In this I joined the ranks of what AA describes as 'the ignorant professionals.'

Flores is clear in his discussion about the nature of addiction, that the first stage with this client group is the recognition that addiction is the primary illness, not the presenting symptom, thus 'alcoholism is the horse, not the cart of mental illness.' From this flows the argument for the abstinence mode, as opposed to the 'moderation movement', and Flores shows considerable compassion as he describes the struggle of the addict not with drink but with managing sobriety. He also points out that addicts, especially those who have undergone traditional therapy, are often well able to intellectualise their reasons for drinking and their inability to stop. The power of groupwork is its potential to move away from trying to uncover psychological pathology and instead 'identify the defences and characterological deficits that prevent compliance with abstinence and recovery' (p14). In this Yalom's emphasis on the intrapersonal and interpersonal aspects of group life seems absolutely appropriate, as is psychodynamic theory whose concept of false-self formation is seen as relating to the core belief of many addicts and alcoholics that they are unworthy or defective.

Flores keeps returning to his emphasis on the success of AA in offering continuing care through identification, support and sharing of common concerns and that this is based absolutely on the centrality of abstentionist principals. Flores here usefully stresses Yalom's curative factors, especially Universality, Instillation of Hope and Cohesiveness and links these to AA's belief that alcoholism is 'a spiritual emergency' demanding in turn a programme that is quasi-revivalist and transcendental in emphasis.

Flores develops his argument with passion invoking a wealth of sources ranging from Greek philosophers, Socrates and Epicuras, to literary figures, T.S. Eliot, Camus, Hemingway and Hermann Hesse, as well as the philosophers, Nietzsche and Frankl. But what is missing from this discussion is how this relates to what AA actually does, apart from a brief discussion of the important of 'the life history' in meetings and an insight into AA as 'a transitional object'.

This is a significant oversight. The text's sub title promises the integration of Twelve-Step and Psychodynamic theory but the emphasis throughout is on how psychodynamic theory can adapt to the needs of the addicted, and the principles of AA, rather than on the reverse of the process, how AA, and other self help groups, might usefully draw on psychotherapy theory. Thus, when Flores is discussing therapy groups he offers numerous vignettes that powerfully illuminate theory. The AA groups, however, are not discussed in any detail and the members remain stubbornly not just anonymous but invisible. This may be inevitable but it does identify a notable weakness in an otherwise impressive and useful book.

Jeremy Weinstein, Course Director, MSc Social Work, South Bank University, and independent trainer/groupworker, currently training with the Gestalt Centre (London)

Notes for Contributors

Articles are welcome from all who have an interest in work with groups (whether as practitioner, trainer, academic, researcher, user or consultant), and who wish to contribute to the development of groupwork theory and practice.

Types of articles

A wide range will be welcomed including:

- groupwork practice accounts which describe and reflect on group purpose, process, experience and outcomes;
- the significance of the context of groupwork (organisational, societal, policy);
- education and training in groupwork skills, methods and models (including consultation and supervision);
- group process and interventions in work groups and teams;
- issues of power and oppression in groups: the significance of race, gender, class, disability, sexual orientation and other factors in group process, and for anti-oppressive practice;
- research, monitoring and evaluation of groupwork;
- new developments: ideas for practice, ways of understanding group processes, concepts, models and approaches;
- international/European groupwork accounts/developments/comparisons/issues.

Structure and style

Please note the following points when preparing your article;

- the 'story' of groupwork practice which includes the members' own words and experiences can be very powerful;
- the use of anti-oppressive language and terminology is expected;
- please include a brief summary at the beginning, of not more than 150 words.

References

These should be quoted in the text by putting in brackets the author's name and year of publication. They should then be listed in alphabetical order at the end of the article as follows, please pay special attention to the punctuation and use of upper case letters in the examples below:

Books - authors surname, initials, date (in brackets), title of book (in italics), place of publication, publishers.

e.g. Barlow, D. and Lancing, D. (1994) *Groupwork Publications*. London: Daffodil Press.

Articles - authors surname, initials, date, title of article (within single quotes), title of journal (italics), volume, issue, page numbers. e.g. Einstein, A. and Freud, S. (1920) 'The groupwork unconscious', *The Journal of the Future*, 24(2), pp.101-124.

Please note that it is the responsibility of authors to ensure that the referencing is done correctly before submitting the manuscript. Remember to double check that the date in brackets in the text corresponds to the date cited in the references list at the end.

Length of papers

The normal range is 2500-4000 words, but the editors will consider longer pieces on merit. There is also a place for briefer contributions on new developments, responses to previous articles, and other material of special interest.

Form of submission

Please supply 4 copies of your paper initially, and keep your disk for the potential publication stage when it will be needed by the publishers. When you send your disk, please give full details of the software package used. If your paper is accepted for publication, a further 3 copies of the final version will be required. Once accepted for publication, the author(s) will receive a paper indicating all the publishers' housestyle requirements, so that these can be incorporated into the final text/disc.

Please note: All papers should be sent in the first instance to The Editor, Groupwork, c/o Whiting and Birch Ltd, PO Box 872, 90 Dartmouth Road, London SE23 3HL, England.

Assessment for publication

When articles are first received the editors make a decision on potential suitability for the journal. Articles are sometimes rejected or returned to authors for major review at this stage. Otherwise, they are sent (anonymously) to two members of the journal's panel of assessors for their comments and views on publication. The editors make the final decision on publication, taking into account the views of the assessors. All authors receive personal feedback on decisions taken.

Book reviews

All books for review should be sent to the book reviews editor, c/o the publishers.

GROUPWORK

Volume 10 Number 3 1997-98

SUBSCRIPTION, ADVERTISING AND BUSINESS ENQUIRIES
Should be addressed to the publishers, WHITING & BIRCH LTD, PO Box 872, Forest Hill, London SE23 3HL. TEL: 0181-244-2421 (Int'l +44181 244-2421).
FAX: 0181-244-2448 (Int'l. +44181-244-2448)

SUBSCRIPTION RATES
British Isles £37.50, North America US$85, Elsewhere £47.50
Special reduced rates apply as follows: Individuals to private address: £19.00 British Isles, North America, US$37.50 Elsewhere £25.00.
Special reductions for members of AASWG.
Groupwork is published three times a year.

PAYMENT
Should accompany order. Cheque or banker's draft (made payable to WHITING & BIRCH LTD) may be in any convertible currency to the relevant amount. Direct transfer can be made to our Girobank account (no. 5440564). The following credit cards are also accepted: Mastercard, Visa, Diners Club, American Express. Quote card number, expiry date and give cardholder's name and address if different from delivery address.

GROUPWORK is cited in: *Applied Social Sciences Index & Abstracts, Sociological Abstracts, Bibliographie Zeitscriftenliteratur aus allen Gebieten des Wissens, Social Care Update, Social Work Research & Abstracts, Special Educational Needs Abstracts.* and *Studies on Women Abstracts.*

PUBLISHED BY WHITING & BIRCH LTD, LONDON. ISSN 0951-824X
Printed in the UK by Watkiss Studios Ltd

Exploring Worker Responses to Critical Incidents

Marian F Fatout[1]

The very heart of working with groups is the worker's guidance in helping members focus and work through the issues which are affecting them. This article identifies the worker's mind set, knowledge and understanding essential to responding in a meaningful helpful way. Often the meanings of the members' behaviours are not immediately available for understanding. A series of critical incidences may be necessary before the latent content becomes evident to the practitioner. The pre-session preparation, the social worker's immediate responses and analysis are important in understanding the real underlying meanings of behaviour. Example and suggestions are made which are intended to enhance the social worker's awareness and skill in this area.

While the social worker was distracted by a conversation with another child, seven year old Billy slyly poured punch down the worker's skirt. Why did this behaviour happen? What was its purpose? How did the worker respond? A practitioner would identify this event as a critical incident.

The very heart of working with groups is the practitioner's ability to guide the group and its members in ways which allow group processes and the mutuality which develops to benefit the members. Worker interventions at critical points are essential to the success of the group and members. It is only with knowledge and understanding of the meaning of member, sub-group and group behaviour that this can be

1. Professor, School of Social Work, Louisiana State University. Address for correspondence: School of Social Work, Louisiana State University, Long Fieldhouse, Baton Rouge, Louisiana 70803, USA

accomplished. The concept 'critical incident or event' is often used in the literature to focus on this area. An understanding and expansion of this literature is imperative to improve the practitioner's ability to work with groups.

The Nature of a Critical Incident

A critical incident is an event in the group that represents a significant point of choice for the members and the practitioner (Anderson, 1997; Cohen & Smith, 1976). It may be a comment, demand, question or non verbal behaviour directed at the social worker, at a member or subgroup within the group by another member or subgroup. It may be an interaction between members overheard by the worker such as a conversation. It may be an event taking place or even a period of silence in which an expectation or demand is made of the worker.

An incident or event is viewed as critical when it is seen as a 'turning point' or the most helpful single event in a session (Yalom, 1995) or as described by Donigian and Malnati (1987) as potential barriers or potential opportunities for group and member growth:

> The essential property of a critical incident is that it is judged important enough for a group leader to consciously consider whether to act in a specific way that is assumed to have an important impact on the group (Cohen and Smith, 1976, p114).

Obviously the practitioner views the event as critical by definition, but one might wonder if members also see the same significance in the incident. A striking agreement between the practitioner and families, with whom he was working, was found in an early study (Sherman, 1972). There was agreement in the subject matter, content and the stylistic manner in which they were reported. Yalom (1995) used patients' reporting of critical incidents within the sessions to determine 'turning points' for them. His research in this area resulted in the 'curative factors' which he has identified.

The importance of this concept is stressed by Davis and Reid (1988, p306), who state that by analysing events, practitioners can gain an understanding that 'illuminates a particular case or accumulated general knowledge and practice wisdom about timing and consequences of interventive strategies, processes of client change, and professional supervision and education.'

Uses of this Concept

Analysis of clinical events has been a part of competent and thoughtful practice for many years (Cohen and Smith, 1976; Davis & Reid, 1988). As early as 1954, the concept of critical incident, was used by Bach in attempting to articulate the characteristics and functions of group leadership. Others working in this area (Berzon and Solomon, 1966; Fiebert, 1968; and Miles, 1965) further elaborated this work attempting to specify the nature of the leader's role and the changes over time.

A major focus of study of critical incidents has been in the area of identifying problems related to the developmental stages of a group. The importance of this procedure is that as critical incidents are recognised they can be 'made to systematise and deal with those issues to promote effective group development' (Cohen and Smith, 1976, p118). Kottler (1994), Corey, Corey, Callanan and Russell (1988) and Donigian and Malnati (1987) were primary writers promoting the importance of this process. The group worker's response, or conscious decision not to respond to a critical incident, is recognised in the literature. The practitioner's response is seen as a determinant of the effect that the incident will have on the group's development (Donigian and Malnati, 1987).

Critical incidents were also studied as they applied to a variety of theoretical approaches or models of practice (Churchill, 1974; Cohen and Smith, 1976; and Corey, 1990). In reviewing this literature it becomes clear that worker responses are at least partly determined by the practitioner's knowledge and beliefs about human behaviour and methodological practice issues.

Edelwich and Brodsky (1992) focused on critical incidents as common problem behaviours that therapists had to deal with throughout the life of the group. Issues such as absences, lateness, grievance, anger, rescuing and avoiding conflicts all recurred again and again and were the themes for critical events needing worker interventions.

Garvin (1997) identified critical incidents as major content in writing group records. The focus of the record might be an event that affected the whole group or a part of that group.

It is evident that the concept of critical incident has been very meaningful for both researchers and practitioners in attempting to understand and explain the interactions in groups. Supervision, teaching, learning and understanding are often centred on discussions of critical incidents in practice situations.

The Critical Incident and Change

The worker's response to a critical incident is not only seen as a determinant of the effect that an incident has on the group's development but also on the experience of sub-groups and members of that group. It must be noted that a single critical event cannot be viewed as a therapeutic factor as Yalom (1995) reminds us. For an incident to be change promoting, the experience must be honest and spontaneous but in addition through reasoning the implementation of the incident must be understood. In a study it was found that critical incidents without the cognitive component did not distinguish successful from unsuccessful members in respect to change (Lieberman, Yalom, and Miles, 1973).

Worker's Response

To take the first step in this change producing process it is essential that the practitioner be as knowledgeable as possible, and aware of issue(s) which may cause critical incidents. The charge to the practitioner is emphatically stated by Kottler (1994, p147) 'Within a single instant, all our training and preparation must come into play; a split-second decision must be made as to the best way to handle the situation; and we must live with the consequences forever.' The importance of the worker's response is further underscored by Cohen and Smith (1976) as they emphasise the importance of the intervention in terms of the path which the group and/or members may take as a result of the specific worker response or lack of response.

Preparation for Meaningful Responses.

'All human behaviours have purposes' is a generally held belief in the profession. There may be clear overt reasons for the behaviour or the motivation underlying human behaviour may be unconscious. 'The speaker may believe he wants to communicate one idea but, through body language, tone, and word choice, may actually communicate something else' (Brandler and Roman, 1995).

Understanding motivation for behaviour becomes even further complicated in groups. Here, there are many communicators and many observers and the person who speaks or acts may be communicating for another or other group member(s). Latent material in groups may be strongly influenced by the needs of individual members, sub-groups, or the group as a whole. The practitioner too may have unconscious resistance to dealing with certain material that may be presented by the group.

Pre-Session Preparation

In order to focus and understand the process occurring in the group, with the members and the worker himself/herself it is essential for the practitioner to have supervision through out the life of the group. These sessions may be utilised in a variety of ways including sensitising the practitioner to the members communications, either verbally or non-verbally.

Another step which may be helpful in preparing oneself for a group session with an awareness essential to understanding and responding to critical incidents in the most helpful manner is a period of pre-session preparation. The purpose of reviewing before each session is to create an *open* awareness. One aspect of this open awareness involves what Middleman and Woods (1990, pp24-26) refer to as looking with 'planned emptiness.' or cultivating 'an area in one's mind that is reserved for the unknown, that is ready to accommodate the new, perhaps alien, idea and experience it, rather than rationalise it away or avoid it' (p24). This is a 'route toward being open to restructure or even discard ideas, rather than only building on the old ones' (pp25-26).

Another facet of open awareness is described as 'tuning in' by Schwartz (1962). 'Tuning in' involves 'playing out' in one's mind or with colleagues what and how members may be thinking and feeling in that up-coming session. This really involves an attempt to develop empathy with the members and the group as a whole in their time, space, and at their level of experience.

It is essential that the practitioner not make a *decision* about what can be expected. The purpose of this process is to expand the worker's openness about seeing and hearing what members are feeling and saying.

Areas for focus in pre-session preparation are:

- **Factors in the group**
  - History of the group with emphasis on the last 3 sessions
  - Sub-group and member interactions, stresses and conflicts
  - Awareness of members' behavioural problems evident in past sessions
  - Awareness of the group stage
  - Purpose and goals of the members and the group
  - The potential hazards of the planned content and or environment in which the session is to take place

- **Factors originating outside the group**
  - The worker's readiness to deal with specific content as presented in the group
  - Ethnicity, level of maturity, and socioeconomic status (values) of the members and the practitioner
  - Significant events or occasions which are occurring in the lives of members (holidays, graduations, industrial lay-offs, seasons of the year, unresolved conflicts in the family or work situation)

All of these factors would be a part of the ongoing assessment of the group and the members. By recalling and creating a heightened awareness of group factors, individual patterns, needs, and goals, the worker will have created a more *open* mental thinking environment for an in depth understanding of potential latent issues being posed by members in the form of critical incidents. An example of understanding latent content in a critical incident is as follows.

There were two more sessions before this group of young

> adolescent boys were to terminate. As a special event they had planned an outing to a national forest preserve. They had brought their lunches and planned to hike around the park. In preparation for the trip, the boys had been told that there was a ban on fires in the park because of hazardous conditions.
>
> After the boys arrived at their destination, they split into sub-groups to try the various hiking trails. They seemed to be having fun telling each other of their adventures. At the end of the day as the boys were in the agency van returning home, they noticed smoke coming from within the park. It was later found that the fire had been set by one of the sub-groups just before they prepared to leave. The fire was discovered quickly and extinguished by the park rangers.
>
> There were two major areas of latent content driving this critical incident. These were boys who had been in difficulty with the police, some on probation and a couple who had been in camps for delinquents. A major issue was that the group was going to end. As could be expected with termination, the boys were sad and did not want the group to end. They had been brought together because of their negative behaviour, so getting into difficulty again was a way of demonstrating that they still needed the group.
>
> The other major factor involved was that one of the members, Raymond, was going to be sent to another state to live with his father. By getting into trouble again he hoped to be placed on probation and remain in the area with his friends.

The worker knew that termination was a crucial group stage which required careful planning and implementation. This was a long term group which had been meeting for almost two years. The members had always been aware of the approximate date that the group would end. For the last three months, there had been continual reference to the fact that it would soon be terminating. In the last four weeks there had been a great deal of focus on discussing and planning for the ending by the total group. The worker was aware that an appropriate activity to prepare the members for participation outside the group was something which they could do alone. Since the boys wanted a final celebration, the picnic and hike in the park seemed especially appropriate to meet the needs. There were still two more sessions available to finish dealing with their feelings about ending.

The worker had not realised that members still had not

sufficiently dealt with their feelings. As a result they found it necessary to express them through acting-out behaviours. Through this experience he learned that with groups of emotionally disturbed and delinquent members it was prudent to plan termination programs in familiar settings, perhaps repeating activities they had done successfully, previously.

The worker had not been aware of Raymond's situation and thinking in this session. It was only after this incident that the worker could help him find other options for dealing with his problem.

As a result of this experience, the worker with the help of his supervisor, determined that it was essential to extend the duration of the group for a few weeks allowing for representatives of the park service to make the boys aware of the dangers of forest fires. This also allowed more time for the members to express and work through some of their feelings about endings.

Worker Responses during the Session

After careful preparation before the session, it is essential that the areas for focus are kept in mind and that the practitioner continues to analyse aspects of critical events as they happen. Ability to quickly recognise and identify a critical incident will vary greatly depending on the practitioner's preparation, alertness, and knowledge. Some critical events can not be ignored; they demand some sort of immediate action. Billy's pouring punch down the worker's skirt is an example of this type of demand for some action by the practitioner. Others are much more subtle and may be overlooked in terms of the gravity of their meaning.

Billy was a member of a group of severely abused latency age children. All of the children were in need of attention by the workers. In this instance, the worker's attention had been diverted to another child for a moment. The pouring of the punch was Billy's attempt to regain her attention. This incident alerted the worker to the need to help Billy gain attention through more appropriate ways. After the clean-up that day, ways of gaining positive attention became the focus. This became a goal in working with him in future sessions.

As significant events are recognised, the worker's response in a manner which helps to deal with the real issue(s) involved is crucial. At the same time, the process of quick thinking necessary to accomplish this may be exceedingly complex. Steps, tools, and models have been developed attempting to assist the practitioner in this process of understanding and responding effectively to the identified events.

Cohen and Smith (1976, pp. 123-154) developed a method for analysing a critical event which is very helpful for review in hindsight. It may be used as a tool for analysis during the session and before responding only by the most skilled practitioners because of its complexities. A tool developed by Brandler and Roman (1995, p. 30) may help the worker to identify the latent content underlying the incident. The categories which need to be identified on a chart help to create a recognition by the worker of possible individual and group issues involved in the incident.

A concept most useful in further understanding the worker's response to a critical incident is the reflection-in-action as described by Schon (1987). When something the worker has said or done fails to meet his/her expectation he/she may brush it aside, 'selectively inattending to the signals that produced it' or respond by reflection (Schon, 1987, p. 26). Reflection can occur in two ways, either by looking back on the outcome or by pausing in the midst of action to think about the situation. This latter form of reflection is referred to by Schon as action-present. This is a period of time during which the worker can still make a difference in the situation at hand. The practitioner can still reshape what he/she is doing while he/she is doing it. This is to 'reflect-in-action.' In this process the worker thinks about why he/she responded in this way and restructures strategies of action based on an understanding of the current situation. The importance of this concept is that this review of what we know 'leads to on the spot experiment and further thinking that affects what we do—in the situation at hand and perhaps also in others we shall see as similar to it' (Schon, 1987, 29).

In a sense, in working with people there is often a kind of conversation that occurs. One in which there is input and listening on the part of both sides until the two parts can gain a mutual understanding. In the incident which follows, the worker and the group can come together in their understanding of the issue of concern.

A group of early adolescent girls had planned for months to go to a popular amusement park. The group was composed of mostly Mexican-American members and two 'Anglo' members. The social worker with this pre-delinquent group was also 'Anglo'.

The group had gone together in an agency van and planned to meet at noon inside the park then go outside to eat lunch together in the van. First, only four of the members met the worker as planned, a sub-group of five Mexican-American members was still missing. After awaiting the return of the others, with no success, the five of us went to the van. There we found the other five members anxiously waiting. They were non-committal about why they had not followed our plan.

As we sat in the van eating our lunch the five members began to talk about seeing 'some kids' dancing on the hood of a car. This car was parked near our van. After some discussion about whether the owners would see footprints in the dust on their car, the girls giggled and said that they had been the dancers. The worker commented about how frustrated they must have been about the mix-up in plans, thinking that this must have been the cause of the behaviour. There was no response. There was no damage to the car and lunch was finished. One of the more aggressive members of the sub-group rolled foil from her lunch into a large ball and threw it from the back seat. As planned, it hit the worker squarely in the back of the head. The member apologised profusely, saying that she was trying to throw it out the window. She seemed to want to be assured by the worker that it had hurt to be hit in the head in this way (even though it had not).

As the worker began to talk of returning to the park to ride rides for which they still had tickets, the sub-group was clear that they were not going to return and the others were ambivalent. Finally, one of the girls asked the worker, 'Why are all of the people that work here Anglo?' Now, the practitioner was clear about the latent message underlying all of this unexpected behaviour, such as, leaving the park, dancing on the hood of a car, wanting to hurt the Anglo worker, and now not wanting to return to the park. They were angry at the discrimination and racism, as it was perceived by them.

It was only as the latent issues, racism and discrimination, unfolded that the social worker was able to ascertain the meaning of the first behaviour in a series of behaviours. The girls had been 'acting out' beginning with not meeting the worker and group as planned and continuing on through the session.

A discussion of this situation and their feelings about it developed as the group sat in the van after lunch. The worker became aware that they were correct in their observations of the lack of minorities employed in this setting. We talked about the geographic location of the park and the racial ethnic population of this area, which was almost all 'Anglo'. The girls were not ready to delve into this issue at great length at this time they were tired and upset. The members decided that they wanted to return to their community and not return to the park that afternoon. This was done as they requested.

This was the beginning of a series of sessions focused on racial and ethnic commomalities and differences and their feelings about them. The members initiated exploration of this area in a variety of ways and the practitioner used community resources to help the girls experience and learn about others living in near-by communities.

Summary

The social worker's responses to the group and its members is basic to his/her ability to guide the systems toward agreed upon goals. Competent practice requires that attention be focused in this area. There is a body of literature which centres on events in groups which necessitate some response from the worker or a decision not to respond. This literature alerts the practitioner to the underlying meaning of these critical incidents and provides areas for focus in understanding and responding in ways which are most helpful to the group and the members.

A major task for the worker in priming him/herself for a session with the group is the pre-session preparation. Areas for review, both internal and external to the group and its processes are identified. A 'state of the mind' important for pre-session preparation includes two aspects. One is 'looking with planned emptiness' (Middleman and Wood, 1990) and the other is 'tuning in' (Schwartz, 1962).

During the session tools to provide analysis of events as they happen are identified (Brandler and Roman, 1995; and Cohen and Smith, 1976) A concept which is very important in understanding latent issues in critical incidents is that of 'reflection-in-action' (Schon, 1987).

Some may dismiss the importance of knowledge about responding to critical incidents by suggesting that interventions by the worker are a matter of worker style or intuition. Schon's response to this could be 'One might recognize the existence of professional artists capable of making sense of unique or uncertain situations, but there is no way to talk sensibly about their artistry—except, perhaps, to say that they are following rules that have not yet been made explicit' (1987, 35).

References

Anderson, J. (1997) *Social Work with Groups: A Process Model.* New York: Longman

Bach, G.R. (1954) *Intensive Group Psychotherapy*. New York: Ronald Press

Berzon, B. and Solomon, L. (1966) 'Research frontier: The self directed therapy group: Three studies', *Journal of Counseling Psychology,* 13, 4, pp491-497

Brandler, S. and Roman, C.P. (1995) 'Uncovering latent content in groups', in R. Kurland & R. Salmon (eds) *Group Work Practice in a Troubled Society*. New York: The Haworth Press

Churchill, S.R. (1974) 'A comparison of two models of social group work: The treatment model and the reciprocal model' in P. Glasser, R. Sarri & R. Vinter, *Individual Change Through Small Groups.* New York: The Free Press

Cohen, A.M. and Smith, R.D. (1976) *The Critical Incident in Growth Groups: Theory and Techniques*. San Diego, CA: University Associates

Corey, G. (1990) *A Manual for the Theory and Practice of Group Counseling*. Pacific Grove, CA: Brooks/Cole

Corey, G., Corey, M.S., Callanan, P.J. and Russell, J M. (1988) *Group Techniques*. (Revised edition), Pacific Grove, CA: Brooks/Cole

Davis, I.P. and Reid, W.J. (1988) 'Event analysis in clinical practice and process research', *Social Casework*, 69, 5, pp298-306

Donigian, J. and Malnati, R. (1987) *Critical Incidents in Group Therapy.* Monterey, CA: Brooks/Cole

Edelwich, J.L. & Brodsky, A. (1992) *Group Counseling for the Resistant Clients.* New York: Lexington Books

Fiebert, M.S. (1968) 'Sensitivity training: An analysis of training interventions and group process', *Psychological Reports,* 22, 8, pp829-838

Garvin, C.D. (1997) (3rd. ed.) *Contemporary Group Work*. Boston: Allyn and Bacon

Kottler, J.A. (1994) *Advanced Group Leadership*. Pacific Grove, CA: Brooks/Cole

Lieberman, M. A., Yalom, I. D., & Miles, M. B. (1973) *Encounter Groups: First Facts.* New York: Basics Books

Middleman, R.R. and Wood, G. G. (1990) *Skills for Direct Practice in Social Work.* New York: Columbia University Press

Miles, M.B. (1965) 'Changes during and following laboratory training: A clinical experimental study', *Journal of Applied Behavioral Science*, 1, pp215-242

Schon, D.A. (1987) *Educating the Reflective Practitioner* San Francisco: Jossey-Bass

Sherman, M.H. (1972) 'Some dimensions of style in family therapy', *Psychotherapy: Theory, Research and Practice*, 9, pp67-75

Schwartz, W. (1962) 'Toward a strategy of group work practice', *Social Service Review*, 36, 3, pp268-279

Yalom, I.D. (1995) *The Theory and Practice of Group Psychotherapy*. New York: Basic Books

A Critical Analysis of a Support and Clinical Supervision Group for Interpreters Working with Refugees Located in Britain

Rachel Tribe[1]

This paper has two aims: firstly to document the facilitation of a support and clinical supervision group for interpreters working with refugees in Britain, and secondly to observe how the dynamics of working as interpreters in partnerships with health professionals may have impacted upon the group content and process for both the interpreters and facilitators.

Working within a triad as opposed to a dyad changes the dynamics and experience for all three parties. This paper will briefly detail the process that the organisation went through in better integrating the interpreters into the clinical group and thus improving service delivery. This was achieved through establishing a support and supervision group for interpreters / bicultural workers. This paper considers some of the issues, dilemmas and experiences arising from this group over a five year period. [1]

The Organisational Context

Out of the Medical group of Amnesty International, a small charity was formed in 1985 to provide health services to people who had been tortured or suffered organised violence. The

1. Job title. Senior Lecturer
Address for correspondence: Psychology Dept, University of East London, Romford Road, London E15 4LZ. England.

Groupwork Vol. 10(3), 1997-98, pp.196-214

majority of the clients are asylum seekers. In 1997 the organisation saw 2500 people from 65 countries, speaking 46 languages. It is believed that lack of fluency to speak European languages should not act as a barrier to accessing services, (Shackman, 1985; Tribe, 1999) therefore a team of interpreters/ bicultural workers are part of the multi-professional health team. A small core staff team is augmented by a larger group of voluntary and sessional health practitioners.

A philosophy and practice have evolved which attempt to meet the needs of the whole person, family and community. The work includes a range of medical and psychological therapies, medico-legal assessments and documentation in addition to advice, training and consultancy to other agencies as well as working with colleagues around the world undertaking similar work.

Client Group

Eighty percent of the clients are asylum-seekers, 29% have been granted refugee status or have been allowed to remain exceptionally in the UK. They are seeking refuge in Britain under the terms of the 1951 UN Convention Relating to the Status of Refugees. This states that a refugee is anyone who has

> A well-founded fear of persecution for reasons of race, religion, nationality, membership of a particular social group or political opinion, leave their country of origin and are unable to avail themselves of the protection of that country.

Clients may have, not only been severely tortured, or subject to organised violence but may be suffering from the trauma of exile - separation from loved ones, and the loss of country, job, identity and the ability to communicate and be understood through language. (Venables & Rodriquez, 1991).

Contextual Dilemmas

Self disclosure and openness in communication take on a

totally different resonance for refugee clients compared to other patients because such very characteristics may have led them to being imprisoned in the first place. Clients may not trust a bicultural worker because they may assume that their compatriot holds different political views to their own, or they may just be frightened and suspicious as a result of their experiences in their country of origin (Tribe, 1999).

For someone coming from a repressive regime information can be an extremely dangerous thing which could place family members remaining in their country of origin at risk of torture or imprisonment. Alternatively clients may assume the opposite and assume that the bicultural worker will be happy to take on considerable responsibility in assisting them in Britain. Issues relating to the potential different roles of an interpreter have been written about by Baker, (1981); Shackman, (1984); Freed, (1988); and Raval, (1996). Role clarification and management may require considerable thought by the organisation and its workers.

Defining Boundaries and Barriers within the Triad

Two of the three members of the triad will at some point in the health consultation be literally excluded from the triangular relationship through non comprehension of the others spoken language. Raval, (1996) notes that some NHS mental health workers were concerned about feeling that 'interpreters took over' the session and of loss of emotional affect when working with an interpreter. The bicultural worker is the one that first hears the client's words and emotions. As well as interpreting the words, the bicultural worker has to emotionally process these words and meanings for themselves. A common complaint from interpreters is not to be treated merely as an 'interpreting machine.'

Health professionals in their desire to provide a good service to their client, and to understand what they are saying may temporarily forget this. (Faust & Drickey, 1986). Given that many bicultural workers employed at the centre are themselves refugees and may have had similar experiences to the clients it is particularly important that this is heeded. The bicultural workers are employed on a sessional basis by the centre, having undergone a rigorous selection procedure. The task of the bicultural worker is a complex and sophisticated one requiring a range of skills over and above the ability to speak two languages fluently. (Alpert & Marcos, 1976; Baker & Grainger, 1999).

Working as or with an interpreter is likely to be particularly difficult when the three members of the group have not clarified the boundaries between themselves. The bicultural worker may unknowingly overstep the mark that the practitioner has set down and may become more active, summarising on behalf of the client or deciding what the client has said is not important and therefore interpreting only the gist or part of it. (Freed, 1988). A number of writers have noted some of the dilemmas and challenges associated with working with interpreters, (Sabin, 1975; Launer, 1978; Marcos, 1979; O'Neil, Koolage, & Kaufert, 1988; Phelan & Parkman, 1995), as well as the positive opportunities and benefits which may accrue in this situation. (Raval, 1996).

All three members of the triad may feel overwhelmed by the information they hear as the clients have come through many horrendous experiences. On occasions each triad member may try and protect the other two from this in some way.

Case Study

I remember being asked to see Ms Ali who was obviously extremely angry about the way she felt she had been treated in Britain. Ms. Ali had made a serious and dramatic suicide attempt in a government building to try and prevent being returned to her country of origin. This attempt had left her badly handicapped and made her own self care difficult. She spoke very little English.

A 'friend' had become her voice and advocate to the outside world. In our first meeting in which Ms Ali was trying to get me to access certain resources for her, it was obvious from her non-verbal communication that she was extremely angry with me. On reflecting this back the interpreter who had obviously become accustomed to speaking for the client rather than on her behalf told me that the client was not angry, but was on the contrary very happy and would like to thank me. This message appeared to me to be in direct contradiction to what I could observe, and appeared to be what the interpreter, for some reason, thought I would like to hear.

The interpreter in this case had broken all boundaries and was acting as a barrier to any real verbal communication between myself and the client. After much persistence and work by the three of us we were able to overcome these difficulties and conduct meaningful communication.

History of the Interpreters group

It was to try and consider some of the difficulties and dilemmas experienced by the three members of the triad, but particularly the bicultural workers who were undertaking very demanding work and to provide a better service to clients that we decided to try and start a support and clinical supervision group. We were concerned that the interpreters were viewed not as equal team members, but as lesser members with many health professionals seeing them as 'a necessary nuisance' which got in the way of their 'real clinical work'. It is no coincidence that the majority of health professionals were white middle class males, and the majority of the interpreters were black refugee women with the inequalities of power commonly associated with this dynamic. Issues of racism, patriarchy, colonial legacies and financial disparities between the developing and developed parts of the world unfortunately form part of the context in which we all operate. We wanted to offer support to the interpreters with the extremely difficult work they were undertaking as well as offering the opportunity to be members of a clinical supervision group and provide space to reflect and enhance their practice.

We loosely would have used the following definition of supervision;

> The supervisor's role is not just to reassure the worker, but to allow the emotional disturbance to be felt within the safer setting of the supervisory relationship, where it can be survived, reflected upon and learnt from. (Hawkins & Shohet, 1989, p3)

As group facilitators we took the interpreter's support and supervision group to the regular group supervision sessions offered by the organisation. We found this very useful, we also wished the work of the interpreters to be positioned as central to the organisation's work rather than as tangential or incidental.

Development of the Group

For five years the author and a colleague ran a support and supervision group for the bicultural workers. Most of the bicultural workers had no experience of being group members, while as group facilitators we had never run such a group before. Many of our early meetings were taken up with considering and defining the limits and parameters of the group.

The group ran for one and a half hours. Attendance at the group was paid on the same basis as interpreting work. It was initially run on a monthly basis, but at the request of the bicultural workers, it changed to meeting every two weeks. This changed the nature of the group quite considerably and was beneficial for the group process. During this period considerable changes took place in relation to the employment, role and confidence within the organisation of bicultural workers. The group had a major influence by providing a forum for discussing the experience of being an interpreter, building relations between interpreters and for resolving problems. A measurable artefact of the group has been the recent production of a formal code of practice for bicultural workers and for clinicians working alongside them.

Group Composition

The bicultural workers come from 28 countries and speak 20 languages. Over sixty percent of the interpreters are women. Their motives for becoming a bicultural worker vary from the wish to help members of their own community/political group or ethnic group through to the need to earn money. The majority are between thirty and fifty, most are educated to university level and they hold a variety of religious and political views

Group Facilitators

We were two British born white women employed as mental health practitioners by the organisation who do not possess the necessary expertise to work as bicultural workers ourselves. Our gender and race inevitably affected the dynamics of the group in a number of ways, for example our positioning by others within a society which privileges gender and race in a particular way. Issues of racism and sexism need constant consideration. We were not refugees or new entrants to British society and had no first hand understanding of this experience. In addition we had a different contractual position within the organisation, we were secure in our employment and therefore might be viewed as being within a more powerful position than the interpreters who were paid on a sessional basis. We might be viewed as representing the host organisation or organisational culture and practices. Also we, as facilitators often found ourselves at some level representing a link/fence between the organisation and interpreters and vice versa. This tension was not always a comfortable one and at times we felt torn between who and what we were representing to the 'other ' group. (The interpreters or the other health professionals). A similar or parallel process and tension to that frequently felt by interpreters working within the organisation.

Group Attendance

As most of the interpreters are refugees themselves and experiencing many changes in their lives this meant that initially the membership of the group varied which slowed down group cohesion and effected the group life. For the last two years the membership has barely altered and some have attended for the duration. At each meeting approximately twenty bicultural workers now attend. In many ways the group is too large but to split the group into two would be divisive and would counter the process of a team identity.

Group Goals and Tasks: Disparate Aims and Objectives

The evolution of the group meant that it was initially charged with a number of rather disparate tasks, including:

- financial affairs
- training
- management
- induction

as well as that of supervision and support. The latter two were seen as the central components by the two facilitators as this was in line with their own professional objectives and groupwork training.

At the beginning of the group discussions often focused on rates of pay and other practical issues, when we, the facilitators, were more interested in talking about the psychological implications of the work. Although we realised that without the financial component many of the interpreters might not be offering their services to the organisation and we were the only formal access point to the organisation which they had. As facilitators this also forced us into a more directive approach than we would have chosen as the practical issues were mainly rooted in policy which we had to then pass on to group members. This set a style precedent which it proved difficult for us to change.

We decided as a compromise to have a period at the beginning of the group where practical issues could be discussed before moving into a more therapeutic mode. This required considerable negotiation, as some of the participants wanted to move immediately into the therapeutic mode, while others felt that the practical issues were more important. We have recently been able to shed responsibility for the financial aspects of the work and the group has been able to move into a new realm.

It took some time for the bicultural workers to feel able to criticise the organisation in any way and initial sessions of the group were taken up with group members acting in an almost sycophantic manner. A contributory factor to this behaviour was the fact that they are employed on a sessional basis and were worried that any complaints they made might result in them losing their jobs. Slowly the group members came to realise that this was a safe place for them to talk and the group content began to change.

Dilemmas for the Group Facilitators

We sometimes found ourselves in the difficult position of being, on the one hand group facilitators and on the other, co-workers with the interpreters. In additional we frequently heard complaints about our peers, some of whom felt very threatened by a support and supervision group for interpreters. It was also difficult for the interpreters to discuss openly difficulties they might have been experiencing working with us, the facilitators in our role as health practitioners.

Although there were many related dilemmas, there were also a number of positive components in that we were able to act as a voice on behalf of the bicultural workers to others in the organisation. We were able to give realistic feedback about what response they might expect to requests and comments. We were also able to offer a real understanding of the client group and organisational philosophy in which they were working.

Group Process

One of the difficulties associated with working as a bicultural worker at the organisation is competition for work amongst speakers of the same language. Inevitably some practitioners choose to work with particular interpreters more than others because they are particularly skilled and the health professional finds them comfortable to work with. In addition, the organisation could get a sudden influx of clients from, for example, Bosnia and thus the Bosnian interpreters will get a lot of extra work for a time. This is a basic inequality of this system and although the bicultural workers were asked if they could contrive a more equitable system, one could not be found. This disparity of work set up certain rivalries and the group offered a forum where these type of problems could be aired openly.

The issue of gossip, jealousy and lack of trust between

certain bicultural workers has been an area which has concerned us at two points in the group's life. We have spent considerable time examining this and the wider refugee community politics that the problem appears to reflect, which are frequently dogged by political divisions and fear based on traumatic experiences or potential experiences back home. In addition the issue of organisational transference has been a common theme.

Other common themes related to issues of power and to feelings of guilt when a bicultural worker felt that a client was not telling the truth and they had to decide what to do, if anything about it. Perhaps most importantly the group provided somewhere for the bicultural workers to discuss problems, experience peer support and gain some element of cohesion. Members now report that if they feel distressed after an interview they can either talk about this in the group, or they can call on another member of the team to give them some support and advice. The bicultural workers report feeling more contained and that things have improved.

They have also learned strategies for coping from each other and different ways of working. The group has at times moved from the emotional terrain to a problem-solving one. At different times the group has felt sluggish and sleepy, traumatised, angry and persecutory, and also as a place of warmth, support, spontaneity and friendship.

Attempted scapegoating of individuals has occurred and many dissatisfactions with working conditions expressed, the latter has to some degree been ameliorated by changes in working practices. One example of this was that interpreters repeatedly felt that health professionals did not understand the complexities and difficulties of their task and often made unrealistic demands of them. Initial attempts at discussion around this area did not meet with the success we would like, so it was decided that we would ask for one of the regular clinical meetings to be given over to this issue. After much discussion about the most appropriate and effective use of this forum we decided to develop a small role-play which would literally illustrate some of the difficulties involved in the role and would hopefully enable the health professionals to 'see' for themselves how some of the dilemmas presented themselves. Plenty of time for discussion and debate was built into this afternoon's work. The afternoon proved a great success with the role-play raising a number of serious issues in an accessible, informative, non-threatening and humorous way. The play appeared to enable many of the health professionals to view the situation from the interpreter's viewpoint and see how they might better work together rather than in parallel, as well as the interpreters to understand some of the dilemmas and pressures faced by the health professionals, many of whom were volunteers offering time to the organisation as well as holding down full-time jobs elsewhere. The role-play became integrated into the organisation's history and was subsequently used as part of the induction process for new staff.

Changes in working practices started as small changes, for example the interpreting staff being included in the list of staff contributing to the organisation's work, then they obtained their own waiting room rather than having to linger in reception, corridors or sit in the client's waiting room with all the role and boundary confusions this caused. Other changes have led to a paid post for an interpreter's co-ordinator being established. These changes have come about through the advent of the bicultural workers group which has provided a forum for the members to express dissatisfactions to develop a collective identity and power and come up with possible resolutions. The group helped raise the profile of the interpreters as important team members and helped to change their place within the organisational culture. From being invited in only to interpret, they now attend regular clinical and referral meetings, thus establishing a permanent presence and important role within the organisation.

Leadership

As group facilitators we were working from a Psychodynamic base, we were not leaders as defined within much of the literature, having said that there is no doubt that we were ascribed and had power within the organisational structure. (If using, for example - French and Raven's (1959) typology of five bases of power;- reward, coercive, legitimate, expert, and referent power). In addition we knew most if not all of the interpreters when the group started, while many did not know each other.

Initially we were expected to 'lead' the group, but over time the group developed its own way of operating which was much more democratic. The group development might be framed within Tuckman and Jensen's (1973) model of group functioning, which contains four major stages, these are of forming, norming, storming, and performing.

One of the most noticeable themes was the rivalry over leadership among the bicultural workers. They had no organisational need for a leader, although a psychological need was frequently expressed, in that the group members frequently asked one of two group members to take on this role. There was competition for the role of leader between two members, one from Africa and one from the Middle East. In meetings there would sometimes be either tacit or open encouragement by some of the other group members for one of the contenders.

At the beginning we largely represented the interpreters to the wider staff team, this later changed and they represented themselves. We might be defined as 'Central People' in a group work context as defined by Redl (1942) and developed by Heap (1996), although this was a support and supervision group and not a therapeutic group. As the group life developed and the interpreters got to know one another better and to form a group identity the group dynamics changed. The issue of designated group leaders and how this relates to naturally evolving leaders, is one that has been discussed at length in the literature, with little agreement (Verba, 1961; Feidler, 1965). Issues of leadership with any group are always complex and evolving. If the dimensions of task and socio-emotional leaders are further considered (Bales, 1950; Verba, 1961), the dynamics become even more complex. This group, as stated earlier had a number of roles to fill, support and supervision, in addition to developing a code of practice, enhancing the role of the interpreter within the organisational culture and perhaps a training function about the nature of the variety of facets of the organisation's work.

It is perhaps important to note that we as group facilitators had run groups together before and felt extremely comfortable working together, we always tried to find time to meet before the group meetings and to debrief afterwards

Cultural Differences

Cultural differences were a frequent subject of discussion, and were sometimes used to express anger at the insensitivity of the British.

One example was that of a doctor who, on being presented with back ache by her patient, informed her that this pain was caused by stress and would not respond to medication or any type of medical intervention. The doctor suggested the patient would benefit from swimming. The client had apparently become extremely upset about this, asking if the doctor was trying to make her community (Shiite Muslim) reject her as a 'scarlet woman' by showing her body in such a brazen manner. The practitioner then suggested she joined a tennis club which was again culturally inappropriate.

The bicultural worker described how angry she felt on behalf of the client and how she became the apex of the discussion as both practitioner and client wanted her to explain their position to the other one. This interface also raised difficult feelings for the bicultural worker who, although born into the client's community, felt she had taken on many of the strictures of the West and would herself have gone swimming or played tennis. Thus issues relating to her own personal boundaries were raised.

Group Life and a Shared History

The above story became one of the group's own jokes or shared history and the doctor became known within the group as 'tennis' for several months afterwards. It also became the group's shorthand way of dealing with cultural misunderstandings in either direction. On occasions when these were discussed the group climate bordered on the hysterical with group members competing to relate similar experiences. The hysterical laughter seemed to be about getting permission to express these incidents in a safe and contained environment.

It is also important to note that cultural misunderstandings can also occur between clients and bicultural workers. This is particularly likely to happen when one of them comes from a rural community and has undergone little formal education, while the other comes from an urban area and has had a high level of formal education.

One of our African bicultural workers explained how she became confused when, in the middle of a session, the client started to talk about the size of the moon and using some terminology she did not understand. She realised after some moments that the client was talking about her period. She said: 'I was meant to be her interpreter, but we literally did not speak the same language'.

What is Being Interpreted?

Words and meanings are often not interchangeable between languages and certain words do not exist in other languages. Different cultural strictures may apply. Eva Hoffman, a Polish refugee, writes:

> You're welcome' for example, strikes me as a gaucherie, and I can hardly bring myself to say it - I suppose because it implies that there's something to be thanked for, which in Polish would be impolite. Even the simplest adjectives sow confusion in my mind; English kindliness has a whole system of morality behind it, a system that makes 'kindness' an entirely positive virtue. (Hoffman, 1989)

Also words do not seem to stand for things in the same way they do in one's mother tongue. To quote Hoffman again:

> When my friend Penny tells me that she's envious, or happy, or disappointed, I try laboriously to translate not from English to Polish but from the word back to its source, to the feeling from which it springs. Already in that moment of strain, spontaneity of response is lost. And anyway, the translation doesn't work. I don't know how Penny feels when she talks about envy. The word hangs in a Platonic stratosphere, a vague prototype of all envy, so large so all-encompassing that it might crush me - as might disappointing or happiness.. (Hoffman, 1989)

Dilemmas

The organisation offers a wide variety of perspectives, ranging from western medicine through to complementary practices such as reflexology, an unusual situation in a British health context. Thus a great deal is asked of our bicultural workers who may have to move from a formal medical examination, where the emphasis is on literal translation to a psychotherapy session or an aromatherapy consultation where the feelings and emotions predominate.

There will always be dilemmas associated with moving from one context or role to another, the different interpreting roles have been named the advocate/link worker, literal, and the community interpreter (Saunders, 1994). Most health providers will use one predominant model of interpreting, in the organisational context of this paper several may be used. One of the ways we dealt with this was by developing a code of practice which recommends that the health practitioner and interpreter meet together before the consultation with the client to discuss how they are going to best work together and to discuss any other issues which may be pertinent to the consultation about to take place. They also spend some time after the consultation reviewing their work together and considering future joint working. In addition regular attendance by interpreters at clinical meetings where these issues are discussed ensures a heightened and continuous awareness and sensitivity to the issues of interpreter modality.

From a Dyad to a Triad

What is it that is different when instead of the traditional therapeutic dyad it is replaced by a triad which includes an interpreter? The interpreter is essential if any meaningful communication is to occur between the patient and the therapist, but all parties are likely to feel, at some level, a wide range of emotions towards the other two.

The English expression 'two is company, three is a crowd' perhaps touches on the essence of this. Interpreters may feel they are in some way acting on behalf of one or other of the parties (client or practitioner), and, rarely, for both. The interpreter may feel that, as they share a language, a culture and maybe politics with the client, and that there is a strong alliance between them. Alternatively they may feel that they are representatives of the organisation and therefore share an alliance with the worker. All three participants are involved in this process and the client will certainly sense these and they will effect the dynamics of the consultation.

It has been suggested that one of the individuals in a triad or triangular relationship will always feel excluded. As therapists we are used to working behind closed doors, unless we are family therapists where there is a highly ritualised and accepted series of interventions by those behind the screen. Having a third person in the room may raise all sorts of feelings of being watched or judged at work and can generate fears of not being a 'good enough' therapist. Some practitioners see the use of an interpreter as hindrance or a barrier to their work, and either avoid using them or try to maximise their presence in the room.

A bicultural worker is never a neutral presence in the room and will always become an object of transfer. She or her can also inadvertently become part of the therapeutic system.

There may be many benefits from employing a bicultural worker. These include the fact that the presence of a fellow national or member of a familiar community can increase feelings of trust and belonging which the client feels towards the agency and practitioner. It has been suggested (Saxtroph & Christiansen, 1991) writing about Middle Eastern families living in exile in Denmark that bicultural workers may act as a positive role model for clients. The

cultural understanding which the bicultural worker brings into the therapeutic communication may bridge the gap between health professional and client. It may also enhance the health professional's understanding of the client's history and culture.

Conclusion

In summary, the nature of the client group necessitates the use of interpreters/bicultural workers if any meaningful communication is to occur. The paper has noted some of the dilemmas this may produce, including boundary and barrier conflicts felt by all members of the triad. Issues of transference and how the bicultural worker may inadvertently become part of the therapeutic system were commented upon. Also the difficulties of translating words and meanings from one language to another were considered.

The formation and subsequent role of a support and supervision group for bicultural workers were discussed as well as the dilemmas this raised for the organisation, the facilitators and group members. The group took some while to become an accepted part of the Foundation's work, but is now seen as an integral part. Its inception has been seen as a positive addition to our practice and is felt to be essential by the bicultural workers. The group has provided a forum for the bicultural workers to talk about the difficulties they experienced while working at this organisation. It has provided a safe place for interpersonal difficulties to be discussed and for practical difficulties to be resolved.

Note

1. Throughout this paper the term 'Bicultural Worker' will be used to describe someone whose primary task is to interpret for a client the spoken word, cultural symbols and beliefs to a health practitioner. This differs from an interpreter whose primary task is to interpret only the spoken words. Different countries and nationalities may use these terms differently. The term 'Practitioner' will be used to describe someone who is working as a health worker. The primary focus in this paper is on the support and clinical supervision group from one of the facilitator's perspective as it would be inappropriate to write on behalf of the Bicultural group members.

References

Alpert, M. and Marcos, L.R. (1976) 'The phenomenon of language independence strategies and risks in psychotherapy with bilingual patients', *American Journal of Psychiatry*, 133, pp1275-1278

Baker, N. (1981) 'Social work through an interpreter', *Social work*, 26, pp391-397

Bales, R.F. (1950) *Interaction Process Analysis*. Reading, Mass: Addison Wesley

Faust, M. and Drickey, M.D. (1986) 'Working with interpreters', *Journal of Family Practice*, 22, 2, pp131-138

Feidler, F.E. (1967) *A Contingency Theory of Leadership Effectiveness*. New York: MacGraw-Hill

Freed, A. (1988) 'Interviewing through an interpreter', *Social Work*, pp315-319

French, J.R.P. and Ravens, B. (1959) 'The bases of social power', in D. Cartwright (eds) *Studies in Social Power*. Ann Arbor: Michigan Institute for Social Research

Grainger, E. and Baker, M. (1999) 'An investigation into the role and work experience of the interpreter', in R. Tribe and H. Raval (1999) *Undertaking Mental Health Work Using Interpreters*. London: Routledge

Hawkins, P. and Shohet, R. (1989) *Supervision in the Helping Processions*. Milton Keynes: Open University Press

Heap, K. (1996) 'The groupworker as central person', *Case Conference*, 12, 7, pp20-29

Hoffman, L. (1989) *Lost in Translation*. London: William Heineman

Launer, J. (1978) 'Taking medical histories through interpreters: Practice in a Nigerian out-patient department', *British Medical Journal*, Sep 30th, pp934-935

Marcos, L. (1979) 'Effects of interpreters on the evaluation of psychopathology in non-English speaking clients', *Journal of Psychiatry*, 136, 2, pp171-174

O'Neil, J., Koolage, W. and Kaufert, J. (1988) 'Health communication problems in Canadian Innuit communities', *Arctic Medical Research*, 47, pp374-378

Phelan, M. and Parkman, S. (1995) 'Work with an interpreter', *British Medical Journal*, 311, pp555-557

Raval, H. (1996) 'A systemic perspective on working with interpreters', *Clinical Child Psychology and Psychiatry*, 1, 1, pp29-43

Sabin, J.E. (1975) 'Translating despair', *American Journal of Psychiatry*, 132, pp197-199

Saxtroph, V. and Christiansen, J. (1991) *Working with Refugee Families from the Middle East in Denmark*. Presented at the III International Conference of Centres, Institutions and Individuals concerned with the Care of Victims of Organised Violence. Santiago: Chile

Saunders, M. (1994) *Issues and Practice of Interpreting*. London Interpreting Project

Shackman, J. (1985) *The Right to be Understood. A Handbook on Working with Interpreters*. London: The National Extension College

Tribe, R. (1998) 'What can counselling psychology offer in situations of civil conflict and war overseas', *Counselling Psychology Quarterly*, 11, 1, pp109-115

Tribe, R. (1998) (in press) 'Therapeutic work with refugees living in exile: Observations on clinical practice', *Counselling Psychology Quarterly*

Tribe, R. (1999) (in press) 'Some observations on using interpreters/ bicultural workers when working with refugee clients, many who have been tortured', *British Journal of Medical Psychology*

Tribe, R. and Raval, H. (1999) *Undertaking Mental Health Work Using Interpreters*. London: Routledge

Tuckman, B.W. (1965) 'Developmental sequence in small groups', *Psychological Bulletin*, 63, pp384-99

Tuckman, B.W. and Jenson, M.A. (1977) 'Stages in small group development revisited', *Group and Organizational Studies'*, 2, pp419-427

Venables, M.and Rodriquez, P. (1989) *A Spanish-speaking Psychotherapy Group for Exiled Male Victims of Torture and Political Violence*. Presented at the III International Conference of Centres, Institutions and Individuals Concerned with the Care of Victims of Organised Violence. Costa Rica

Verba, S. (1961) 'Leadership: affective and instrumental', in *Small groups and Political Behaviour*. Princeton, NJ: Princeton University Press.

Feminist Groupwork with Lesbian Survivors of Incest

Patricia A. Groves[1] and Connie Schondel[2]

Lesbian survivors of incest can benefit from participation in a group composed specifically for lesbian survivors, members feel safer to explore issues that are pertinent to their lives
Using a feminist approach enables group workers to operate from facilitator and catalyst roles for change and avoid being perceived as experts. A feminist groupwork approach with lesbian survivors will be presented. The group process will be explored detailing how the facilitators minimize false dichotomies enabling the participants to assume responsibility for themselves and the direction of the group, and emphasizing the importance of removing the label of being a victim to survivor to thrivor. Furthermore, the workers assisted the members in seeing their strengths that have developed as a result of their abuse experiences, for example, helping the victim to re-label behaviors such as dissociation not as bad or as a psychiatric symptom, but rather as adaptive responses to abusive environments.
Emergence of themes in the groupwork process will be described. For instance, the interdependence of the dynamics of homophobia and being a survivor, trust and its relationship to social stigma and discrimination, family secrets and maintenance of the message about silent, denial and minimizing the pain around silence, oppression and isolation. The authors' approach to healing lesbian incest survivors was intricately connected to the ability of lesbian women to come together and form a strong healthy community able to address the destructive forces of oppression and homophobia.

1. Associate Professor and Director of Social Work Program, University of Toledo. 2. Until her recent untimely death, Connie Schondel was Associate Professor, Dept of Social Work, University of Toledeo.
Address for correspondence: Dept of Sociology, Anthropology and Social Work, University of Toledo, 2801 W. Bancroft St, Toledo, OH 43606, USA

Groupwork Vol. 10(3), 1997-98, pp215-230

Introduction

The incidence of sexual abuse has been well documented in the literature (Russell, 1986; Tackett-Kendall, Williams, & Finkelhor, 1993). In addition, a variety of treatment modalities has been utilised to address the victimisation process experienced by abused women (Faria & Belohlavek, 1984, Patten, Gatz, Jones, & Thomas 1989). Female adult survivors experience a wide range of difficulties including fear of intimacy and mistrust of others, feelings of low self esteem and inadequacy, extreme isolation, and sexual dysfunction (Swink & Leveille, 1990). To address these problems, individual and groupwork treatment approaches have emerged. These methods help survivors to work through feelings about abuse and to develop healthy life management skills (Bergart, 1986; Gordy, 1983).

This article examines the therapeutic issues raised in a group by lesbian women who are coping with the repercussions of childhood sexual abuse. The focus of the therapeutic group was around incest issues and the societal oppression of lesbians which combine to create identity confusion and disrupted adult functioning.

Feminist Groupwork and the Role of Facilitator

Groupwork has been found to be a valuable intervention when working with incest survivors (Knight, 1990). The theoretical framework of feminist social work presented by Vandenberg and Cooper (1986) complements the purposes of a mutual aid group for lesbian women who are survivors of incest. The feminist perspective emphasises the elimination of false dichotomies, reconceptualising power, honoring process, validating renaming, and believing that the personal is political.

A critical element in the formation of the group was the creation of a context that facilitated the empowerment of group members. The feminist model of social work was utilised as the guiding principle to promote a supportive environment for the women. The facilitators were both lesbian women and survivors of childhood sexual abuse. While it was important to maintain professional boundaries, false dichotomies between members and facilitators were avoided. The thread of shared experiences as women and survivors assisted in binding the group together. Roles of the facilitators included maintaining safety, preserving the boundaries of discussion, and facilitating the interaction among members. Group members were able to feel a sense of control over their group and its process (Groves & Schondel, 1996).

The facilitators of the group reinforced feminism by the effective use of selves in modelling concepts such as 'breaking down false dichotomies. Healing was emphasised as a process which we, as women, as lesbians, as survivors all experience. As professional facilitators, we brought a set of skills, experience, and self awareness to the group.

One way to break down secrecy was for co-facilitators to share, as appropriate, their own experiences. This broke through the barriers of secrecy and helped to decrease the dichotomous nature of the therapeutic relationship. While it was important to decrease barriers, it was also important to maintain boundaries and to maintain enough professional distance to be effective as a group facilitator. Personal sharing was tailored to the needs of the group while personal issues of facilitators were not brought into the group. By the facilitators sharing that we were both lesbians and survivors of incest, the group members were able to feel a connection to the facilitators and to develop a sense of all of us as a group of women working to promote our healing journey. The knowledge that the facilitators had been through some of the same experiences and shared the pain and similar feelings gave the members hope and encouragement. It is important to use caution when sharing such information as the group exists for the benefit of the members and not the facilitators. It is recommended that sharing be limited to brief statements of one's past experiences, rather than cathartic expressions and that current conflicts be avoided.

Co-facilitation of the group enabled the facilitators to model effective interactions. By expressing differences of opinion or viewpoint, the members were able to observe two people being able to accept each other even though they did not share the same perspective. This is an important issue for lesbian incest survivors, who often grew up in families where differences were not accepted or tolerated.

Co-facilitation lessened the transference and the development of dependence upon one therapist. Different responses from each facilitator, helped to point out that there are different ways to cope and to respond to the lesbian survivor experience.

Group Formation and Composition

An essential element in formation of the group was the creation of an environment that facilitated empowerment of group members. As VandenBerg & Cooper (1986) have suggested that the feminist model was utilised because it emphasises the process of empowerment through the elimination of false dichotomies, reconceptualising power, valuing process, validating the renaming process, and believing the personal is political.

In addition, the feminist model is consistent with the Code of Ethics of the National Association of Social Workers (1997).

The group evolved from the clinical practice of one of the facilitators who deals primarily with lesbian women. While heterosexual women have had opportunities to meet in support groups, lesbian women have had limited opportunities to experience effective groupwork intervention (Groves & Schondel, 1996). In the authors' experience, the homogeneity of an all lesbian group is more effective than placing a lesbian woman in a primarily heterosexual group. Lesbian women often report having difficulty establishing trust with heterosexual women survivors because of their fears of homophobic reactions of other members (Groves & Schondel, 1996). In addition, the lack of common relationship experiences further alienate the lesbian survivor.

Lesbian incest survivors often view themselves with hate based on the incest experience combined with the surrounding environment which reinforces the negative stereotypes and the shame associated with being a lesbian. This group experience would enable the participants to redefine themselves as strong surviving individuals as well as similar to other women confronting like circumstances and problems. It also provided the members with opportunities to receive validation for the oppressive experiences as well as helping members to develop positive means to confront these experiences.

In addition to inviting appropriate individuals from the

practice of one of the facilitators, participants were recruited through an advertisement placed in a local gay/lesbian newsletter . Since the lesbian community is small and women are often familiar with each other or their partners, it was made clear that it was acceptable that members knew each other prior to the group. Since this group dealt with individual issues, both members of a couple were not able to participate. In several instances, when both individuals in the relationship were survivors, they needed to decide who was going to participate in the group. The facilitators agreed to make this rule because a couple in the group could present a united front in relation to other members or one partner could feel exposed and 'ganged up' on by the rest of the group. Because the facilitators and members were aware of the need for couples to deal with the impact of incest on the relationship, another group was offered specifically for couples (Groves & Schondel, 1996).

Another rule that the facilitators initiated was a prohibition on sexual relationships developing between group members. Incest survivors often have learned from their childhood experiences that relationships can only be sexual or that a sexual offer could not be refused. The co-leaders supported friendships among members that were not sexual in nature. Members were asked not to become involved in sexual relationships while they were members of the group. This limitation helped the members learn and maintain boundaries necessary for an environment where all members could feel safe. If a sexual relationship developed, the members were asked to leave the group at the end of the set of sessions. Processing this occurrence by all members would be vital in order to bring understanding and closure.

The facilitators decided that a group of six to eight members would enable members to present diversity of ideas and also allow for intimacy to develop among the members. The group consistently remained at six, with two members leaving the group after the completion of a set of sessions. One member left the group for one set of sessions and returned for the following set. A new member was recruited to replace another member who decided to terminate after the initial set of sessions.

Group Structure

The group met weekly for three sets of twelve week sessions. This gave members the opportunity to make a commitment for one set of sessions and to decide whether to continue and commit to another set. This model enabled members to feel a sense of control over their involvement with the group. If the group became too intense or if a member had conflicting commitments, she had the opportunity to quit after the twelve week session. If a member chose to terminate with the group after keeping her commitment for the twelve week set of sessions, she could share her reasons for leaving with the group and thus reduce her feelings of guilt associated with leaving and separation and reduce the surfacing of abandonment issues in other members. The group could process these feelings when they did surface in relation to a member making a decision to terminate with the group.

The facilitators requested that group participants be involved in decision making about the operation of the group. The facilitators presented a list of areas for potential discussion. These included feelings of anger toward perpetrators and other care givers, feelings of abandonment, trust issues, the interplay of the incest experience with the coming out process, and sexuality. The members decided to use these areas as a broad guide to keep the group focused and to use a round robin method of raising concerns for discussion each week. It was the responsibility of the facilitators to assist the group in staying on track in relation to the overall plan for the group.

Group Development

During the initial session, group members introduced themselves and clarified who knew each other prior to the beginning of the group so members were clear that some members did already know each other. The feminist model and overall goals of the group were discussed and the members decided how to conduct the group sessions. The need for confidentiality was also discussed. This issue was of particular significance to a group where members and partners of members knew each other.

As Yalom (1985) has reported, individuals often enter therapy feeling alone with their problems, thoughts, impulses, and fantasies. Lesbian women are often unaware of their internalisation of oppression and discrimination. The following structured activities were used to help identify commonality, bonding, and identification between and among group members.

The facilitators identified myths and stereotypes about lesbians (Schecter, Hart, & Ritchie, 1988). These myths were written on individual sheets and hung about the room. The participants were asked to choose the one myth with which they most identified. The same process was used with myths related to being a survivor of incest. These activities promoted an awareness of internalised oppression and enabled the participants to see the commonality in their beliefs about themselves and others. These exercises provided boundaries which promoted sharing while ensuring safe emotional distance to be maintained. The initiation of these activities by the co-facilitators also demonstrated their role in maintaining a safe environment for members.

During the first set of sessions, the members were able to gain trust and to move into the first working stage by being able to discuss common feelings and issues. As the group progressed into the second set of sessions, a deeper level of intimacy was achieved and the members were able to risk sharing issues which might differentiate them form other members. An activity utilised during this set of sessions was to have members bring pictures of themselves in childhood as a means to get in touch with their 'inner child.' As the group entered the third set of sessions, even greater intimacy was achieved and the members were able to reveal fears and concerns about sex and sexuality. By the end of the this set and at the point of termination, the members had reached the maturation stage and were able to separate from the group and to maintain contact with other members offering mutual support.

Therapeutic Issues

As the group progressed, the key therapeutic issues became evident. These issues were the interdependence of the dynamics of 'homophobia' and 'being a survivor,' a sense of isolation and feeling different from others, a lack of trust in self and others, a tendency to deny or minimise the impact of one's experiences, feelings of shame and self depreciation, maintenance of family and lesbian community secrets, negative feelings about one's sexuality, and experience with abusive relationships.

Interdependence of the Dynamics of 'Homophobia' and 'Being a Survivor'

Because being a lesbian and being an incest survivor are both viewed negatively by society, they share common dynamics. It is impossible to separate the impact of one from the other. For example, a common societal myth is that rape or incest will make a girl become a lesbian. The internalised mythical beliefs held by each member had to be worked through in order for her to become comfortable with her lesbian identity. Even though a woman may present herself as confident in her lesbianism, she often holds underlying self hatred which must be confronted in order for healing to occur.

The exercise identified earlier enabled members to see how their internalised beliefs about being lesbian and being a survivor often interacted, resulting in behaviours which were unhealthy. Members frequently reported having had a series of unhealthy relationships with women, often involving the use of drugs and/or alcohol. Some women had experienced destructive relationships with men as a way to deny their lesbianism. Once achieving sobriety, they needed help and support to develop healthy and intimate relationships and to feel positive about their lesbian and survivor identity.

Sense of Isolation and Feeling Different from Others

The issue of isolation emerged as women were able to begin building bonds within the group. They shared the existential crisis of being dually different. Knight (1990) discussed the fear of incest survivors that her 'real', 'bad' self will be discovered if she gets too close to others. Among heterosexual incest survivors the group members had felt the fear of exposure as lesbians, and among lesbians, members feared being exposed as incest survivors. This lack of validation from others, added to the sense of aloneness. Members were unable to develop a positive self identity when they felt their lives were segmented and full of secrets. It is impossible to develop a sense of personal integrity if one believes one's life to be a lie. Through the experience of coming together in this group members, for the first time were able to feel acceptance and understanding from others.

As the barriers of isolation were broken down, members began to open up and trust one another. This process evolved as individuals began to share their stories with each other and were heard, often for the first time. Generally, lesbian survivors have been reinforced not to trust others because of the social stigma and discrimination related to being a lesbian and a survivor (Finkelhor, D. & Browne, A. 1985).

As members began to share stories, their commonalities became clear. One woman told about her abuse by a grandfather and how she felt responsible for being abused because her mother told her this is how men are when she attempted to get help from a grown-up. Another member reached out her hand and offered support indicating that she had similar feelings and how wrong it was for adults to give this message to children who were being victimised.

Lack of Trust in Self and Others

In addition, they have been reinforced not to trust their perceptions of events that occurred. Their experiences were not validated by significant others in childhood. The ongoing denial of reality leads to a sense of powerlessness. This powerlessness impairs the sense of efficacy of coping skills resulting in the expectation of being revictimised. This expectation may lead to the inability to assess the safety of situations and creates a high risk of subsequent victimisation (Finkelhor & Browne, 1985).

Lesbians are at risk for further victimisation as they reveal their lesbianism as a part of the coming out process. Confusion may result about when and to whom one can safely come out. For example, coming out in the workplace may realistically threaten employment, or may lead to harassment from co-workers.

Lesbian survivors who have previously been in relationships

with men may upon the realisation of being lesbian, assume that relationships with women are automatically safe. Also, the myth that female partners are incapable of being abusers (Groves, P., 1991). Several participants related being in lesbian relationships that were abusive. That experience assisted members to share openly their sense of shame and receive validation and support from the other group participants. For several members, the fact that they were victims of domestic violence at the hand of a woman was a completely new awareness. One member was shocked when confronted by this fact and responded that she truly believed she deserved the abuse from her female partner because women could not be abusers. The members shared strategies for identifying potential abuse, particularly by strong needs for power and control over one's partner and offered to provide emotional support if any member found herself in such a situation. Issues such as jealously, control over the type of clothing worn, isolation from friends and family, and financial control were discussed.

Denial and Minimising One's Experiences

The issues of denial and minimising surfaced throughout the three (12) week sets of sessions. Denial is one of the common coping strategies in the early coming out process (Groves & Ventura, 1982). Simultaneously, minimising and denial are utilised by survivors to avoid the pain associated with their victimisation (Patten et al, 1989). For example, during one of the group sessions, a participant began to question whether she was a lesbian. The group helped her to process this denial and was beneficial in her resolving her identity confusion. Minimisation was exemplified during the session where participants shared childhood pictures and experiences. One member brought a picture of when she was six years of age and totally bald because she would pull her hair out. She minimised the pain associated with this picture by laughing and creating jokes about herself. The group responded with laughter to her humour, thus further minimising the pain. The facilitator responded to the group with tears in her eyes, indicating that she felt that this little girl was in a great deal of pain, having to pull out her own hair and having no one respond to her.

When confronted by a facilitator, the group members re-examined their reactions and allowed themselves to get in touch with the feelings of pain associated with abuse.

Feelings of Shame and Self Depreciation

A major therapeutic issue confronted by all the participants was the shame and guilt associated with being a lesbian and a survivor. Having broken through the denial, participants could begin to deal with the internalised self hatred and shame. Sgroi (1982) has identified the negative self image and low self esteem resulting from this shame as the 'damaged goods' syndrome. This was illustrated in the group as two members vocalised their hatred of their child within. 'Child ' was identified as evil and bad and deserving of abuse. Both of these participants had patterns of self abuse which they were able to identify as stemming from the need to punish this bad child. The other participants pointed out that all children are inherently lovable and offered a variety of suggestions to assist these members to become more self nurturing.

Maintenance of Family and Lesbian Community Secrets

Another issue which emerged during the group was the maintenance of family secrets. It is typical in families the incest, often intergenerational is kept as a family secret. The survivor learns that discussion of her incest experiences are taboo within and outside of the family. This silence around the experience and the accompanying feelings further alienates the survivor from family, friends, and community.

Similarly, being lesbian is a topic which families and society often refuse to discuss. Again, the individual is silenced. When one individual holds these two secrets simultaneously, they become intertwined, intensifying the feelings of being different from others. Lewis (1984) has pointed to the difficulties created by the family silence around being lesbian. Unlike racial minorities whose differences are visible and shared by families, parents of lesbians do not teach their daughters skills for coping with a hostile environment.

The anger experienced may be more likely to be turned inward without support for identifying its roots in societal oppression. For the incest survivor, this experience of silence and lack of teaching of coping skills is repeated. Therefore, the lesbian survivor is placed in a position of 'double jeopardy'.

One group member shared her experienced of being shunned by her family, first in childhood because she was abused, and later in adolescence because she revealed her lesbianism to her parents. As an adult, she became intimately involved with a woman who strongly denied her lesbianism. As part of this denial, the group member felt coerced by her partner to date men and to act and look 'feminine' which ran counter to her own identity. She developed severe depression and made several suicide attempts as a result of the self hatred which was intensifies by feeling unacceptable to family and even to her lesbian partner. When other members shared similar painful experiences, the group members began to feel empowered and recognised that they were indeed lovable as people. Once the members began to realise that they had been victimised by an oppressive society, they were able to become aware of how this oppression has permeated the lesbian community. All minority groups need to protect themselves from the destructive messages of the majority community. In the lesbian community, this has led to silence (Lobel, 1986) around negative issues which do exist. There is strong community denial of partner abuse, rape, and drug and alcohol abuse. In addition, it only very recently that professional journals have begun to address these subject areas. The group members recounted experiences of feeling unable to share their stories of incest or other abuse in the community and with professionals from whom they sought help.

Counsellors frequently lack the necessary information to help lesbians cope with these taboo subject areas. One group member reported that her previous therapist had reinforced her belief that her lesbianism was a result of her incestuous childhood and that she should try dating men as a way of healing from her childhood incest. She terminated with this therapist after several frustrating attempts to date men. She described herself as feeling totally worthless at that point in her life. Another member went to counselling because she had been battered by her partner. The counsellor told her that the problem stemmed from poor communication, and she was given ideas for becoming more direct in asking for her needs to be met in the relationship. As she became more assertive, the abuse became more intense. The facilitators were able to point out that abuse is directly the responsibility of the abuser, regardless of gender. It can be dangerous to provide couple counselling when on person is being victimised. The group members were able to utilise this information to empower themselves to exit relationships where they felt they were being abused. They also felt more able to be in charge of relationships with therapists. One of the strategies of the feminist model used for this group was to encourage members to question the therapists. The individual is in charge of her own journey; we can facilitate the process, but we do not have all the answers. Each woman must travel her own road and she is the best source of knowledge about herself.

Negative Feelings about Sexuality

Sexuality and sex was an uncomfortable topic for members and became the culminating area for group discussion. It was only towards the end of the last set of sessions that members trusted each other enough to reveal themselves in this area. The subject would frequently come up in earlier sessions, but member would shut down when they felt that they might have to reveal thoughts and feelings around topics related to sexuality. In addition, the awareness that the group would soon terminate may have enabled some members to take greater risk to disclose their discomfort about being sexual.

One participant disclosed her unwillingness to perform sexual activities that were associated with her past abuse. Because she had been unable to talk about these issues with her partner, the couple had completely stopped all sexual intimacy. The group was able to help her address the pain around these experiences, and to feel strong enough to share her feelings with her partner. Through discussion, she gained the voice to say 'no,' and she and her partner were able to talk about what sexual activities might be comfortable for both.

Another member shared her discomfort about feelings of sexual arousal. She dealt with these by carefully avoiding anything which might bring them on. If this mechanism failed, she would dissociate and allow her partner, and sometimes others to have sex with her, resulting in intense shame and internalised self hatred. The group was able to explore ways of becoming more aware of the body, and to recognise that sexual feelings are a part of healthy adult functioning, and that allowing one's self to indulge in the expression of these feelings is a means of self nurturing.

The group was also able to give members permission to say no to sexual overtures and to think of intimacy as being attainable with or without sexual activity. For example, the member who had difficulty in saying no to her partner or others was able to learn to set limits and to achieve intimacy in non sexual ways. This became particularly important in her being able to develop nonsexual friendships with lesbian women.

Experience with Abusive Relationships.

Several group members were able to share their experiences with abusive partners, both male and female. Lobel (1986) and Renzetti (1992) have documented the existence of partner abuse in lesbian couples. It is important not to make the assumption that sexual abuse causes individuals to enter into and remain in abusive relationships in adulthood. The group members who had experienced abuse from intimate partners in adulthood indicated that the feelings of shame associated with being abused in childhood made it more difficult address the abusive relationship in adulthood. One member stated that she realised that as a child she was not responsible for what had happened to her, but as a adult she had great difficulty letting go of the guilt and responsibility for the abuse, saying 'As an adult I am responsible for what I allow to happen to me.' By sharing these feelings, the members were ultimately put the abusive relationships in perspective and let go of the guilt and shame.

Being able to acknowledge that abuse had occurred in adulthood was difficult for members. The abusers' messages that the victim was to blame and not to share relationship matters with others were entwined with the similar childhood messages from perpetrators, thus making disclosure more difficult. Again the power of sharing in the group led members to be more open about their experiences. One member was able to start a discussion group to address issues of violence in the lesbian community.

Implications for Practice

This paper has presented a model for effective groupwork with lesbian incest survivors. Whether one is a lesbian or heterosexual therapist, it is important to review the therapeutic issues raised in this group. Survivorship brings a set of issues that need to be addressed in the treatment process. Being a lesbian survivor brings in new issues as well as the intensification of the common survivorship issues. Feminism implies honesty and willingness to share one's self as appropriate. It is not necessary to be a lesbian or to be an incest survivor in order to successfully facilitate a group for lesbian survivors. What is important, however, is the willingness to examine your own feelings and experiences and to share these insights with the group as appropriate.

References

Bergart, A.M. (1986) 'Isolation to intimacy: Incest survivors in group therapy', *Social Casework,* 67, pp266-275.

Minnesota Coalition for Battered Women (1990) *Confronting Homophobia: A Manual for Battered Women's and Anti-Sexual Assault Programs*. Lesbian Advocacy Committee, Minnesota Coalition for Battered Women

Finkelhor, D. and Browne, A. (1985) 'The traumatic impact of child sexual abuse: A conceptualization', *American Journal of Orthopsychiatry,* 55, 4, pp530-540

Faria, G. and Belohlavek, N. (1984) 'Treating female adult survivors of childhood incest', *Social Casework*, 65, 8, pp465-470

Groves, P. (1991) An Analysis of Physical Conflict in Lesbian Relationships. Unpublished doctoral dissertation. Columbus: Ohio State University, College of Social Work

Groves, P. and Schondel, C. (1996) 'Lesbian couples who are survivors of incest: Groupwork utilizing a feminist approach', *Social Work with Groups* 19, 3/4, pp93-105

Groves, P. and Ventura, L. (1982) 'The lesbian coming out process: Therapeutic considerations', *Personnel and Guidance Journal*, 62, 3, pp146-148.

Gordy, P. (1983). 'Groupwork that supports adult victims of childhood incest', *Social Casework*, 64, 3, pp300-307

Kendall-Tackett, K., Williams, L., and Finkelhor, D. (1993) 'Impact of sexual abuse on children: A review and synthesis of recent empirical studies', *Psychological Bulletin*, 113, 1, pp164-180

Knight, C. (1990) 'Use of support groups with adult female survivors of childhood sexual abuse', *Social Work*, 35, 3, pp202-206

Lewis, S. G. (1979) *Sunday's Women*. Boston, MA: Boston Press

Lobel, K. (1986) *Naming the Violence: Speaking out About Lesbian Battering*. Seattle: The Seal Press

NASW (1997) *NASW's Code of Ethics*. Silver Spring MD: National Association of Social Workers

Patten, S., Gatz, Y., Jones, B., and Thomas, D. (1989) 'Posttraumatic stress disorder and the treatment of sexual assault', *Social Work*, 34, 3, pp197-203

Renzetti, Claire M. (1992) *Violent Betrayal: Partner Abuse in Lesbian Relationships*. Newbury Park: Sage.

Russell, D. (1986) *The Secret Trauma: Incest in the Lives of Girls and Women*. New York: Free Press.

Sagroi, S. (1982) *Handbook of Clinical Intervention in Child Sexual Abuse*. Lexington, MA: D.C. Health.

Schechter, S., Hart, B., and Richie, B. (1990) 'Building women's leadership: A training manual for activist in battered women's programs, rape crisis services, and women's centers', in *Confronting Homophobia: A Manual for Battered Women's and Anti-sexual Assault Programs*. Lesbian Advocacy Committee, Minnesota Coalition for Battered Women

Swink, K.K., and Leveille, A. E. (1986) 'From victim to survivor: A new look at the issue and recovery process of adult incest survivors', *Women and Therapy*, 5, pp119-141

Van den Bergh, N. and Cooper, L. (eds.) (1986) *Feminist Visions for Social Work*. Silver Spring, Md: National Association of Social Workers

Yalom, I. (1985) *Theory and Practice of Group Psychotherapy*. New York: Basic Books

'Don't worry, it's just a stage he's going through': A reappraisal of the stage theory of group work as applied to an open model treatment group for men who abuse women

Tom Caplan[1] and Harle Thomas[2]

This paper reviews various stage theories in terms of their implications for a treatment group model for men who abuse women, and uses case examples from the McGill Domestic Violence Clinic's treatment group for male perpetrators to present its own five-stage model. The stages include: (1) safety; (2) social; (3) inclusion; (4) collaboration; and (5) continuity. Men who are violent need to address the issues of relationship building; their stage work may be more appropriately conceived of in terms of 'process' rather than in terms of 'power and control.' The open model treatment group, where men enter and exit at their own pace, may not be adequately described by a stage theory built on the concept of a whole group moving simultaneously through discrete stages. An open group model may better reflect the real world if conceived of as an individually paced process with permeable 'stage' boundaries through which group members achieve mutuality.

1. Adjunct Professor, McGill University School of Social Work and Director, McGill Domestic Violence Clinic
2. Social Worker, Montreal General Hospital and Clinician and Group Worker, McGill Domestic Violence Clinic
Address for correspondence: Domestic Violence Clinic, McGill University School of Social Work, Montreal, QC, Canada, H3A 2A7

Introduction

One major concept discussed in the various theories about group work is the development of an interactive process between the members. This group process has been described by Garvin (1974) as the vehicle by which social skills and appropriate behaviours in relationships are modelled and assimilated. Many models for doing group work are based on a stage theory that, in describing group process, identifies seemingly discrete developmental phases that occur in groups. The Mediating Model (Schwartz, 1971) includes four stages: tuning-in, contracting, work/transition and termination. The Toronto Model (Currie, 1983) and the Windsor Model (Buckley, Miller and Rolfe, 1983) have beginning, middle and end stages. The classic five-stage Boston Model (Garland, Jones and Kolodny, 1978) lists pre-affiliation, power and control, intimacy, differentiation and separation as epigenetic stages in the life of a group. While the Boston Model format is widely recognised in describing group dynamics, the structuralist nature implicit in such a distinct Eriksonian (1963) categorisation of a growth process has been reappraised by other theorists.

Schiller (1995), for example, would modify its application to working with groups of women. Schiller argues that strengthening relationships, inclusion, and interpersonal empathy are critical aspects of group work with women, and she proposes that alternative descriptions of group stages include these aspects of interactive experience. Shapiro (1990) extended the original 'frames of reference' component of the Boston Model to incorporate contemporary social, political and cultural processes that occur in a post-structuralist context. He points out that:

> Different group-types may imply different processes of development according to what is considered the appropriate degree of permeability of group and interpersonal boundaries, and of time and space boundaries, and the appropriate distribution of member/member and member/worker status and power. (p14)

That different group-types exist suggests that a variety of stage theories may need to be formulated to describe them. We propose that further exploration of stage theory might also target open group models. Many social work theorists of the past appear to have used the term 'group work' in a generic sense, implying that group work has typically been defined by closed membership and time-limited formats. Shapiro (1990) describes contemporary 'unstructured groups' as '. . . a group development type used in an attempt to counteract what is perceived as a process engendered by the social structure prevailing in Western society.' (p15) In particular, Eddy and Myers (1984) found that most groups for men who abuse women (male perpetrators) last approximately 10 to 30 weeks and are structured along meeting cognitive-behavioural and psychoeducational objectives (See Pence, 1983, for example). Tolman and Bennett's review (1990) reveals similar findings. However, Edleson and Syer's report (1990) lists a 'self-help' category for violence treatment groups, modeled roughly on Alcoholics Anonymous peer support concepts, that suggests a precedent for open model treatment groups for male offenders. The advantages of long-term and open membership groups for male perpetrators are listed in Edleson and Tolman (1992) as well.

This paper describes a stage theory for our open model treatment group for men who abuse women, and this theory is based on a number of considerations that merit discussion:

1. The open model treatment group, where men enter and exit at their own pace, may not be adequately described by a stage theory built on the concept of a whole group moving simultaneously through discrete stages.
2. Men who are violent, in particular, need to address the issues of relationship building, and their stage work may be more appropriately conceived of in terms of 'relational process' rather than in terms of 'power and control.'
3. Yalom (1985) describes groups as microcosms representing the macrocosm of the real world; open model group work experience may better reflect the real world if conceived of as an individually paced process with permeable stage boundaries through which group members achieve mutuality.

In rendering this account of our experience with male offenders in open-ended group therapy we hope to describe what we see are possible advantages to our model. However, we cannot substantiate our claims based on outcome indicators other than with what we have observed ourselves in relation to clients in group, conversations with their partners and with statements made by clients returning to the group as guest speakers. This is not unlike the experience in British group work with male offenders described by Bensted, Brown, Forbes and Wall (1994). Orlinsky, Grawe and Parks (1994) state the following:

> The quality of the patient's participation in therapy stands out as the most important determinant of outcome. The therapeutic bond, especially as perceived by the patient, is importantly involved in mediating the process-outcome link. The therapist's contribution toward helping the patient achieve a favorable outcome is made mainly through empathic, affirmative, collaborative, and self-congruent engagement with the patient ... (p361).

Finally, we wish to point out that our narrative shows a more positive reflection of our experience treating male offenders. It is important to acknowledge that a number of men do drop out of the group, stay in the group and make little progress or show their ambivalence about treatment. In our experience these clients appear to represent a minority. We feel that our treatment method faces a certain set of challenges as do other approaches, yet the principal focus of this writing is to demonstrate a stage model wherein the interrelatedness of all group participants is optimal. A more in-depth examination of the issues of conflict resolution, interpersonal skill building, client and therapist resistance, etc., are the context of a different paper (see Thomas and Caplan, 1997). We feel that the primary limitation of our approach is based on the relative experience, or inexperience, of the group worker.

McGill Domestic Violence Clinic

The proposed open model stage theory has been developed over the past five years in the McGill Domestic Violence Clinic's (MDVC) treatment group for male perpetrators. This group can be described in Lang's (1979) terms as the following:

1. 'Loose-knit:' Men enter immediately (as space allows) and

take responsibility for terminating their participation in the group.

2. 'Permanent:' The group operates year-round as opposed to being 'time-limited.'
3. 'Leader-dependent' as opposed to 'autonomous:' While the group strives to be self-directed, it relies on the presence of a professional facilitator to provide continuity. The worker promotes group process to the point that treatment has the quality of self-help (Kurland and Salmon, 1992).
4. 'Person-centred' as opposed to 'high conformity:' Emphasis is placed on self-paced treatment goal achievement by the client.

The MDVC treatment group is facilitated by a man and woman co-therapy team, and the average membership for the weekly two-hour sessions is ten clients. Based in Montreal, the MDVC group is distinguished by its racial, cultural and socioeconomic diversity.

Domestic violence in Canada appears proportionately equivalent to Great Britain and the United States in terms of the magnitude of its scope and the shortcomings of its corrective measures (Bensted et al., 1994; Dwyer, 1995; and Thomas, 1995). The Canadian criminal justice system defines domestic violence, that is, the physical assault of one intimate partner against another, as a felony. This law was enforced in all Canadian provinces by 1986. However, the provincial courts administer justice differently. For example, British Columbia invokes court-mandated treatment for men who batter (Dutton, 1995); Quebec prohibits it. Throughout Canada treatment for men who abuse women is often (but not always) a condition of peace-bond, probation or parole agreements (Thomas, 1995). Many clients arrive for treatment by 'self-mandate,' i.e., their partners have left them or threaten to leave. The clinic recommends that each participant attend a minimum of 15 consecutive weekly sessions, and members tend to stay longer to continue the process. Some members return to the group after leaving; they come back for a few maintenance sessions or longer if there has been a relapse (Jennings, 1990). The clinic maintains an 'open door' policy.

Finally, the MDVC utilises an eclectic approach to treatment that builds on the emergent theme(s) of any given meeting to develop cognitive-behavioral, psychoeducational or peer relations work within the session. Collaboration on problems

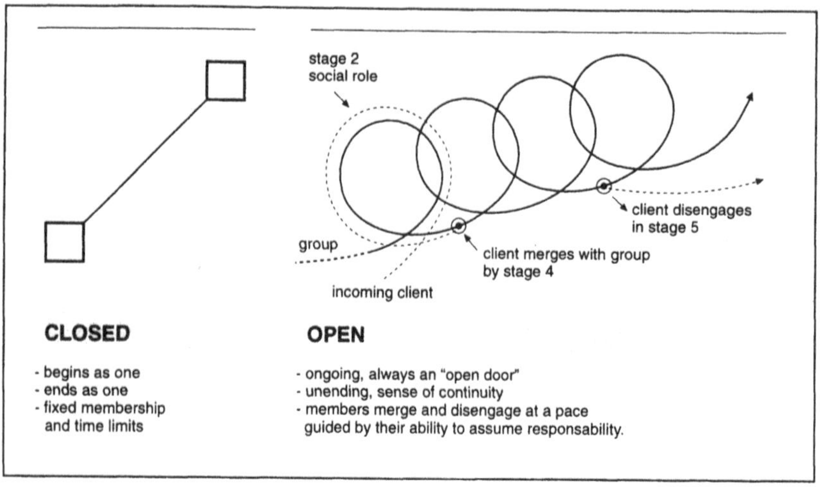

Figure 1. Closed Group compared graphically to Open Group

and solutions is the hallmark of this self-directed group process (Mullender and Ward, 1991) within which clients are continuously invited to take responsibility for their treatment (Jenkins, 1990). Yet, the co-facilitators consistently monitor levels of safety and comfort within the group as well as facilitate discussion (when necessary) to maintain the members' focus on treatment goals (Caplan and Thomas, 1995).

The MDVC Open Group Stage Model

Our primary assumption about this open group model, based on our experience, is that there is no beginning, middle or end to the process of this group as a whole entity. While the group is in a continuous state of flux as new members enter and older members leave, the overall operation of the group appears homeostatic. Clearly, there is development in the group as a whole with change occurring horizontally across time (social and ideological development); however, vertical growth in the group as a whole (beginning, middle and end) is less apparent. Based on this assumption, this paper proposes that there are two parallel stage processes evolving simultaneously, one from the point of view of the group as a whole and the other from the point of view of each individual client. (See Figure 1). For heuristic purposes each of these points of view will be discussed separately with the understanding that the actual experience of the open group model is dynamically interactive between these two areas.

The Group Stage

Assuming that the MDVC group as a whole is in an ongoing state of coalescence, the group continues at what Schwartz (1971) and Shulman (1992) described as the 'working' stage, a stage in which safety (Caplan and Thomas, 1995) appears to be generally extant. Safety would be found in demonstrations of empathy, inclusion, validation, communication and the encouragement to risk new and different behaviours. The group stage is also described by a variety of collaborative efforts among group members. The authors want to clarify the understanding of empathy and collaboration within the context of treating offenders so that in no way will such terms be misinterpreted as collusive. Empathic interventions seek to promote emotional safety for offenders that will engender appropriate behaviour towards women. The meaning of collaboration in this context centres on ownership of the responsibility for abuse of women and the ongoing efforts to authentically address that problem. Other forms of empathic or collaborative interjections such as playing the role of victim, self-pity or woman-bashing are challenged directly by the mentors and group facilitators.

The strongest component in this facet of the group process is peer modelling or mentoring. Because the MDVC group convenes year-round, there has never been a time when there was not at least two or three mentors in the group. Almeida and Bograd (1990) have written of the advantages of sponsorship between male perpetrators, that is, having seasoned clients with well-adjusted attitudes and behaviours become mentors for clients who are at the beginning stages of therapy. This concept of linking newcomer to mentor is operationalised in the MDVC model by the continued emergence of such mentors within the group setting. Further, the MDVC model nurtures the important positive effect that such a dynamic has on maintaining the continuity of this ongoing stage of intimacy and working. Mentoring is a significant part of group therapy; and such activity leads to the development of hierarchy in the group. However, we wish to be clear that such hierarchy is achieved by merit which our clinic defines as relational work through authentic concern for achieving treatment goals and not by power and control which our clinic defines as veiled threats, pedantic postures and scapegoating.

A new member introduced to a closed group already in progress might be perceived as an invasive element; group cohesion recently developed may be threatened by such a dynamic. The experience within the MDVC ongoing group appears to be different. In a group which has been made to feel safe through mentoring, the newcomer might have a better chance of being looked upon as a colleague. In effect, group 'safety' is not at issue, but rather it is group 'comfort' which is challenged (see Caplan and Thomas, 1995). While there might be a brief uncomfortable sizing-up period, the positive peer relationships incumbent in groups with long-term clients tend to carry the group over this awkward phase since the older members have bonded through shared growth experiences.

The Incoming Client Stages

1. The 'Safety' Stage

The incoming client stages of our model begin with the introduction of one or more new members to the already existing group. In this first stage such a client's experience is similar to what has been described by Garland, et al., (1978) as the 'pre-affiliation' stage. Here, individual clients present with a sense of concern as to whether they are going to be able to trust the group process enough to engage in the treatment. This concern can generate increased feelings of fear, anger and ambivalence for male perpetrators. While these offenders dominate their relationships through acts of violence, coercion and isolation toward their partners, such men often perceive themselves as emotionally frustrated in relationships and punished by others in authority (Edleson and Tolman, 1992). The majority of new clients enter the offender treatment group in some state of recent crisis.

The MDVC Model appears to lessen the 'we/they' power differential between client and therapist; senior members in the group bridge the gap between preconceived dichotomies of control by modelling acceptance of the treatment process.

Further, the notion that there can be hope for change is concretely represented in those seasoned members who greet new members with sincerity and empathy. In our experience the frequency and depth of the disclosure of emotional vulnerability is directly proportional to the degree of safety promoted in the group (Orlinsky, et al., 1994). Typically, an older and more established group member will challenge a new member in a supportive manner about his preconceptions regarding group treatment.

> **Example:** John (to new member): 'You remind me of when I first came here. I was really 'pissed off.' Now I know I was just afraid that I would be hammered out for doing what I did to my wife.'

The newcomer often responds with reduced defensiveness which suggests that he is beginning to develop a sense of safety in the group. The group process also profits; such an empathic interaction models the style of relational work that is significant to the therapy.

2. The 'Social' Stage

The second stage of the MDVC Model proposes that the client does not necessarily jockey for power and control as in the Boston Model but rather follows a dynamic which has more in common with Schiller's (1995) 'establishing a relational base.' Not unlike Schiller's theory, the MDVC Model perceives that new members are struggling to find a place of safety in the group through relating to others. Because men who are violent bring with them feelings of disenfranchisement, relational incompetence and emotional dysfunction, we believe that there is greater therapeutic effectiveness in promoting concepts of relational inclusion than there is in perpetuating notions of individualised men in power struggles. One conclusion drawn from the research of Orlinsky et al. (1994) is that the variation of treatment approaches is a less significant outcome indicator of success in treatment than the strength of the relationship built between the therapist and the client.

The assumption that group members struggle for power and control suggests that group process would be evaluated by practitioners within parameters of stereotypical descriptions of masculine behaviour, which Erikson (1963) described as 'autonomy' and 'mastery.' We do not deny that power and control as a masculine construct exists and is both culturally determined and widespread. We are mindful of feminist theory building regarding the use of power in male inter-relationships (Thorne-Finch, 1992). Assumptions include the ideas that men as a group are programmed to be superordinant, analytical and to abjure emotional disclosure. Men are often seen to relate to one another as competitors vying for 'top dog' status in a rigidly limited hierarchical environment. Male offenders are often described as such, and traditional group work with these perpetrators (see Pence, 1983) tends promote the direct confrontation of members who 'act out' using these behaviours.

However, social construction theory posits that experience becomes shaped by the way in which it is defined and not the other way around (Berger and Luckmann, 1966). One could argue, therefore, that it is all the more important for violence treatment theorists to conceive of group process in terms of Surrey's (1991) 'self-in-relation,' which counterpoints the premise that 'autonomy' and 'mastery' are the *desired* outcomes of development. Sternbach (1990) supports the assumption that men in a group are more than capable of relating through disclosure and emotional process, particularly when group structure develops the opportunity for men to do so. The MDVC examines the power and control issues offenders bring into the group as misguided attempts at behaviourally appropriate relationship-building. Interventions are designed to support the perpetrators' initial interpersonal risk-taking rather than threatening to reinforce the offenders' negative world-view that punishment is a significant part of any intimate relationship.

Jenkins (1990) explains that being powerless means having the inability to act responsibly, and this is how the clinic defines 'powerless.' In our experience, men who carry this sense of powerlessness compensate for the insecurity by use of power and control backed by acts and threats of violence. Paradoxically, the MDVC approach supports the idea that male offenders with issues of power and control benefit therapeutically from verbalising their feelings of powerlessness. Equally paradoxical is the experience that men who are capable of such self-disclosure, that is, to admit their inability to act responsibly, are validated by the group for their contribution to the collaborative effort. Self-esteem, which to the client could be linked to his sense of status in the group, is better generated by such achievement in relationship-building and, as such, is an essential component of treatment for men who batter.

This second stage can be seen as a crossroads for incoming members. The newcomers limited and dysfunctional sense of self is met by collaborative and empathic rejoinders from the group. In Schwartz's (1971) 'contracting' stage these struggles to belong often centre around questions of identity. Protection of self is maintained while figuring out how to relate to others in the group, and to this purpose new clients usually assume a social role. The social role serves as an initial bridge between the individual and the group as a society (Biddle, 1986; Shapiro, 1990); and most group members assume what they consider to be socially acceptable manners in an effort to connect with others in the group.

While it is undeniable that the more insecure newcomers in the offender treatment group may assume control-seeking roles (distancer/victim) in an effort to find safety, most others will take on more relationship-oriented roles (information/opinion seeking). Often men will assume an 'ideal' role in which they parrot the treatment jargon in order to gain initial acceptance as an exemplary client. These transitional roles are important in allowing clients to move towards the collaborative process at their own pace. Again, maintaining mentors in this open group model has a significant influence on the manner in which newcomers become aware of the safety enhancing function of initially maintaining these social roles. Mentors seldom confront newcomers in a punishing way for using these social roles, instead they reflect on their own struggles as newcomers to find safety and inclusion in the group.

> **Example:** Fred presents as an affable victim. He is often heard to comment: 'You think you've had it rough. I was sent to prison for 12 years while the other guy got off scot-free. I don't know an easy way of doing anything.' George assumes the role of group reporter. He is constantly seeking information from others as if he was going to write an article. He questions, 'Do you think it's possible for a man to truly be non-violent once he has crossed that line?' Jacques assumes the role of co-therapist by saying, 'What do you think is the thing that she does that most often pushes your buttons?'

One assumption about these roles is that while they may

not appear to be significantly introspective, they serve the important and often overlooked function of initiating a relational base. This is a starting point from which men can begin their collaborative work in treatment.

3. The 'Inclusion' Stage

The transitional dynamic of the MDVC Model's third stage describes the point at which a new client has developed enough trust in the process to consider modifying his role. The client becomes less defended in order to test the waters of emotional vulnerability. Having observed the style of mentors working on their own issues in the group, such a client tends to become curious about what that experience would feel like and begins to risk some new behaviours himself. In effect, the client at this stage begins to enter the heart of the group process, where previously he had felt safer in a social role on the group's margin. Sensing this evolution, the senior members of the group tend to meet such a client halfway; they use empathy and validation to encourage the client to shift from the 'ideal' (social role) to the 'real' (able to self-disclose). In effect, the group reaches out and encourages the new member to grab hold, on the assumption that as soon as the new client allows himself to be moved forward through disclosure to even the slightest degree, he is already beginning the process of assuming a new role in the group.

> **Example:** (Ideal/social role) 'I'm having a great week. I know now that I'm never going to be violent again. Now whenever my wife and I have an argument, we sit down and talk it out. I'm really glad I came here.' Or, 'It's important to set limits with yourself. Hitting a woman is wrong. You can't blame her for being angry with you.' Such statements transform into (real/able to self-disclose), 'It was a good week. This is one of the few weeks that I felt I really wanted to come in. I am constantly worried that I might relapse. I hope it isn't always going to be this much work.' Or, 'I had a situation come up this week, and I'm not sure if I handled it as well as I could have. I wonder if I could get some feedback from the group?'

As this inclusion process occurs, the group generates an atmosphere of renewed commitment and strengthened cohesion. The included client gains appreciation as one who is prepared to face the authentic issues of his violence and work towards accomplishing appropriate therapeutic goals. The senior client gains a sense of validation that the process works and is working through him.

4. The 'Collaboration' Stage (Equivalent to the 'Group' Stage)

The empathy already extant in an ongoing group will help the newcomer to feel safe enough to begin this fourth stage. Feeling in the same boat, similar to Schiller's 'common experiences' (1995), is a safety building concept. It is the beginning of a new awareness of self and others, and, not unlike the Boston Model's differentiation stage, this phase can be both exciting and terrifying. The terror of self-examination is alleviated by the continuing support from the group through mentoring and therapeutic maintenance of safety. The excitement is generated in incoming clients by the increasing awareness that change may have occurred within them already and that collaboration is producing positive results. Through working together such men become aware that in order to succeed in long-term non violence, not only must they accomplish the behavioral changes that maintain safety in relationships, they must also change their negative view of the world they live in (Goldberg Wood and Middleman, 1992).

Because the work of emotional responsibility includes elements of fear, grief, humility, etc., this stage can also be described in terms of discomfort/comfort. The client, having achieved a sense of safety in the initial stages of the group process, now begins to examine his world view in greater depth (Caplan and Thomas, 1995). Mentoring helps to monitor the level of such discomfort through empathy and affirmation so that clients do not become overwhelmed by the work. We believe that the collaborative process of establishing trust and authentically addressing issues of discomfort are conducive to producing long-term change.

Change that occurs at this point can also be linked to Jenkins' (1990) premise that progress in domestic violence treatment is demonstrated by the clients' acknowledgment that they are responsible and accountable for their behaviour. In the initial group stages the new client often shows that the owning of responsibility for actions, feelings and insecurities, is a 'dangerous' emotional task. A new client might rail against the injustice of the courts, the power of the 'feminist conspiracy' and other projections of his negative world view as an out-of-control, unimportant and disrespected individual with little meaning in society. However, by the time the client has arrived at the stage of collaborative action, the process of bonding around appropriate problem-solving strategies helps him to understand that the responsibility for violence and the prevention of violence is an internal process based on choice. Men no longer deflect constructive criticism (discomfort) away from themselves in order to feel safe. They begin to realize that authentically addressing one's issues of insecurity in the world becomes something which provides growth for the individual, comfort for others and intimacy for the group.

Collaboration is essential for the process of internalisation of responsibility. For many violent men, interaction in the treatment group is their first experience of a safe relationship. Many men who are violent have never had success at an intimate relationship and their fear of intimacy prompts them to defend themselves. Working successfully with others at self-disclosing and emotional vulnerability provides hope that safety is possible in intimate relationships. Further, collaboration lightens the load and normalises the discomfort of having to be emotionally vulnerable in relationships. Mentors play significant roles in clarifying the boundaries of responsibility between equal partners. In twelve-step groups mentoring occurs outside of the group experience and usually on an individual basis. The MDVC model encourages such sponsorship within a collaborative group work experience. In effect, this group process invites men to take responsibility by examining the restraints that have kept them from being responsible in the past (Jenkins, 1990), and such action is as critical to long-term success of the treatment plan as each client's ownership of the problem.

> **Example:** Alan heard a mentor, Marcus, successfully self-disclose. Something that another group member mentioned reminded Marcus of the difficulty he had had in backing away from an argument with his wife, expressing his 'need to be right.' Alan then stated, 'I have trouble backing away, too. I don't think it's that I always want to be right . . . it's more like I need to feel important. Yeah, that's it . . . I'm worried she thinks I'm stupid. I have trouble believing that my opinions are worth the breath.'

5. The 'Continuity' Stage

Leaving a relationship is always a difficult period of transition.

B. L. Stempler (personal communication, AASWG Symposium, October, 1995) has suggested that problems in relationships are primarily located in dysfunctional beginnings and endings. Group members' apprehensions about separation might be exacerbated by a perception that they are being abandoned by the treatment. Predetermined closure might be considered arbitrary and artificial, and this might even create a problematic notion that graduation from treatment has occurred. Our model's approach to a member's separation from the group assumes that each client's self-paced preparedness for leaving counters the perception that our clinic sets time-limited expectations for progress in therapy.

In previous stages the client has used group feedback to test his perceptions of reality. He has desensitised himself to triggers that would have previously shut him down, and he has learned to accept constructive criticism and to negotiate. In effect, the client has attained a higher degree of emotional responsibility in his relationship with the group. Accomplishing these tasks builds the confidence a client needs to address issues of separation; further, the client feels secure in the knowledge that the group continues and is always there should he need it. The open door policy of our group specifies that not only can clients return for maintenance sessions but mentors are encouraged to return to the group to share their treatment experience and the continuity of internalised treatment principles. This open door policy represents a built-in aftercare component that is particularly validating and is expressly representative of continuity in treatment.

Continuity is the natural progression from the preceding four stages in which modelling and mentoring have played a significant part. Many clients who are at this stage have witnessed other mentors before them prepare to leave the group and then do so. Such clients have also seen themselves transformed from a frightened and alienated newcomer to a mentor capable of self-disclosure and accountability. This client has experienced the feeling of accomplishment in helping other incoming clients to achieve a similar sense of responsibility as mentors in the group. In effect, a client at this stage often expresses his confidence that the best teachings of the group are incorporated within himself. He also feels better prepared to leave the group knowing that other mentors that he has helped to empower will continue to carry the torch.

Finally, the natural progression of this developmental

process is that clients use the review of their personal growth in treatment to launch them into advocacy in the world outside of the group. Our assumption is that the client's ownership of separation from the group safeguards the process of internalising treatment goals. We refer to this part of the process as 'the Zen of the group.' Specifically, the client approaches intimate relationships with the same emotional openness and reciprocity that he has discovered works in the group. In general, the client advocates in society by modelling new attitudes, new perspectives on masculinity and increased tolerance for difference in society. It is true that there is some regret when an old friend leaves. However, because the newer mentors are focused on their role, they will now look forward to being considered experts in problem-solving strategies. Having members replace those terminating treatment maintains the group in a secure position to continue the work at hand. Termination of treatment can, therefore, also be a celebration of success as well as an added encouragement for those still in earlier stages of development. For this reason the continuity stage could just as well be called the 'hope' or 'legacy' stage.

> **Example:** George (in saying goodbye to the group): 'I'd like to come back and check in from time to time. I really feel much better about myself.' Doug responds sarcastically with a smile: 'Yeah, we're really going to miss your punishing remarks.' George laughs and says: 'I assume you've learned to punish yourself?' Doug, in a more serious tone of voice, replies: 'Not really, I've actually learned how to be more self-critical . . . to understand what's going on inside. Thanks George!' George, with some degree of emotion, responds: 'I'm glad there are guys like you still here to help. I know you'll do even better than me.'

Conclusion

All forms of treatment for male perpetrators are important. Saunders (1996) recommends that different group models be developed to fit the needs of different typologies of male perpetrators, from compliant clients to those who are quite recalcitrant. In fact, some offenders that enter treatment at our clinic are so highly defended that they never move beyond stages one or two. However, based on our collective but subjective assessment of changes that group members make throughout the course of treatment and in follow-up, we submit that we have witnessed far more client progress than failure. Feedback from the partners of the male perpetrators under treatment is an important component in assessing outcome. The anecdotal evidence that we have gathered from the clients' partners through telephone conversations appears to corroborate that progress in treating these offenders with our approach has achieved results. The authors wish to be clear that when rendering an account of the interactional experiences in the MDVC treatment group, such an account in no way suggests that one model is 'better than' any other model. There would be little data to substantiate such a claim in any case.

Freeman, Lambert and Nosko (1994) show that the research on treatment group models for men who batter appears underdeveloped. For example, Edleson and Syers (1990) found that facilitated self-help groups for male perpetrators in their study did not compare favourably with more leader-directed, educationally-oriented groups in terms of measured outcomes. However, the self-help groups in the above study were led primarily by untrained, non professional former male perpetrators, which is quite different to the facilitation available in the MDVC model. Also, as Bidgood, Tutty and Rothery (1991) discovered, sample attrition in woman abuse treatment group research is such a significant factor that results cannot readily be generalised. Further, Follingstad (1990) points out that more matched samples with comparable therapeutic interventions and instruments of research measurement are needed to produce clearer outcome research data than are provided by the studies currently available. Finally, one must keep in mind Jennings' (1990) words of caution in drawing conclusions about the effectiveness of offender treatment based on current research outcomes. Jennings suggests that rigid treatment expectations for high conformity and immediate change might in and of themselves be self-defeating.

The purpose of this paper has been to describe an approach which appears to have some advantages in treating men who batter. These advantages include emphasis on all those involved taking responsibility for the treatment process by modelling appropriate problem-solving strategies as well as providing mentoring for newcomers. The group experience has been conceptualised in a stage theory that identifies two distinct but dynamically interactive processes. While the group as a whole continues in an on-going state of collaborative work, the individual client's experience in the group can be described as a five-stage evolution by which the client assimilates the values and work ethic inherent in the treatment. The paper has also highlighted distinctions between this stage theory and others. Building a relational base counterpoints a focus on power and control in describing clients' struggles to feel safe in the group process. Collaborative merit-based hierarchies are preferred over high conformity, leader-directed agendas. And, continuity rather than termination is developed in addressing issues of separation from the group.

The comprehensive research by Orlinsky et al. (1994) indicates that the most compelling predictor of therapeutic outcome is the way in which the client experiences treatment. We hope that this model will encourage theorists and researchers to examine more closely the comparative efficacy of the various treatment models using instruments of measure that best capture the reality of a continuing therapeutic group experience.

References

Almeida, R.V. and Bograd, M. (1990) 'Sponsorship: Holding men accountable for domestic violence', *Journal of Feminist Family Therapy*, 2, 3/4, pp243-259

Bensted, J., Brown, A., Forbes, C. and Wall, R. (1994) 'Men working with men in groups: Masculinity and crime', *Groupwork,* 7, 1, pp37-49

Berger, P. and Luckmann, T. (1966) *The Social Construction of Reality.* Garden City, NY: Anchor Books

Biddle, B.J. (1986) 'Recent developments in role theory'. in R.H. Turner and S.F. Short Jr. (eds.) *Annual Review of Sociology*, 12, pp67-92

Bigood, B., Tutty, L.M. and Rothery, M. (1991) *An Evaluation of the Co-ordinated Family Violence Treatment Programs in the Waterloo Area.* Waterloo, ON: Centre for Social Welfare Studies, Faculty of Social Work, Wilfrid Laurier University

Buckley, L.B., Miller, D. and Rolfe, T.A. (1983) 'A Windsor model', *Social Work with Groups*, 6, 3/4, pp189-195

Caplan, T. and Thomas, H. (1995) 'Safety and comfort, content and process: Facilitating open group work with men who batter', *Social*

Work with Groups, 18, 2/3, pp33-51

Currie, D.W. (Fall-Winter, 1983) 'A Toronto model', *Social Work with Groups*, 6, 3/4, pp179-188

Dutton, D. (1995) *The Batterer: A psychological profile.* New York: Basic Books

Dwyer, D. (1995) 'Response to the victims of domestic violence: Analysis and implications of the British experience', *Crime and Delinquency.* 41, 4, pp527-540

Eddy, M. and Myers, T. (1984) *Helping Men Who Batter: A profile of programs in the U.S.* Austin, TX: Texas Department of Human Resources

Edleson, J.L. and Syers, M. (1990) 'Relative effectiveness of group treatments for men who batter', *Social Work Research and Abstracts,* 26, pp10-17

Edleson, J.L. and Tolman, R.M. (1992) *Intervention for Men Who Batter: An ecological approach.* Newbury Park, CA: Sage Publications, Inc

Erikson, E.H. (1963) *Childhood and Society.* (2nd ed) New York: Norton

Follingstad, D. (1990) 'Methodological issues and new directions for research on violence in relationships'. In D. Besherov (ed) *Family violence: Research and public policy issues.* Washington, DC: AEI Press

Freeman, R., Lambert, K. and Nosko, A. (December, 1994) *Working towards Eliminating Male Violence against Women: A group intervention for abusive men: Pilot project outcome report.* Toronto, ON: Family Service Association of Metro Toronto

Garland, J., Jones, H. and Kolodny, R. (1978) 'A model for stages of development in social work groups'. In S. Bernstein (ed.) *Explorations in group work.* Boston, MA: Charles River Books, pp17-71

Garvin, C. (1974) 'Group process: Usage and uses in social work practice'. In P. Glasser, R. Sarri, R. Vinter (Eds.) *Individual Change through Small Groups.* NY: Free Press

Goldberg Wood, G. and Middleman, R. (1992) 'Recasting the die: A small group approach to giving batterers a chance to change', *Social Work with Groups,* 15, 1, pp5-18

Jenkins, A. (1990) *Invitations to Responsibility.* Adelaide, South Australia: Dulwitch Centre Publications

Jennings, J.L. (1990) 'Preventing relapse versus stopping domestic violence: Do we expect too much too soon from battering men?', *Journal of Family Violence,* 3, 1, pp43-60

Kurland, R. and Salmon, R. (1992) 'Group work vs. casework in a group: Principles and implications for teaching and practice', *Social Work with Groups*, 15, 4, 3-14

Lang, N. (1979) 'Some defining characteristics of the social work group: Unique social form', *Proceedings of the First Annual Symposium on*

Social Work with Groups. Binghamton, NY: Haworth Press

Mullender, A. and Ward, D. (1991) *Self-Directed Groupwork: Users take action for empowerment.* London: Whiting and Birch

Orlinsky, D., Grawe, K. and Parks, B. (1994) 'Process and outcome in psychotherapy: Noch einmal', in A. Bergin and S. Garfield (eds) *The Handbook of Psychotherapy and Behavior Change.* (4th ed) Toronto: John Wiley and Sons

Pence, E. (1983) 'The Duluth domestic abuse intervention project', *Hamline Law Review,* 6, pp247-275

Saunders, D.G. (1996) 'Interventions for men who batter: Do we know what works?', *Session: Psychotherapy in Practice,* 2, 3, pp81-93

Schiller, L.Y. (1995) 'Stages of development in women's groups: A relational model'. In R. Kurland and R. Salmon, (eds) *Group Work Practice in a Troubled Society: Problems and opportunities.* Binghampton, NY: Haworth Press

Schwartz, W. (1971) 'On the use of groups in social work practice'. In W. Schwartz and S. Zalba, (eds.) *The Practice of Group Work.* New York: Columbia University Press

Shapiro, B.Z. (1990) 'The social work group as social microcosm: "Frames of reference" revisited', *Social Work with Groups,* 13, 2, pp5-21

Shulman, L. (1992) *The Skills of Helping Individuals and Groups.* Itasca, IL: F.E. Peacock

Sternbach, J. (1990) 'The men's seminar: An educational and support group for men', *Social Work with Groups,* 13 , 2, 23-39

Surrey, J.L. (1991) 'The self-in-relation: A theory of women's development'. In J. Jordan, A. Kaplan, J. Baker-Miller, I. Stiver, and J.L. Surrey (Eds.) *Women's Growth in Connection: Writings from the Stone Center.* New York: Guilford Press

Thomas, H. (1995) *Montreal's Legal Response to Men's Violence against Women in Intimate Relationships: A comparative study of how domestic violence cases are treated by the criminal justice systems of Winnipeg, Manitoba, London, Ontario and Montreal, Quebec.* Master's Thesis, McGill University Library

Thomas, H. and Caplan, T. (1997) 'Client, therapist and context: Addressing resistance in group work', *The Social Worker,* 65, 3, pp27-44

Thorne-Finch, R. (1992) *Ending the Silence: The origins and treatment of male violence against women.* Toronto, Canada: University of Toronto Press

Tolman, R. and Bennett, L.W. (1990) 'A review of quantitative research on men who batter', *Journal of Interpersonal Violence,* 5, 1, pp87-118

Yalom, I. (1985) *The theory and practice of group psychotherapy.* (3rd ed) NY: Basic Books

Active Learning Programmes to Promote Cognitive Change

Siu-Kau Cheung[1]

This article discusses the application of active learning in designing programmes for cognitive change. Two different approaches are examined, including learning through critical reflective and learning through active practice. The former aims at restructuring members' pre-existing knowledge whereas the latter targets the strengthening of the reception and retention of new information. Specific design steps are explained with illustrative applications. Though cognitive change by itself is seldom sufficient to enhance clients' social functioning, the present suggestions will be valuable when imparting information or combating dysfunctional schemata .

Introduction

Helping clients acquire valid and realistic knowledge is one of the essential components in educational groups, such as sex education, drug prevention (e.g., Gropper et al., 1995), and family life education (e.g., Dennison, 1995; Weizmann, 1991). In support groups for family carers, helping group members understand the family members in need (e.g., the frail elderly) is also vital (e.g., McCallion & Toseland, 1995). Though knowledge per se is not sufficient, having correct information will certainly enhance members' ability to anticipate situations, develop realistic expectations and cope with the situations more effectively.

1 Principal Lecturer
Address for correspondence: Division of Social Studies, City University of Hong Kong, Tat Chee Avenue, Kowloon, Hong Kong.

Surprisingly, there have been few discussions in social work literature on the use of programme activities for cognitive learning. Major discussions examine programmes in terms of the effects of structural dimensions on participant behaviours (Gentry, 1984; Philips, 1989; Vinter, 1985). Others focus on the process dimension and examine how a worker could engage members in the planning and implementation of a program so as to actualise themselves, further their goals, and enhance their potential (Casey & Cantor, 1983; Glassman & Kates, 1990). Though relevant literature acknowledges the various functions of programmes, it is obvious that cognitive learning is underplayed (e.g., Heap, 1979; Whittaker, 1976). In addition, few give in-depth elaboration on how programmes could be designed to achieve those aims and functions.

Among those discussions that detail the principles and procedures of programme design, most of them fall in the domain of behavioural change or skill development. Social learning principles form the theoretical basis for most of these programmes (e.g., Glassman & Kates, 1993; LeCroy, 1987; Lynn & Nisivoccia, 1995; Wong et al. 1996). Apart from these, there are discussions on the use of structured experiences (Anderson, 1980; Kees & Jacobs, 1990) and growth games (Manor & Dumbleton, 1993). These are rooted in the human relations movement and many of the activities are based on the experiential learning model proposed by Kolb (1983). Though they bear some relations to cognitive change, the activities mainly facilitate members to get insight about themselves or the group dynamics rather than some propositional knowledge. To the author's knowledge, there is only one article on designing programmes for cognitive learning by Cherny and Inclan (1980) in the literature. It describes a procedure for teaching facts within a group work context. Unfortunately, it does not explicate the principles on which the suggested procedure is based.

In practice, we observe that many practitioners resort to didactic presentations when propositional knowledge is to be delivered. Despite its apparent time-efficiency, educational research has demonstrated that the learning outcomes are far from satisfactory (see Bonwell & Eison, 1991). In addition, having group members as passive receivers is at variance with the working principles that stress members' participation and active involvement in social group work. As an alternative, active learning is strongly advocated in the educational field in the last decade. The ideas and the principles have great potential for use in social group work. This article discusses the principles and introduces the two forms of active learning that may form the basis for activity design for knowledge acquisition in a group work context.

Active Learning

Active learning is an approach to promote participation and effective learning for a wide range of individuals, including children, adolescents and adults. The theoretical basis can be traced back to Piaget, who emphasised that a child must be 'engaged' in a task in order to achieve cognitive progress (see Smock, 1981). Experience is crucial, and learning occurs as cognitive schemata or structures change to accommodate to new experiential data. There are several features of active learning (Baldwin & Williams, 1988; Bonwell & Eison 1991). First of all, the learner is actively involved in the process. He or she is engaged in activities and in higher order cognitive processes, such as analysis, synthesis, and evaluation. The role of the worker is that of an enabler and facilitator of learning. It assumes that everyone in the group has a positive contribution to make, based on their experience, knowledge, and talents. The focus of learning is not only on imparting knowledge but also on developing learning skills and exploration of values and attitudes.

Despite these common features, two types of active learning can be distinguished: learning through critical reflection and learning through active practice. Distinctions are seldom made between the two types, but actually they are based on different assumptions about learning, serve different functions and follow different design procedures.

Active Learning through Critical Reflection

In most circumstances, group members are not totally ignorant of a topic but hold invalid or unviable premises or assumptions which hamper their functioning. The worker's task is to dispel the myths inherent in their prior knowledge and to help members develop alternative functional and realistic understanding.

In contrast to the didactic approaches, the worker adopting active learning strategy does not attempt to change group members by means of teaching or persuasion. Instead, members are engaged in a process whereby the underlying premises of ideas are assessed and critiqued. The essential component of programme activities include: the presentation of problem situations for members; members' application of prior knowledge to the problem; a dialogical process among the members; and the restructuring of prior knowledge based on the feedback one receives. Because of its less didactic tone, it is an especially good programme strategy for adult learners as they may feel respected in the process. As Knowles (1973) notes, adults tend to prefer self-direction in learning. Critical reflective activity design is highly versatile. It is in accord with the rationalist approaches, such as Beck's (1976) cognitive therapy. When a suitable style of facilitation is adopted, it can also be compatible with the approaches in the constructivist camp (e.g., Mezirow, 1991; Guidano and Lotti, 1983).

Specifically, critical reflective activities can be designed according to the following procedure. First, the worker starts with a needs assessment and helps member think through the reasons for their initially expressed needs (Mezirow, 1991). Members' motives for joining the group are examined in relation to how these lead to some ideal of their self-concept or enhanced functioning. When members see the values of the group and its programmes in pursuing their interests, their motivation to participate in the activities will be enhanced. Next, based on the learning needs of the members, a set of problems is devised. This can be, for example, in the form of true/false statements, multiple choice questions or case problems. In the group meeting, each member obtains the set of problems and works on it individually or in sub-teams. They approach the problems based on their prior knowledge of the topic. At this point, the worker only adopts a procedural role and refrains from giving advice on the 'answer' to the problems.

It is inevitable that members hold different opinions in their approaches to the problems, which to some extent reflect their underlying premises and assumptions. After the members have finished, the worker conducts a sharing of answers with the members. The exact way in which this may proceed would depend on the orientation of the worker. Workers following the rationalist position may raise questions such as 'what evidence supports that view?' 'How could you test that belief?' On the other hand, those taking a constructivist stance may ask the questions such as 'in what other ways could you view that?' 'What are the consequences for you when you think of it that way?' (Granvold, 1996). Through the sharing and discussion, members will become aware of alternative perspectives and receive feedback on their positions. Whatever the worker's orientation is, the discussion has to be conducted in an atmosphere of acceptance and criticism should be avoided. With worker's accentuation of the realistic or viable ideas, the members may reorganise their original ideas about the topic in question.

The application can be illustrated by its use in a support group for carers of the mentally ill. Practice experience reveals that family members frequently hold preconceived ideas about mental illness. Though some of these are valid, misconceptions or myths may also exist. The worker of the group intended to help members acquire correct understanding of mental illness so that they could provide appropriate care to the family members. In the group session, the worker devised a set of statements for members to determine whether their understanding about mental illness is correct or whether they have adopted beliefs or myths about it. Sample items included: 'We must try our best to protect the family member against any possible harm', 'stress is an important factor leading to the relapse of schizophrenia'. Members were asked to indicate their own responses to the questions, and after ten minutes, share their answers item by item with one another. Experience shows that inevitably there would be members holding different opinions about the items. Some members were able to note the problem of over-protection. Some could rightly point out the hazards of stress on a mentally ill person. However, often there were members who misconceived the appropriate caring attitudes. The worker would play a facilitating role, helping members identify dysfunctional ideas, drawing attention to counter-examples, encouraging alternative views to the issue and reinforcing those viable notions. The exercise enabled the worker to utilise the resources of the group and promoted an atmosphere of cooperative learning among the members.

The approach also formed the basis for an activity design in a drug prevention group for adolescents. Adolescents often hold misconceptions about the properties of drugs and the consequences of using drugs. In a session, the worker played a game with the members to combat these misconceptions. Unlike the previous one, movement opportunities and reward were added so as to arouse the members' interest. Before the meeting, the worker prepared a number of questions. For example, one question related to the effects of having soft drugs. Three pictures were presented to the members, depicting different possible sequels of abuse. One described a positive sequel in which the protagonist became very energetic and work-efficient. Another presented that the protagonist grew beautiful and was admired by friends. The third one depicted a gloomy sequel in which the protagonist became weak and pallid. Members indicated their choices by running to three different locations in the room. They were asked to explain their choices. In the process, members' myths regarding drugs were brought to the surface. The worker fostered mutual challenge among the members and in due course brought out the facts related to that topic. Those who got the right answer would get a chip for scoring purpose. Members won by gaining most chips after the several rounds.

Learning through Active Practice

Another kind of active learning, active practice, is frequently adopted in educational practice. It is based on the psychological dictum that rehearsal is the key to increase later recall of an event (see Klein, 1996). Active practice refers to those application exercises where one applies knowledge to problem situations in order to enhance storage of the cognitive elements in long term memory.

Active practice differs from critical reflective learning in that prior knowledge plays a minimal role in learning. The task of the learner is to acquire and retain new knowledge rather than to reorganise existing cognitions. By means of didactic presentations accompanied with audiovisual aids, members are introduced to the subject knowledge beforehand. However, the process does not stop there. Group activities are arranged to help members elaborate and rehearse the cognitive contents in order to strengthen retention. This approach is particularly useful when the group members have little grounding in the subject matter.

Specifically, active practice programmes can be designed as follows: Firstly, the worker must decide on the learning needs of the members, that is, the knowledge that can enhance their social functioning. Then, based on the learning needs, specific learning contents are circumscribed. In the group session, the content is presented to the members by means of a mini-lecture, accompanied with audiovisual aids. Members are then asked to do some activities, such as listing examples, distinguishing examples and non-examples, or applying the concepts in case situations (Yelon, 1996). This may take the form of a quiz, a game, or a discussion. After the activity, members will receive feedback on their answers. At the concluding stage, the main points are summarised. The steps are akin to those adopted in educational settings, but in group work, we emphasise fun, growth and cooperation.

Its application can be illustrated in three group sessions in health education, one for children, one for adolescents, and another for adults. In the children's group, children were informed that they would view a video presentation, followed by a learning game. A twelve-minute video introducing nutritious food was then presented. The children were excited about the challenge of the game and were very attentive during the presentation. After the viewing, a 'fishing' game was introduced. Members were split into two teams and each member held a 'fishing' rod with a magnet at the end of the string instead of a hook. Pieces of paper with names of nutritious and non-nutritious food were used as the 'fish'. A metallic clip was attached to each of the slips. One team was asked to catch the nutritious food whereas the other one, the non-nutritious food. The group which caught more assigned items was deemed the winning team. Essentially, the game provided an opportunity for members to apply and rehearse what they learned from the video presentation. Because of the provision of movement and reward, children enjoyed participation in the game.

In the session for the adolescent group, the twelve-minute video was also presented. However, a different active practice experience was provided. It took the form of a card game, which better fit the style of adolescents. Names of food and nutrition values were written on a set of index cards. In each round, each member received a card turned upside down. On the instruction of the worker, they turned the cards over simultaneously. When a member noticed that his or her own card 'matched' with another member's card (e.g., 'fish' was written on own card whereas 'vitamin A' appeared on another member's card), the member should rush to state the other member's name. Rounds were repeated, and the one member who won in most rounds was given a prize. After the game, the worker asked members to recapitulate the nutritious values of daily food to enhance their retention.

In the group for parents, they were first asked to pick out the food their children normally took in a day before the videotape was presented. They were then asked to note specifically what nutrition these food items possessed when they viewed the video presentation. After the presentation, the parents were asked to pick from cards on which nutrition values were printed and match them with the food items their children consumed daily. Some parents were surprised that the food their children took had such a low nutritional value. Some became aware of the surfeit of fat in the food. The activity, in addition to enhancing their retention of knowledge of nutrition, helped them relate the knowledge to their daily lives. This kind of elaborative rehearsal, in contrast to the maintenance rehearsal in the previous two activities, is particularly effective in enhancing later recall (Craik & Lockhart, 1986).

Similarities and Differences

It can be noticed that both approaches share basic features of active learning as mentioned previously. Members are involved in the learning process and they are the major resources for mutual stimulation. In addition, with the game design, members obtain multisensory experiences which will enhance their memory of the subject. Thus, both are effective approaches which can be used in a group work context.

The two approaches differ in a number of ways. Firstly, they target different levels of cognitive change. Critical reflective activities aim at restructuring existing thoughts, which are at a higher, schematic level. On the other hand, active practice is about reception and retention of new information, which occupies a lower level in the hierarchy of cognition. Second, the sequences of learning events also differ. In critical reflective activities, problem situations are presented first and feedback follows; whereas in active practice, knowledge input precedes application to problems.

Workers must exercise caution in designing and

implementing both kinds of activities. A worker may inadvertently adopt a position of superiority when conducting the games, especially for those pertaining to active practice. This may lead to the imposition of worker's ideas, which can be problematic, unethical and inimical. From a constructivist point of view, reality is invented, constructed largely out of meanings and values of the observers (Allen, 1993). Social workers should always possess such awareness and exercise humility. However, I do believe that there are propositions in health and cognitive sciences that adequately describe the patterns and processes in most if not all people. The critical issue is to ensure that the knowledge we introduce should offer real, practical solutions backed up by evidence that a good outcome is likely (Launer, 1996).

Conclusion

The paper explains two forms of active learning programmes which can be used in group work contexts. Both of them address cognitive learning, which are scarcely discussed in group work literature. Perhaps, practitioners may put a premium on behavioural change but this should in no way deny the importance of information and cognitive change. Though cognitive change by itself is not sufficient in most cases, it may be helpful for clients who lack the knowledge to progress in their pursuits and those whose functioning are hampered by dysfunctional beliefs. Well-designed programmes can arouse the interest of the members, engage them in useful learning processes, foster a cooperative learning atmosphere in groups, and enable members to achieve cognitive changes that in conjunction with other change efforts enhance their social functioning.

References

Allen, J.A. (1993) 'The constructivist paradigm: values and ethics' *Journal of Teaching in Social Work,* 8, 1/2, pp31-54

Anderson, J.D. (1980) 'Structured experiences in growth groups in social work' *Social Casework,* 61, pp277 -287

Baldwin, J. and Williams, H. (1988) *Active Learning: A Trainer's Guide*. Oxford: Basil Blackwell

Beck, A.T. (1976) *Cognitive Therapy and the Emotional Disorders*. New York: International Universities Press

Bonwell, C.C. and Eison, J.A. (1991) *Active Learning: Creating Excitement in the Classroom*. ASHE-ERIC Higher Education Report 1, Washington DC: The George Washington University, School of Education and Human Development

Casey, R.D. and Cantor, L. (1983) 'Group work with hard-to-reach adolescents: The use of member initiated program selection' in R. Middleman(ed) *Activities and Action in Groupwork*. New York: Haworth Press

Cherny, M.J. and Inclan, R. (1980) 'An effective method of teaching facts within a groupwork context' *Social Work with Groups*, 3, 1, pp17-21

Craik, F.I.M. and Lockhart, R.S. (1986) 'CHARM is not enough: Comments on Eich's model of cued recall' *Psychological Review*, 93, pp360-364

Dennison, S.T. (1995) 'The E.S.S.E. group model: A twenty-first century approach for families at risk' *Journal of Family Social Work*, 1, 2, pp57-71

Gentry, M.E. (1984) 'Developments in activity analysis: Recreation and group work revisited' *Social Work with Groups*, 7, pp35-44

Glassman, U. and Kates, L. (1990) *Group Work: A Humanistic Approach*. Newbury Park: Sage Publications

Glassman, U. and Kates, L. (1993) 'Feedback, role rehearsal, and programming enactments: cycles in the group's middle phase' in S. Wenocur et al. (eds) *Social Work with Groups: Expanding Horizons*. New York: Haworth Press

Granvold, D.K. (1996) 'Constructivist psychotherapy' *Families in Society*, 77, pp345-357

Gropper, M., Liraz, Z., Portowicz, D. and Schindler, M. (1995) 'Computer integrated drug prevention: A new approach to teach lower socioeconomic 5th and 6th grade Israeli children to say no to drugs' *Social Work in Health Care*, 22, 2, pp87-103

Guidano, V.F. and Lotti, G. (1983) *Cognitive Processes and Emotional Disorders: A Structural Approach to Psychotherapy*. New York: Guilford Press

Heap, K. (1979) *Process and Action in Work with Groups*. Oxford: Pergamon Press

Kees, N.L. and Jacobs, E. (1990) 'Conducting more effective groups: How to select and process group exercises' *Journal of Specialists in Group Work*, 15, pp21-29

Klein, S.B. (1996) *Learning: Principles and Applications* (3rd ed.) New York: McGraw-Hill

Knowles, M.S. (1973) *The Modern Practice of Adult Education: From Pedagogy to Andragogy (2nd* ed) New York: Cambridge Books

Kolb, D.A. (1983) *Experiential Learning: Experience as the Source of Learning and Development.* New York : Prentice-Hall

LeCroy, C.W. (1987) 'Teaching children social skills: A game format' *Social Work,* 32, pp440-441

Launer, J. (1996) '"You're the doctor, Doctor!": Is social constructionism a helpful stance in general practice consultations?' *Journal of Family Therapy,* 18, pp255-267

Lynn, M. and Nisivoccia, D. (1995) 'Activity-oriented group work with the mentally ill: Enhancing socialization' *Social Work with Groups,* 18, 2/3, pp95-106

Manor, O. and Dumbleton, M. (1993) 'Combining activities and growth games: A systems approach' *Groupwork,* 6, p248-265

McCallion, P. and Toseland, R.W. (1995) 'Supportive group interventions with caregivers of frail older adults' *Social Work with Groups,* 18, pp11-25

Mezirow, J.D. (1991) *Transformative Dimensions of Adult Learning.* San Francisco: Jossey-Bass

Philips, J. (1989) 'Targeted activities in group contexts: The analysis of activities to meet consumer need' *Groupwork,* 2, pp48-57

Smock, C.D. (1981) 'Constructivism and educational practices' in I.E. Sigel, D.M. Brodzinsky and R.M. Golinkoff (edS) *New Directions in Piagetian Theory and Practice.* Hillsdale, NJ: Lawrence Erlbaum Associates

Vinter, R.D. (1985) 'Programme activities: An analysis of their effects on participant behavior' in M. Sundel, P. Glasser, R. Sarri and R. Vinter (eds) *Individual Change Through Small Groups* (2nd ed) New York: Free Press

Weizmann, R. (1991) 'Facilitating adult life transitions through use of groups' in M. Weil, K. Chan and D. Southerland (eds) *Theory and Practice in Social Group Work: Creative Connections.* Binghamton, NY: Haworth Press

Whittaker, J. (1976) 'Differential use of program activities in child treatment groups' *Child Welfare,* 55, pp459-467

Wong, S.E., Morgan, C., Crowley, R. and Baker, J.N. (1996) 'Using a table game to teach social skills to adolescent psychiatric inpatients: Do the skills generalize?' *Child and Family Behavior Therapy,* 18, pp1-17

Yelon, S.L. (1996) *Powerful Principles of Instruction.* White Plains, NY: Longman.

Reviews

Women Survivors of Childhood Sexual Abuse
Judy Chew
Binghampton, NY, Haworth Press, 1998, 160pp
ISBN 0 7890 0110 1 (hbk) US$39.95
ISBN 0 7890 0284 1 (pbk) US$14.95

This book discusses the rationale and potential benefits of using group work with women survivors of childhood sexual abuse as a way of helping women on a journey of healing. The author is concerned with the journey beyond survival; moving on from the 'victim' position many women take on themselves or are labelled with. She summarises the conditions which promote the process of recovery and healing, and makes the point that therapy should access the strengths and resiliencies which have enabled women survivors to develop healthy living, as well as respecting their experiences of victimisation and suffering.

The book aims to fill a gap in the existing literature by providing a practical text in 'how to' conduct a group of this nature, one which bridges theory with practice. The author explores the theoretical and philosophical bases to understanding childhood sexual abuse and describes in detail a group work programme which will be of interest to people who work with women survivors.

The author describes the background to setting up the groups, which drew its members from women who were attending college in Canada where the author works. The main part of the book provides a detailed description of the content of each of the thirteen sessions in this program, with a final chapter on 'self-care for the therapist'.

There is a lot of emphasis on creating a safe and secure atmosphere for the group members, which is very important for a group of this nature. Detailed guidelines of the group are set out, and ways of debriefing after the exercises and at the end of the sessions. The programme includes group discussion, mini-lectures, structured exercises, and journal writing. Many of the exercises involve relaxation and visualisation/guided fantasy, and the use of poetry and symbols, which are powerful techniques. The author could have given a stronger caution that when using these techniques one has to be aware of the powerful emotions they may evoke in people. There is a spiritual, philosophical base to the group work programme, which the author acknowledges at the outset to the reader and to prospective members, and which she addresses more openly and in more detail in the final chapter.

The author addresses the possible pitfalls of some of the exercises. In particular she sets out some clear guidance for the middle sessions which involve disclosure of each women's 'personal story', and explains how and why this process can be helpful to the women in a handout entitled 'Why Telling is Transformative'. The programme is very full. There are handouts, stories and poetry to inspire the women, a journal to be kept, and homework to be done.

My concerns are about whether this programme would meet the needs of women who are not drawn from the university population. This kind of group might work for educated, middle-class, white women but would the content be as relevant or suitable for poor or uneducated women, or women from different ethnic backgrounds? I was also surprised at the absence of an analysis about the outcome of the groups. There are no statistics as to how many women have attended or how many groups have been run. A one page evaluation/feedback, which would have given us more information about how the women thought they benefited from the group.

Although it has its limitations, all in all this *is* a useful book for social workers, groupworkers, therapists and others who work with women survivors of sexual abuse. I liked the quotes used at the beginning of chapters, and some of the visualisations and poems were quite moving. It is difficult to convey what the process of a group actually means to the participants, but the book does provide a well thought out and detailed group work programme, which could be adapted. The philosophy is positive and the emphasis is on the strengths and resilience of women to achieve what the groups are called, going: 'Beyond Survival: Discovering Pathways to Healing.'

Lorraine Schaffer
Lecturer in Social Work
Brunel University

Voices from the Field
Albert Alissi and Catherine G. Corto Mergins (eds)
Binghampton, NY, Haworth Press, 1997
ISBN 0 7890 0138 1, US$49.95, 181pp

This is a collection of papers from the Sixteenth Annual Symposium of the Association for the Advancement of Social Work with Groups, held in Connecticut, USA.

In an introductory paper, Konopka takes us back to her Second World War European roots and the crucial 'connectiveness' which makes us human. She reminds us that 'social work cannot be restricted to alleviating individual problems, but must also include community action and social reform' (p7). She emphasises the need to 'mean something', and the way in which groups can achieve this for individuals. Maier's introductory chapter makes links between social group work and developmental group care.

Lee et al describe Empowerment Groups in the setting of an agency serving homeless women and children in an inner-city; these groups are both individually-oriented (helping women to find affordable housing). The chapter ends with the description of a sociodrama performed at the Symposium which enacts the severe levels of inequality in the United States.

Kurland and Salmon ask what happens when the norms of the leaders and the members in a group collide, when all the other systems seem pitted against the leadership, or antithetical to it. In other words, how do we deal with a situation when the ideas that members use to guide and sanction behaviour in the group are very different from the leaders'. This is particularly evident in groups of adolescents, where the communication nor may be the 'put-down', but it is also evident in more subtle ways when the culture of group members is at variance with the group workers' (for example, not to talk about taboo subjects). This chapter provides very useful, concrete advice to group workers in this kind of situation and (implicitly rather than explicitly) uses a systems framework to explore the best point for action - with the useful lesson that this is not always inside the group, but with people (such as parents) outside the group.

Crown and Gates describe groupwork with juvenile sex offenders, using a combination of cognitive and behavioural methods to help the perpetrator 'to acknowledge his feelings, deal with them in a more appropriate way and develop a plan for what to do if and when he has the urge to re-offend' (p57). Their stance as group leaders is vend revisiting issues that are resistant to change, means that the lessons to be learned about how to develop, interpret and implement policy, go far beyond the example in either time and place described so well in this book.

Sheila Kesby
University of Kent

Teaching a Methods Course in Social Work with Groups
Roselle Kurland and Robert Salmon
Alexandria, VA, Council on Social Work Education, 1998
ISBN 0 87293 060 2, £20.80, 219pp

Securing a place for social groupwork within social work education in the United States is the main purpose of this teaching resource. Indeed, it is worth reading Appendix B: 'Issues Confronting Group Work', first. Readers will find that social groupwork in the United States is struggling with problems similar to those confronting us in Britain. The marginalisation of groupwork in practice and in social work education has reached an alarming level. Yet, in the United States groupwork is fighting back.

Groupworkers in the United States have been united within the Association for the Advancement of Social Work with Groups (AASWG) for a long time now. So - they have been able to approach the American equivalent of the British CCETSW (CSWE) with a very clear agenda. As a result, the American Council on Social Work Education accepted the need to publish a series of books aimed at helping social work educators teach social group work, and this is only the first volume.

Any review of this book has to take into account the survival struggle underpinning its creation. Various underlying issues must have guided the authors when they prioritised materials and decided the level at which to pitch it for a foundation module of a BA course in social work. Since I practice and teach in Britain, I may not be sensitive enough to these issue. So, my review can address only the relevance of this volume to British social work educators.

The purpose of this volume is described as two-fold: to increase students' appreciation of knowledge, values, and skills of social group work, and to increase the students' comfort in group work practice (p. 2). I think that most educators will agree with these goals for a foundations course.

Written in a very down to earth in-house style, this is an immensely rich teaching resource. Huge number of teaching assignments and exercises are generously offered and each of these is written-up in minute detail. A twenty eight pages bibliography, divided into twelve topics, is offered as an Appendix.

The material itself is organised as eleven teaching units. The first two units: Launching a Course, and The Evolution of Group Work, provide an introduction. Then the sequence is ordered according to stages of a group's development: Pre-group Planning and Group Formation, Beginnings, Middles, and Endings. In-between these stages, major groupwork issues are introduced. The Problem-Solving Process in Group Work Practice follows the Beginnings. Group Roles, Dealing with Conflict and Difference, and The Use of Program Activities follow the Middles. Group Work versus Casework in a Group follows Endings.

A number of Appendices are added: Assignments, Process Recording, A Model of Planning for Social Work with Groups, The Problem-Solving Process, and three tables describing what the authors consider the common stages of group development: beginning, middle, and ending.

How can this vast range of resources help British educators?

As the authors themselves are at pains to emphasise, even American teachers will have to modify the materials to suit each particular class, and that certainly holds true for teaching in Britain. Of course many terms will have to be virtually translated, and specific contexts of practice will have to be introduced.

Beyond these cultural differences, the basic logic; of focusing on common features that often appear in many different groups, is accepted by many who teach at this very introductory level. Ordering the topics according to the stages of group development is, again, very common practice among groupwork teachers nowadays. The question is whether Beginning, Middle, and End is a very good order. My experience is that students who are taught this framework easily impose their own ideas of 'the middle' on groups whose middle periods differ very markedly. Consequently, their practice accounts often appear quite arbitrary and this artificiality raises serious questions about their practice. The question of common groupwork stages seems to me somewhat more complex, and other solutions may be available.

Another question is about the teaching methods used. The authors encourage 'diversity of means' (p.xi), but emphasise the priority of supportively challenging students' thinking, within

John Dewey's model of problem solving. That model emphasises extensive exploration of various facets of each problem before searching for solutions. While intuitively this choice feels right to me too, it would have been helpful to hear why the authors consider this framework to be so very clearly the best.

As for the contents: there is so much to celebrate here. The units about Group Roles, The Use of Program Activity, and Group Work versus Casework in Groups, are just three examples of heart-warming texts that many will value. Yet, I have to say that some sections left me somewhat puzzled. Hartford's definition of a small group as 'at least two people' is described as 'most helpful' (p.ix). Is it? Is there no QUALITATIVE difference between a dyad and a triad? Family therapists are acutely aware of the difference. Many adult dyads face a crisis with the arrival of the first child as this event turns a couple into a family. It seems to me that even beginning students can be helped by understanding the added complexity that arises when three (rather than two) people begin to interact. Neither was I entirely sure that the teaching about scapegoating (pp76-86) was clear enough. These authors write so lucidly about groupwork versus casework in a group (pp147-156). Yet, when it comes to scapegoating they do not seem to encourage students to explore FIRST whether the dynamics of the-group-as-a-whole has produced this problem. Surely, if that is the case, pragmatically 'solving' the scapegoating of one girl will just delay the appearance of another scapegoat later on.

The lack of any reference to effectiveness research is also quite surprising. Yet, these are all minor quibbles.

As mentioned at the beginning, the main point of this book is the contribution that AASWG made to presenting teaching materials which could and should be reintroduced into the mainstream of social work education. Does it suggest the need for a groupwork association in Britain too?

Oded Manor
Principal Lecturer in Social Work
Middlesex University

Notes for Contributors

Articles are welcome from all who have an interest in work with groups (whether as practitioner, trainer, academic, researcher, user or consultant), and who wish to contribute to the development of groupwork theory and practice.

Types of articles

A wide range will be welcomed including:

- groupwork practice accounts which describe and reflect on group purpose, process, experience and outcomes;
- the significance of the context of groupwork (organisational, societal, policy);
- education and training in groupwork skills, methods and models (including consultation and supervision);
- group process and interventions in work groups and teams;
- issues of power and oppression in groups: the significance of race, gender, class, disability, sexual orientation and other factors in group process, and for anti-oppressive practice;
- research, monitoring and evaluation of groupwork;
- new developments: ideas for practice, ways of understanding group processes, concepts, models and approaches;
- international/European groupwork accounts/developments/comparisons/issues.

Structure and style

Please note the following points when preparing your article;

- the 'story' of groupwork practice which includes the members' own words and experiences can be very powerful;
- the use of anti-oppressive language and terminology is expected;
- please include a brief summary at the beginning, of not more than 150 words.

References

These should be quoted in the text by putting in brackets the author's name and year of publication. They should then be listed in alphabetical order at the end of the article as follows, please pay special attention to the punctuation and use of upper case letters in the examples below:

Books - authors surname, initials, date (in brackets), title of book (in italics), place of publication, publishers.

e.g. Barlow, D. and Lancing, D. (1994) *Groupwork Publications*. London: Daffodil Press.

Articles - authors surname, initials, date, title of article (within single quotes), title of journal (italics), volume, issue, page numbers. e.g. Einstein, A. and Freud, S. (1920) 'The groupwork unconscious', *The Journal of the Future*, 24(2), pp.101-124.

Please note that it is the responsibility of authors to ensure that the referencing is done correctly before submitting the manuscript. Remember to double check that the date in brackets in the text corresponds to the date cited in the references list at the end.

Length of papers

The normal range is 2500-4000 words, but the editors will consider longer pieces on merit. There is also a place for briefer contributions on new developments, responses to previous articles, and other material of special interest.

Form of submission

Please supply 4 copies of your paper initially, and keep your disk for the potential publication stage when it will be needed by the publishers. When you send your disk, please give full details of the software package used. If your paper is accepted for publication, a further 3 copies of the final version will be required. Once accepted for publication, the author(s) will receive a paper indicating all the publishers' housestyle requirements, so that these can be incorporated into the final text/disc.

Please note: All papers should be sent in the first instance to The Editor, Groupwork, c/o Whiting and Birch Ltd, PO Box 872, 90 Dartmouth Road, London SE23 3HL, England.

Assessment for publication

When articles are first received the editors make a decision on potential suitability for the journal. Articles are sometimes rejected or returned to authors for major review at this stage. Otherwise, they are sent (anonymously) to two members of the journal's panel of assessors for their comments and views on publication. The editors make the final decision on publication, taking into account the views of the assessors. All authors receive personal feedback on decisions taken.

Book reviews

All books for review should be sent to the book reviews editor, c/o the publishers.

Appendix: Contents of *Groupwork* Volumes 1-13

Volume 1 (ISBN 9781861770554)
Groupwork practice with hard to reach clients: A modality of choice Lawrence Shulman
The worker and the group process: A dilemma revisited Ken Heap
Race and groupwork: Some experiences in practice and training Ros Muston and Jeremy Weinstein
A group for white women with black children Clare Rhule
Structured activities with adolescent boys Rod Craig
Supporting voices: Groupwork with people suffering from schizophrenia Lynda Randall and Wendy Walker
Groupwork books published in Britain 1980-86 Harold Marchant
Swimming upstream: Articles on groupwork in social work journals 1986-87 Nano McCaughan
Preparing the client for social groupwork: An illustrated framework Oded Manor
Groups for older people in residential and day-care: The other groupworkers Lorraine Bernard, John Burton, Phyllis Kyne and June Simon
'But 1 don't want to lead a group!' Some common problems of social workers leading groups Ken Reid
Programming skills in social groupwork. Sue Ross and Andy Thorpe
A model for evaluating groupwork Michael Preston-shoot
Groupwork as the method of choice with black children in white foster homes Audrey Mullender
Short term groupwork in the treatment of chronic sorrow. A Norwegian experience Gerd Kramm Engebrigtsen and Ken Heap
Revisiting open groups Michael Henry
Social action groupwork as negotiation: Contradictions in the process of empowerment Eamonn Keenan and John Pinkerton
'Nowt to do and always getting into trouble'. The Bulwell Neighbourhood Project: A social action response Bill Badham, Michael Bente and Pauline Hall
A team development exercise John Taylor, Di Miles and John Eastgate
'The brothers and sisters group': A group for siblings of children with physical disabilities Anne Badger
Groupwork with adolescents: Abstracts Alison Skinner

Volume 2 (ISBN 9781861770561)
Challenging familiar assumptions: Preparing for and initiating a self-directed group Audrey Mullender and David Ward
Doing something with our lives when we're inside: Self-directive groupwork in a youth custody centre. Bill Badham (Ed.). Bob Blatchford, Steph Mcartney and Malcolm Nicholas
Using contracts in groupwork Michael Preston-shoot
Targeted activities in group contexts: The analysis of activities to meet consumer need Julie Phillips
Designing cancer groups for maximum effectiveness Barry M. Daste
Decision-making in therapeutic groups Marian F. Fatout
Confronting human finitude. Groupwork with people with AIDS George S. Getzel and Kevin F. Mahony
Organising accountability for social groupwork: More choices Oded Manor
A group for black and white sexually abused children Marie Lebacq and Zaffira Shah
Learning about groupwork. Jenny Lumley and Harold Marchant
Establishing a feminist model of groupwork in the Probation Service Tara Mistry
A way forward: A group for refugee women Rachel Tribe and Jane Shackman
Searching the literature on women's groups Cathrine Fitzgerald
Open grief groups: the resolution of complicated loss Marianne Davidsen-Nielsen and Nini Leick
Groupwork with the spouses of seriously ill patients Janine Favier
Supportive groupwork for dialysis patients Lizzie Bollmann
Supportive groupwork with young arthritic mothers Amy Østertun Geirdal
Staff development through groupwork in Polish

community agencies: 'The Centres Of Culture' Jerzy Szmagalski
Self-help groups as basic care in psychotherapy and social work Jürgen Matzat
Family group treatment in drug abuse Anna Casanova Torras
Groupwork As Early Intervention In High Risk Families Rigmor Grette Moe

Volume 3 (ISBN 9781861770578)
Social work with groups in multicultural contexts Kenneth L. Chau
Siblings in groups: Children of separated/divorced parents Sandra Regan and Jan Young
Groupwork techniques in a residential primary school for emotionally disturbed boys Peter Clarke and Amanda Aimable
The role of groupwork in research with people with learning difficulties Jan Walmsley
Groupwork training: A case study Andrew Kerslake
Beulah Rothman: An appreciation Oded Manor
Starting the journey: Enhancing the therapeutic elements of groupwork for adolescent female child sexual abuse victims Eileen Craig
Evaluating success in groupwork: Why not measure the obvious? Anne Peake and Olive Otway
Investigating groupwork: A Case study using a group approach in the initial stages of child sexual abuse investigation Sarah Allum
The Forgotten parent: Groupwork with mothers of sexually abused children Helen Masson and Marcus Erooga
Work with male sex offenders in groups Malcolm Cowburn
Protection, control, treatment: Groupwork with child sexual abuse perpetrators Marcus Erooga, Paul Clark and Mai Bentley
Group treatment for women sex offenders against children Sharon Barnett. Francesca Corder and Derek Jehu
Selected article abstracts on child sexual abuse and groupwork Julia Cramp and Helen Armstrong
Self help groups: A minefield for professionals Ulla Habermann
Facing the challenge of developing group services for high risk families Alice Home and Lise Darveau-Fournier
Groupwork with parents of sleepless children Rona Robertson
Culture' groups in prison Graham Towl
Groupwork with a difference: The group 'mosaic' in residential day centre settings Allan Brown
Groupwork in residential settings for elderly people Audrey Mullender

Volume 4 (ISBN 9781861770585)
Empowerment through mutual aid groups: A practice grounded conceptual framework Judith AB. Lee
Making authority accountable: The experience of a statutory based women's group Helen Bodinham and Jeremy Weinstein
Towards a model of social groupwork practice with marginalised populations Margot Breton
Working creatively with children Eugene Clerkin and Belinda Knaggs
The termination phase in groupwork: Tasks for the groupworker Sue Ross
Miami, October 1990 Oded Manor and Dave Ward
Black/white co-working in groups Tara Mistry And Allan Brown
Groupwork and oral history: Raising the consciousness of young people during social transition Sandra Drower
The use of photographs as a projective and facilitative technique in groups Merav DeVere And Ossi Rhonne
Facilitation in self-directed groupwork Dave Ward and Audrey Mullender
Evaluative study of groupwork for stress and anxiety Rhona Birrell Weisen
A long-term support group for chronic schizophrenic outpatients: A quantitative and qualitative evaluation Julie Cwikel And Adina Oron
Using groups in working with offenders:
A survey of groupwork in the Probation Service of England and Wales Brian Caddick
A Miskin Model of groupwork with women offenders Marion jones, Mary Mordecai, Frances Rutter and Linda Thomas
Evolution and accountability Ten years of groups in a day centre for offenders
Judith Earnshaw
The Telford Motoring Offenders Education Project Kathryn Hutchins
Groupwork in the Luton Probation And Bail Hostel Catherine Mulvie
The Newcastle intensive probation programme A centralised approach to groupwork Jane Mackintosh

Meeting prisoners' needs through groupwork Mike Ashe
Groupwork in the Probation Service: Care or control in the 1990s Paul Senior
Selected abstracts on groupwork with offenders John Hodge
Derek Carter 1934-1991

Volume 5 (ISBN 9781861770592)
Groupwork from across the Atlantic: Its identity and diffusion Catherine Pappell
Groupwork in Europe: Past, Present, Future Ken Heap, Diakonhjemmet School of Social Work, Oslo
The groupwork consultant's role in facilitating work groups Alan Turkie, Independent
Evaluation For The Improvement Of Groupwork Practice Kenneth H Gordon, School of Social Work, King's College, Western Ontario
Groupwork in a residential home for older people: Building on the positive aspects of group living Gun Lewis, Officer in Charge
Groupwork with Youth Gangs in Hong Kong T Wing Lo, City Polytechnic, Hong Kong
On empowerment, partnership and authority in groupwork practice: A training contribution Michael Preston-Shoot, School of Social Work, University of Manchester
Groupwork with involuntary clients: Remotivating strategies Cyrus S Behroozi, Indiana University School of Social Work
Handling conflict: Groupwork with violent offenders Rob Canton, Carolyn Mack and Jeff Smith, Nottinghamshire Probation
The dream in groupwork practice Iain Edgar, Dept of Social Work, University of Northumbria
Support groups for older people: Is homogeneity or heterogeneity the answer? Susan Rice and Catherine Goodman, Dept of Social Work, California State University, Long Beach
The group turns inward: A consideration of some group phenomena as reflective of the Northern Irish situation Jarlath Benson, Psychotherapeutic Groupworker, Belfast
Groupwork with bereaved children Nuala Harmey and Bernie Price, Medical Social Work, Temple Street Children's Hospital, Dublin
Reminiscence groupwork with older people Faith Gibson, Dept of Social Work, University of Ulster, Coleraine
Social workers and psychologists as facilitators of groupwork with adults with a learning difficulty: A survey of current practice Heno Schonfield and Mary C Morrissey, Senior Social Workers, Dublin
Groupwork with teenage cancer patients Nicola Martin Medical Social Worker in Oncology, and Eddie O'Neill, Paediatric Oncology Social Worker, Mater Hospital, Dublin
Bereaved by suicide: Setting up an 'ideal' therapy group in a real world Imogen O'Connor, Therapist, Dublin Rape Crisis Centre

Volume 6 (ISBN 9781861770608)
Groupwork versus *casework in a group* Roselle Kurland and Robert Salmon, Hunter School of Social Work, New York
Why groupwork is not put into practice: Reflections on the social work scene in Denmark Ulla Habermann, Director, Volunteer Centre, Denmark
Away with the experts? Self-help groupwork in Germany Jürgen Matzat, Psychologist, Klinik für Psychosomatik und Psychotherapie, Justus-Liebig-Universität, Gießen
Groupwork with siblings of children with special needs: A pilot study Georgina Ferraro and Julie Tucker, Senior Family Project Workers
Neutralisation of group control in youth gangs T Wing Lo, City Polytechnic, Hong Kong
The large group: The heart of the system in group care Adrian Ward, Dept of Social Work, University of Reading
Working with a family group of bereaved children Sheila Finlayson, Child Advisory Social Work Service, City of Birmingham Education Dept
A comparative study of four family bereavement groups Estelle Hopmeyer, and Annette Werk, McGill School of Social Work, Montréal
An asian mothers' group Lynne Muir Director, MEd Programme in Community Education and Hardev Notta, Acorns Hospice for Children, Birmingham
A Cruse family circle Joyce Rimmer, Birmingham Cruse
Coping with trauma Frank Parkinson, former Army chaplain
From group meeting to therapeutic group Bernadette Duffy. Social Care Worker, Dublin and Brian McCarthy, Lecturer in Psychology, Dublin Institute of Technology
Group therapy with adults with learning difficulties who have committed sexual offences Elisabeth

Cormack, Young People's Centre , Northern Ireland

Critical incident analysis and its application in groupwork David Henchman and Susan Walton, Avon Probation Service

Life history work with a group of people with learning disabilities Dorothy Atkinson, School of Health, Welfare and Community Education, Open University

Art therapy: Creative groupwork for women. Olive Otway, Lecturer in Social Work, University of Keele

Groupwork with parents of learning disabled adolescents. Helen Gobat, Independent Social Worker

Groupwork with deaf people. Kavita Kohli, Social Worker, Hounslow Social Services s

Combining activities and growth games: A systems approach Oded Manor, Middlesex University, and Miriam Dumbleton, Care Manager, Westminster Social Services

Volume 7 (ISBN 9781861770615)

The linguistic and cultural barriers to cross-national groupwork Paul Taylor, Lecturer in Community Education, University of Tours, France

Partnership in training and practice with refugees Jill Reynolds, School of Health, Welfare and Community Education, Open University and Jane Shackman, Social Worker, The Medical Foundation for Care of Victims of Torture

Men working with men in groups: masculinity and crime John Benstead, Gloucester Probation, Allan Brown, School of Social Work, Bristol University, Carlton Forbes, and Rick Wall, Avon Probation Centre

Working *with religious communities* Geraldine Grindley, Dublin City University

Issues of empowerment: Anti-oppressive groupwork by disabled people in Ireland Maire Ni Chorcora and Eddie Jennings, DET and Nuala Lordan, Dept of Applied Social Studies, University College Cork

A Psychotherapeutic group for boys who have been sexually abused Gary Dixon formerly South London FSU and Michelle Phillips, Clinical Nurse Specialist, Camberwell Child Guidance Centre

Groupwork and black women: Viewing networks as groups Marcia Francis-Spence Centre for Applied Social Studies, University of Durham

Staying alive in difficult times: The experience of groupwork with mothers of children who have been sexually abused Deb Dobbin and Sarah Evans, Independent Social Workers

A time for women: An account of a group for women on an out of city housing development in Leicester Claire Wintram, Independent Trainer, Kerry Chamberlain, National Health Service Administrator, Marlene Kuhn, Midwife and Jo Smith, Woman with a Disability active in support and campaign groups , Leicester

Groupwork for mental health: Providers utilising the enchanted self concept Barbara Becker Holstein, Psychologist, Long Branch, New Jersey, and Doreen Laperdon-Addison, Movement Educator and Professional Dancer

Promoting positive images:. The role of groupwork in promoting women managers within organisations Judy Fawcett, Independent Consultant and Trainer

Using a facilitated self help group for women whose children have been sexually abused Olive Otway, Dept of Social Work, Keele University, and Anne Peak, Principal Psychologist, Oxfordshire

'All I've got in my purse is mothballs' the social action women's group Sandra Butler, Dept of Social Work, University of Nottingham

Silence in working across difference: Groupwork in a youth and community work training context Janet Batsleer, Youth and Community Work Section, Manchester Metropolitan University

Ourselves and others Helen Gobat, Independent Social Worker

Groupwork with young mothers Caroline Norman, Project Worker, St Gabriels Family Centre, Brighton

Groupwork for parents of young people in trouble: A proposal Mark Drakeford, Dept of Applied Social Studies, University of Wales, Swansea

A dramatic view of groupwork Jeremy Weinstein, Dept of Social Work, South Bank University

Anger management groupwork with prisoners: An empirical evaluation Graham J Towl and Polly Dexter, Forensic Psychologists, HM Prison Service

Volume 8 (ISBN 9781861770622)

'Cycling Over Everest' Groupwork with depressed women Pamela Trevithick, Dept of Social Work, Bristol University

Groupwork in Croatia: Experiences with older refugees Marina Adjukovic, School of Social Work, University of Zagreb, Milena Cevcizovic

and Ksenija Kontak, Psychologists, Society for Psychological Assistance, Croatia
Group dialogue within prisons Peter Garrett, Centre for Action Research in Professional Practice, School of Management, University of Bath
Establishing community meetings in a children's home Adrian Ward, Dept of Social Work, University of Reading
Groups for children who have lived with domestic violence: Learning from North America Audrey Mullender, Centre for Applied Social Studies, University of Durham
Facilitating enquiry and action learning groups for social work education Hilary Burgess and Imogen Taylor, School for Policy Studies, University of Bristol
Developing critical conversations about practice Mark K Smith, Research Fellow and Tutor, YMCA George Williams College
Dialogue and reparation in the large whole group Alan Turkie, Independent and Lecturer in Youth and Community Work, Goldsmiths' College
Using groupwork methods in social work education Margaret O'Dee, Social Work Studies, Salford University
An outdoor treatment programme for a group of first year sixth formers Derrick Rowland Coverdale consultant
A Strategy for groupwork education and training in a social work agency Mark Doel, University of Sheffield and Catherine Sawdon, Training Officer, Wakefield Social Services
Managing the tension between being task-centred and being anti-oppressive Marcia Francis Spence and Beverley Prevatt-Goldstein, Centre for Applied Social Studies, University of Durham
Teachers, learning, ego and groups Leslie Silverlock and Marion Silverlock 'Groups Work'
Creative short term group therapy in a managed care environment Barry M Daste, Louisiana State University School of Social Work
Groupwork to facilitate family reconstitution: A social work response Jan Hadlow, Keynes College
Social groupwork practice in Hong Kong: Application of western ideas in an asian population Debbie O B Lam, University of Hong Kong
Time and space to grieve: A bereavement group for children Sister Margaret Pennels, Northampton General Hospital NHS Trust
An integrated feminist-socioeducational model: Groupwork with nurses in Hong Kong Elaine Au Liu, City University of Hong Kong

Volume 9 (ISBN 9781861770639)
Living with loss: A bereavement support group Sheila Thompson, School of Social Work, McGill University
A collaborative group approach for urban parents Mary McKernan McKay, Teresa Garcia, Joseph Scally and Lori Martinez, Institute for Juvenile Research, University of Illinois, Chicago
Groupwork with male 'domestic' abusers: Models and dilemmas Audrey Mullender, Professor in Social Work, University of Warwick
'Without the group, I'd still be eating half the Co-op': An example of groupwork with women who use food Jill Ball and Annemarie Norman, , Northern Initiative on Women and Food, Newcastle
The use of sculpt in social groupwork education Nuala Lordan, University College, Cork
Groupwork into the future: Some personal reflections Allan Brown, formerly University of Bristol
Ethical issues in practice: Participatory social research and groups George Taylor, Dept of Social and Community Studies, De Montfort University
Enhancing research usefulness with adapted focus groups Alice M. Home, Professor of Social Work, University of Ottawa
Focus groups and familiar social work skills: Their contribution to practitioner research Pat Walton, Lecturer in Post-Qualifying Studies (Child Care)
Focusing on groups in social policy research Paul Swift, Project Researcher, School for Policy Studies, University of Bristol
Exploitation or empowerment? Gaining access to young people's reflections on crime prevention Strategies Alan France, Research Fellow, University of Warwick University
A youth and community work approach to practitioner research into sensitive issues Steve Kenny, Dept of Applied Community Studies, Manchester Metropolitan University
Black community members-as-researchers: Working with community groups in the research process Simon Dyson and Mark Harrison, Director, Centre for Social Action, de Montfort University,
Empowering research process: Using groups in research to empower the people Asnarulkhadi

Abu-Samah, Doctoral student, University of Nottingham
Storming as transformation: A case study of group relationships Oded Manor, Middlesex University
An art therapy group for young people with eating difficulties Janet Fitzsimmons, Social Worker and Rosemary Levy, Art Therapist, Barnet Social Services Children and Families Health related Social Work Team
Intervention in the decision-making of youth gangs Francis W L Lee, Dept of Social Work, Chinese University of Hong Kong, T. Wing Lo and Dennis S W Wong, Dept of Applied Social Studies, City University of Hong Kong
Support groups for families of confused elders: Issues surrounding open peer-led groups Elizabeth Hughes Schneewind, Independent Social Worker
Drama and groupwork: Overcoming the 'double whammy' Philip Moore, Actor and Groupworker, Cumbria Probation
Psychosocial assistance to refugee and displaced women in Croatia Nina Pecnik, School of Social Work, University of Zagreb and Mira Miskulin, Programme for Refugee Women, 'Sunflower' Centre for Grassroots Relief, Zagreb

Volume 10 (ISBN 9781861770646)
Teleconferencing group counselling: Pre-group public phase Sandra Regan, Senior Lecturer in Groupwork, School of Social Work, University of New South Wales,
Suddenly the light went on: Using groupwork to empower returning students Roni Berger, Assistant Professor, School of Social Work, Adelphi University
A group's journey through separation and loss: Therapeutic groupwork with children as a social work intervention Maria Neary and Geraldine Brandon, Thamesmead Family Service Unit
Implementing a novel groupwork model: Application of an innovation-developmental process Jerome R. Kolbo, University of S Mississippi, Kimberly Horn, W Virginia University and Elizabeth Randall, University of S Mississippi
Applying a strengths, competence and empowerment model Anna Nosko, Family Services Association of Toronto and Margot Breton, University of Toronto
Effective groupwork packages and the importance of process David Henchman and Susan Walton, Freelance Trainers and Probation Officers
Using the sensory orientation group with a frail elder population Norma Thomas, Professor, Center for Social Work, Widener University, Pennsylvania and Suzanne Coleman, Social Worker, Bryn Mawr Terrace Nursing Home, Pennsylvania
Research into practice does go: Integrating research within programme development Rob Harry, Staff Dev't Manager, Patricia Heggarty, Probation Officer, Cathy Lisles, Freelance Researcher, Richard Thurston, Research Mgr, Mid-Glams Probation and Maurice Vanstone, Lecturer, University of Wales, Swansea
Brief group therapy and the use of metaphor Christian C Sunderland, Clinical Social Worker, Cardston Clinic, Alberta
We'd like you to come back Hilary Hopkin, Social Worker, Royal Liverpool University Hospital
The use of music in group work with out-patient alcoholic couples: A pilot investigation Wilfred A Gallant, Assoc. Professor of Social Work, Melanie D Galant, Research Asst Human Services Research Unit, Kevin M Gorey, Assoc. Professor of Social Work, Michael J Holosko, Professor of Social Work and Sammi Siegel, Director of Music Therapy, University of Windsor, Ontario
Exploring worker responses to critical incidents Marian F Fatout, Professor, School of Social Work, Louisiana State University, Baton Rouge
A Critical analysis of a support and clinical supervision group for interpreters working with refugees located in Britain Rachel Tribe, Senior Lecturer, Psychology Dept, University of East London, Romford
Feminist groupwork with lesbian survivors of incest Patricia A Groves, Director of Social Work Program and Connie Schondel, formerly Associate Professor, , University of Toledo, Ohio
Don't worry, it's just a stage he's going through: A reappraisal of the stage theory of group work as applied to an open model treatment group for men who abuse women Tom Caplan, Adj. Professor and Director, and Harle Thomas, Clinical and Groupworker, McGill University Domestic Violence Clinic
Active learning programmes to promote cognitive change Siu-Kau Cheung, Principal Lecturer,

Division of Social Studies, City University of Hong Kong

Volume 11 (ISBN 9781861770653)
Crossing bridges: Groupwork in Guyana Judith A B Lee, Professor, Dept of Social Work, Florida Gulf Coast University
Working with polarities, roles and timespirits: A process oriented approach to emotions in the Group Bogna Szymkiewicz-Komalska, Asst Professor, Inst of Applied Social Sciences, Warsaw University
It ain't (just) what you do: It's the way that you do it: Working towards effective practice in probation groupwork Alan Hayden, Jonathan Hopkinson, Janeen Sengendo and Elisabeth von Rabenau, Probation Officers, Cambridgeshire Probation
A Group intervention for children of incarcerated parents: Initial blunders and subsequent solutions David W Springer, Asst Professor, Elizabeth C Pomeroy, Asst Professor and Toni Johnson, Doctoral Student, School of Social Work, University of Texas, Austin
Expressing our anger: Hindrance or help in groupwork with adolescents? Andrew Malekoff, Director or Program Development, North Shore Child and Family Guidance Center, Roslyn Heights, New York
Technical errors or missed alternatives: An interview with Catherine Pappell
Groupwork with the mothers of teenage mothers Catherine Dennison, Research Psychologist and Helen Ingledew, Family Centre Worker, Trust for the Study of Adolescence
Men united: Fathers' voices Jennie Fleming, Research Fellow, Centre for Social Action, de Montfort University and Zbyszek Luczynski, Broader Initiatives Development Worker, Nottingham City Council
Parent education groups: Using cultural literature during engagement phase Gwenelle Styles O'Neal, Assoc Professor of Social Work, West Chester University, Pennsylvania and Janis Coombs Reid, Vice President of Academic Affairs, Atlanta Metropolitan College, Georgia
Action methods and interpersonal· processes in groups: An exploration of psychodramatic concepts Annie Huntington, Lecturer, Dept of Social Work, Salford University
Building solutions in groupwork with parents John Sharry, Senior Social Worker, Dept of Child and Family Psychiatry, Mater Hospital, Dublin
Crossing the great gap: Groupwork for personal growth John Rowan, Group and Individual Psychotherapist
When actions speak louder: Groupwork in occupational therapy Linda Finlay, Associate Lecturer in Social Psychology, the Open University, Leeds
Help as mutual aid: Groupwork in mental health Oded Manor, Principal Lecturer in Social Work, School of Social Science, Middlesex University
No Group is an island: Groupwork in a social work agency Mark Doel, Professor of Social Work School of Social Work and RNIB Rehabilitation Studies, University of Central England and Catherine Sawdon, Training Officer, Wakefield Social Services
Breaking the culture of silence: Groupwork and community development Jacky Drysdale, Lecturer in Social Work and Rod Purcell, Lecturer in Community Development and Adult Education, University of Glasgow
Values as Context: Groupwork and social action Mark Harrison, Director, Centre for Social Action and Dave Ward, Professor and Head, Dept of Social and Community Studies, De Montfort University

Volume 12 (ISBN 9781861770660)
Punishment and the question of ownership: Groupwork in the criminal justice system Liz Dixon, Senior Lecturer in Criminal Justice Studies, University of Hertfordshire and Probation Officer, ILPS
Picking up the Pieces: Groupwork in Palliative Care Pam Firth, Senior Social Worker/Head of Family Support, Isabel Hospice, Welwyn Garden City
Developing the professionals: Groupwork for health promotion Ellen E Reverand, Senior Manager (Learning and Professional Development) and Louis B Levy, Acting Director, Health First, London
Learning beyond the classroom: A role for groupwork? Marion Silverlock, Education and Training Consultant, Somerset
Evolving the curriculum: Groupwork and community based learning Lynne Muir, Course Director, MA in Community Based Learning. , Centre for Education ·Development, Coventry
Using workshops on loss for adults with learning

disabilities Sue Read, Vicky Papakosta-Harvey and Sal Bower

Groupwork with schizophrenia: Clinical aspects Susan E. Mason, Associate Professor of Social Work, Wurzweiler School of Social Work, Yeshiva University, New York

Multi-family group interventions with schizophrenia Jane Hanvey Phillips, Doctoral Candidate, and Jacqueline Corcoran, Assistant Professor, School of Social Work, University of Texas, Arlington

The mixed-based nature of self-help groups in Finland Marianne Nylund, Researcher, Doctor of Social Sciences, Dept of Social Policy, University of Helsinky

Teenagers' experiences of a health promotion project Frances Maggs-Rapport, Senior Research Fellow, Mary Seacole Research Centre, De Montfort University

Working with natural groups of youth-at-risk: An RGC approach Francis Wing-lin Lee Assistant Professor, Dept of Social Work, University of Hong Kong

The strengths perspective in reminiscence groupwork with depressed older adults Alison C. Rishty Advanced Standing MSW Candidate in Clinical Practice, Columbia University

Using fieldwork experience as a tool for teaching: A multi-layered approach Barbara Worden, Assoc. Professor of Social Work, Southern Conecticut State University

Volume 13 (ISBN 9781861770677)

Using technologies in groupwork . Part I: Face-to-face groups, and *Part II: Technology-based groups* Paul R. Smokowski, Director of Distance Education, Maeda Galinsky, Kenan Distinguished Professor, School of Social Work, University of North Carolina at Chapel Hill, and Kristin Harlow, Social Work Practitioner

Researching our own practice: Single system design for groupwork Paul Johnson, Asst Professor, Dept of Social Work, University of S. Maine. Aaron Beckerman, Professor Emeritus and Charles Auerbach, Professor, Wurzweiler School of Social Work, Yeshiva University

Facilitating group beginnings. I: A practice model, and *Part II: From basic to working engagement* Alf Lizzio, Lecturer, and Keithia Wilson, Senior Lecturer, School of Applied Psychology, Griffiths University, Brisbane

To share or not to share: Dilemmas of facilitators who share the problem of group members Marian Maram, Assistant Director of Field Education, and Susan Rice, Professor and Undergraduate Program Coordinator, Dept of Social Work, California State University, Long Beach

In their own voices: Play activities and art with traumatised children Bruce St. Thomas, Psychotherapist/Art Therapist, Westbrook Street Psychotherapy Associates, Portland, and Paul Johnson, Assistant Professor, Dept of Social Work, University of S. Maine

Groupwork with children and adolescents using lifegames Isabelle C. Streng, Chartered Clinical Psychologist, Erasmus Medical Centre, Rotterdam, The Netherlands

Closing a cultural divide: Enhancing mutual aid while working with groups in Hong Kong Fanny L.W.C. Liu, Senior Lecturer, Division of Social Studies, City University of Hong Kong

Strengths and weaknesses of self-help groups in mental health: The case of Grow Kam-shing Yip, Associate Professor, Dept of Applied Social Studies, Hong Kong Polytechnic University

Using groupwork in community mental health: Practitioners' views Ben Papps, Lecturer in Clinical Psychology, Institute of Psychiatry, London., Oded Manor, Principal Lecturer in Social Work, Middlesex University and Jerome Carson, Senior Lecturer in Clinical Psychology, Institute of Psychiatry, London

Hearing voices: Learning to engage the group Terry Conway, Senior Social Worker, Kneesworth House Hospital, Royston

An isle full of noises: Enhancing mental health through the Music Workshop Project Tony Gillam, Early Interventions Team Leader, Merdian Family Interventions Programme, South Worcestershire Early Interventions Service

Henderson Hospital: Greater than the sum of its sub-groups Dr Kingsley Norton, Director, Henderson Hospital and Reader in Psychotherapy, St George's Hospital Medical School

Groupwork fit for purpose? An inclusive framework for mental health Oded Manor, Principal Lecturer in Social Work, School of Health and Social Sciences, Middlesex University

Authors' professional affiliations are those at the time of original publication

www.ingramcontent.com/pod-product-compliance
Lightning Source LLC
LaVergne TN
LVHW101442200926
848483LV00001B/28
* 9 7 8 1 8 6 1 7 7 0 6 4 6 *